Buying, Renting & Borrowing In Texas

The rules of the game

Buying, Renting & Borrowing In Texas

The rules of the game

H. Clyde Farrell
& Paul Kens
Attorneys at Law

Illustrated by Ben Sargent

Texas Consumer Association – Austin

Copyright © 1980 by H. Clyde Farrell and Paul Kens

All rights reserved. No portion of this book may be reproduced, by any process or technique, without the express written consent of the copyright owners.

Published by Texas Consumer Association
302 West 15th Street, Suite 202, Austin, Texas 78701

First published in 1980

Printed in the United States of America

10   9   8   7   6   5   4   3   2   1

Library of Congress Catalog Card Number: 80-52895
ISBN 0-937606-00-6
ISBN 0-937606-01-4

To Jim Boyle, our colleague, mentor and friend; and
To Margot Beutler, our editor and muse; and
To Rebecca Lightsey, who kept it together and made it happen.

ACKNOWLEDGMENTS

The authors gratefully acknowledge the generous assistance of the following persons in the preparation of this book: James G. Boyle, an Austin attorney; Craig E. Davis, an Austin attorney; Beverly Gibson, a Houston attorney; Russell M. Green, an examiner with the office of the Texas Consumer Credit Commissioner; Jim Keithley, Assistant Supervisor of Operations, Motor Vehicle Division, Texas State Department of Highways and Public Transportation; Sam Kelley, Texas Consumer Credit Commissioner; Rebecca Lightsey, an Austin attorney and Managing Director of the Texas Consumer Association; Paula Waddle, a Corpus Christi attorney; and, for their assistance in helping us put this book in plain English, we are especially grateful to Linda Breck, H. C. Farrell, Mary Farrell, Carla Underhill, and our editor Margot Beutler. The final product is the work of the authors, who are solely responsible for its content.

Contents

Preface   1

Part One: Buying and Renting Homes

Chapter 1	Buying and Selling Homes	5
Chapter 2	Renting Homes and Apartments	21
Chapter 3	Buying Home Improvements	49
Chapter 4	Foreclosure on Homes	57

Part Two: Buying Goods and Services

Chapter 5	Warranties	65
Chapter 6	Deceptive Trade Practices	77
Chapter 7	Door-to-Door Sales and Mail Orders	87
Chapter 8	Automobiles and Other Goods	93

Part Three: Borrowing Money

Chapter 9	Credit and Collateral	109
Chapter 10	Understanding the Language of Credit	117
Chapter 11	Calculating the Costs of Credit	125
Chapter 12	Credit Bureaus	141
Chapter 13	Equal Credit Opportunity	149
Chapter 14	Repossession	159
Chapter 15	The Homestead and Other Judgment Exemptions	165
Chapter 16	Debt Collection Practices	175
Chapter 17	Financers' Responsibilities	189

Part Four: Enforcing the Consumer's Rights

Chapter 18	Self Help	201
Chapter 19	Lawyers	213
Chapter 20	Consumer Assistance Agencies	223

Notes   245

Suggested Readings   259

Index   261

Preface

In the past, Texas schools have taught their students very little about handling personal finances or dealing with basic consumer questions. As a result, most Texans who have finished school know more about Egyptian pyramids than about Texas mortgages. We may be able to read Spanish or French novels, but we don't understand the contracts and leases we sign.

The authors of this book did not know the rules either before going to law school. Nobody had tried to teach them to us, and the available books were too long and full of legal jargon. That is why we decided to write this book.

Those who do know the rules are the professionals — the landlords, retailers and lenders — with whom the rest of us do business. All too often, we must rely on these very people for consumer advice, and then count on them to play by the rules. Not surprisingly, these people tend to come out on top. Another reason the professionals tend to come out ahead is that they know their legal options, so they know how to get the most out of the resources they have.

Recognizing the need for consumer education, the Texas Senate in 1979 directed the state's colleges and universities to provide courses in the "principles and concepts of consumer education." (S.R. 677, 66th Legislature.) Even before that, the Texas Consumer Association and several other organizations had begun to develop materials and programs for educating consumers. This book is part of that consumer education effort.

A major obstacle to consumer education is the complexity of the legal rules. Consumers *can* learn to cope with these rules, however, if given assistance in identifying which rules are important, and in translating legal terms into plain English. This book provides both kinds of assistance.

The only way to obtain a clear idea of which rules are important is to counsel and represent consumers on a daily basis. The authors of this book are among those few Texas attorneys who have had this experience. As attorneys for legal aid offices in Texas, we have worked with consumers and their legal problems day after day and year after year. From this experience, we have found that certain questions recur so frequently that every consumer needs to have the answers readily available. *Those day-to-day consumer questions are raised and answered in this book.*

In addition to learning what legal questions plague consumers most, we have learned how to answer those questions in clear, concise language. *In this book, legal questions are asked in plain English and answered in plain English.*

This book speaks directly to consumers — to those who are buying, renting and borrowing for personal or family purposes. It should also be helpful to business people and to landlords who need a handy legal reference.

This book, however, should not be used as a substitute for an attorney's professional advice, when such advice is available. Since no two legal situations are alike, an attorney may be able to explain how your situation is different from a similar one discussed in this book. Also, an attorney may be able to suggest rules or alternative strategies that we have not covered here. Throughout this book, we have identified those problems that are most likely to require an attorney's advice.

Few people, however, could afford to have attorneys at their elbows at all times, even if they should want such company. We all must take care of our own "legal" problems to some extent, just as we must take care of our own bodies without constantly seeking medical attention. To the extent that the reader must rely on his or her own judgment about consumer matters, then, this book should be a practical guide to the rules of the game. It should also help the reader know when to consult an attorney, what questions to ask, and how to understand the answers.

The authors have enjoyed practicing consumer law in Texas, and we have enjoyed putting our experiences into this book. We believe it will give the reader a new sense of confidence and personal effectiveness when buying, renting and borrowing in Texas.

PART ONE
BUYING AND RENTING HOMES

Chapter 1
Buying and Selling Homes

Most homeowning families have no larger nor more profitable investments than their homes. Most of us take great pride in our homes, and for good reason. They are not only major financial investments, but are extensions of our personalities as well. Most of us spend more time at home than anywhere else, and invest much time and energy in caring for our homes.

Too often, however, we don't spend enough time and energy in choosing our homes or in negotiating these purchases. Because the basic concepts and rules in buying and selling real estate are unfamiliar to most of us, we tend to leave too many things in the hands of the "experts" — the brokers and lawyers. This chapter will discuss those concepts and rules in a simplified way. While it won't make you into a real estate broker or lawyer, it will help you to understand what brokers and lawyers say so you will be able to use them to your best advantage. Most importantly, this chapter will help you know what questions to ask them.

THE REAL ESTATE BROKER

Since real estate brokers are involved in many, if not most, sales of homes, it is important to know where they can be helpful and where you are better off without them. Hopefully, this discussion will help you decide whether or not you need to employ a broker.

What is a real estate broker?

A real estate broker is a professional licensed to represent others, for a fee, in all types of real estate transactions. A broker will usually employ one or more salespeople who have less formal training but are licensed to assist the broker. With some exceptions,[1] it is unlawful for unlicensed persons to represent others for a fee in real estate transactions.[2]

What services does a broker provide?

A broker handles the details of *appraising* (setting a price on) the property; advertising it; showing it; negotiating a price; helping the buyer arrange financing; and, together with attorneys and title company (if any), preparing for the *closing*, in which the papers are signed and funds change hands.

What does a broker cost?

The most common commission for a broker in home sales, as of this writing, is 6 percent of the sale price. It may, however, be more or less in various neighborhoods and for various types of homes.

Who pays the broker?

The seller usually agrees to pay the broker, whose commission is deducted from the amount due the seller at the closing. Obviously, however, the broker's commission will tend to raise the price paid by the buyer. The buyer may be represented by his or her own broker, in which case the buyer, of course, pays that broker.

When should I sell my home without a broker?

Whether you can do without a broker depends on many circumstances, such as your knowledge of real estate transactions and the time you are willing to devote to making the sale. With the help of an appraiser and an attorney, whose combined fees will ordinarily be a small fraction of a 6 percent commission, many owners can do it successfully. Several books are available to help.[3]

Buying and Selling Homes   7

What terms will the broker want me to agree to?

There are several basic types of *listing* agreements with a broker. The type preferred by most is the *exclusive right to sell*, under which the broker is to receive the commission if the house is sold within a given time, no matter who makes the actual sale.

> Cedrick Squire decided to sell his estate in Forrest Meadows. He agreed to an exclusive right to sell listing with Francois Brocour, designating a 6-month period beginning August 1. On August 2, before Brocour had a chance to promote the sale, Squire decided to sell the property to his brother-in-law. Squire still owes Brocour his commission.

This type of listing has the advantage of putting the broker in a position to invest in advertising and other sales efforts, which may ultimately result in a higher price or faster sale or both.

At the other extreme is the *open listing,* which allows several brokers to attempt to sell the property at a given price. The first to sell earns the commission; or, if the owner sells, there is no commission. Open listings, which can lead to disputes among several brokers as to who actually "sold" the property, are not favored by brokers. Instead, the real estate industry has sought to meet the need for widespread listing through *multiple listing.* Under this system, all cooperating brokers obtain information on property offered by other cooperating brokers. Any of them may then make the sale, and the commission will be split with the broker who obtained the original listing.

THE EARNEST MONEY CONTRACT

The *statute of frauds* provides that an oral agreement for the sale of real estate is unenforceable.[4] The pupose of this is to prevent frauds and disputes that might develop if oral contracts to sell real estate could be enforced in court. The statute of frauds itself, however, leads to injustice if a person makes an oral agreement and spends money believing this to be valid, only to have the other party back out. To avoid this problem, buyers and sellers of real estate usually sign a written contract called an *earnest money contract* before the seller actually transfers title by signing the deed.

8   Buying, Renting & Borrowing in Texas

What is the purpose of an earnest money contract?

The written *earnest money contract* gives the seller the security to take the property off the market by providing an enforceable contract. It also gives the buyer the security to seek financing (lenders require it) and to incur the costs of a title search or title insurance and a property survey. All of these terms will be discussed below. If the buyer tries to back out of the agreement for a reason other than those allowed in the contract, the seller may keep the earnest money, sue for a court order to require the buyer to comply (for *specific performance*), or sue for damages. On the other hand, if the seller tries to back out for an impermissible reason, the buyer may sue for specific performance by the seller or sue for damages. In addition, the contract, if properly drafted, will eliminate later disputes about exactly what is being sold.

Buying and Selling Homes 9

Is professional assistance necessary in preparing the earnest money contract?

Both buyer and seller ordinarily benefit from professional assistance in preparing the earnest money contract. Although so-called "standard" forms are available, items must always be crossed out or added. Preparing a clear and complete contract will help prevent later disputes about exactly what is being sold and on what terms.

What if the seller does not have good title, or the buyer cannot obtain financing?

The buyer can always get out of the contract if the title search reveals defects in the title that the seller cannot or will not *cure*. For example, the seller may need to cure the title by obtaining a formal written release from a mortgage creditor who has not yet been paid off. The buyer can get out of most contracts also if the specified financing cannot be arranged after reasonable efforts have been made.

REAL ESTATE FINANCING

Real estate financing is a major source of investment for many types of financers. Most people think immediately of banks and savings and loan associations as sources of real estate loans, but many other channels are also open to some or all potential buyers.

What are the major sources of real estate loans?

A real estate broker can be very helpful in assisting the buyer to obtain a loan on the best available terms. Major sources of financing include the following: savings and loan associations (a very common source); commercial banks; life insurance companies (through mortgage brokers, or sometimes directly); mortgage banks; credit unions; individual and organizational investors (often through mortgage brokers); *owner financing* (the owner agrees that the difference between down payment and purchase price may be paid in installments, with interest); and *assumption* by the buyer of the debt still owed on the property. Especially when credit is tight, a diligent search for sources of loans and creative structuring of the transaction are often essential to make a sale possible.

What is the difference between an insured loan and a conventional loan?

An *insured* loan is one in which the lender is protected by government-provided insurance against the borrower's default. That is, if the borrower falls seriously behind in the payments, the insuring agency reimburses the lender for the amount owed on the loan. The agency then steps into the shoes of the lender and may foreclose or take other appropriate action. Most such loans are insured by the Federal Housing Authority (FHA loans) or the Veteran's Administration (VA or GI loans). Some insured loans are also available in certain localities for low-income housing.

A *conventional* loan is simply one that is not government-insured. Some conventional loans are, however, insured by private insurance policies with premiums paid by the borrower.

THE TITLE EXAMINATION

There is no document in real estate law similar to the certificate of title to an automobile. Who has what title can be determined only by examining the many documents recorded in the county courthouse which relate to the property.

How can I tell who has title to a particular piece of real estate?

All the events that change title to land — such as the owner's execution of deeds and liens, the creation of tax liens, and the owner's death — should be (but often are not) recorded in papers filed in the courthouse of the county in which the land is located. Thus, when Cedrick Squire signs a deed that says he is conveying certain land to Ava Ricious, Ricious obtains only the title Squire has in the land — if any. Whether Squire has any title, and exactly what "bundle of rights" it includes, is therefore a matter of great concern to Ricious before she buys the property.

How can the buyer be sure the seller has good title?

The buyer can obtain title protection through either a title search by an attorney or a title insurance policy. Either method should provide adequate protection.

A title search ordinarily begins with the preparation of an *abstract of title* by an abstract company. An abstract of title is a volume consisting of copies of all the papers that have ever been filed in the courthouse concerning the land. If an abstract has been prepared in the past, it may simply be supplemented with all the papers filed since its preparation. Instead of ordering an abstract, the attorney doing the title search may go directly to the courthouse and look through all the recorded documents.

A complete abstract will begin with the very first grant of the land by the *sovereign*. In Texas, the first sovereign to grant the title to a particular piece of land was either Spain, Mexico, the Republic of Texas, or the State of Texas. The attorney examines the documents to determine whether they show any defect in the title of the seller. If so, it will usually be possible to cure the defect by various legal procedures. When the attorney issues a *title opinion* stating that there are no defects or that they have been cured, the buyer can close the purchase with greater confidence.

The second method for obtaining protection for the buyer is to purchase title insurance. The title company itself conducts some form of title search before issuing a policy, although this may not be a complete search. Under the terms of the policy, the title company agrees to pay for any loss the buyer may suffer due to someone else's claiming rights in the land. Title insurance is the more common method for protecting the buyer, and many lenders require it.

THE SURVEY

A survey is a map showing the boundaries of a piece of property, according to a particular legal description. Licensed surveyors prepare these documents for a fee.

What is the purpose of a survey?

A survey is one more way for the buyer to be sure just what is being purchased. The seller has described the property by furnishing a legal description and by pointing out the boundaries on the ground. The title examination assures the buyer that the seller actually owns the property described in the legal description. The survey assures the buyer that the property described in the legal description is the same as that pointed out on the ground.

Cedrick Squire told Ava Ricious the north boundary of his estate ran from an implanted plaster cow to a styrofoam frog pond. Ava Ricious gave I. R. Precise, Surveyor, a legal description of the property and asked for a survey. Much to Ava's chagrin, the survey showed that the plaster cow was twenty feet outside the property line. Ava now knows that a dispute over the plaster cow may arise with the neighbor. She will take this problem into consideration in negotiations with Squire.

Is a survey always necessary?

A survey is not always necessary. A recent survey may be available, or property lines may otherwise be clear. Most lenders require a survey, however, and it is the most reliable method for determining exactly what you are buying.

THE CLOSING

A closing is a meeting at which everyone does what he or she agreed in the earnest money contract to do. Essentially, the buyer and the seller sign the legal papers, the required funds change hands, and both buyer and seller sign various papers disclosing the terms of the transaction.

The closing is most often held at the office of the title company. It may, however, be in the office of an attorney or broker. In simple sales, the closing is sometimes handled by mail.

What legal papers are involved in a real estate sale?

The seller signs a *deed*. If several persons own the property, all owners must sign the deed (or sign separate deeds). For example, property purchased during a marriage by either spouse is usually owned by both of them, so both spouses must sign a deed to transfer title.[5] To avoid later questions, both spouses are usually required to sign a deed regardless of actual community property status of the property.

Ordinarily, the type of deed signed is a *general warranty deed*. In this, the seller warrants (guarantees) that the seller's title is good. If it later turns out not to be good, the buyer (or a subsequent buyer) may sue the seller for the economic loss resulting from the title defect. Of course, the seller (and others signing warranty deeds on the same property) may then be unreachable or without funds to pay, in which case the buyer's only protection is title insurance (if any). In a *special warranty deed,* the seller guarantees only that no title defects have arisen since the seller obtained apparent title. This type of deed is rarely used. Finally, in a *quit-claim deed,* the seller makes no guarantees at all. This type of deed is ordinarily used only in family transactions in which the person transferring title is not being paid. When it is used in any other type of transaction, the mere fact that it is used at all may cast suspicion on the title and make the property difficult to sell.

The price shown on the deed is usually "ten dollars and other good and valuable consideration." This is perfectly legal and proper. The purpose of not showing the actual amount of the sale price is to allow the buyer discretion in releasing that information to potential buyers. However, if the sale is financed, the amount financed usually appears on the deed of trust (explained below), which is filed in the courthouse. Thus, a buyer can usually determine this information and, from it, speculate as to what the full price probably was. In many areas, real estate brokers have access to files showing actual sale prices.

When the sale is financed, a *vendor's lien* is reserved in the deed. This is the most favorable form of lien (see explanation below), and whoever does the financing gets the vendor's lien. The deed will then be called a *warranty deed with vendor's lien.*

The additional legal papers (discussed below) have to do with financing. They are signed by the buyer(s) to create the debt as well as the lien.

If the sale is financed rather than immediately paid in full in cash, the buyer signs a *promissory note.* This contains the exact amount of the principal, the interest rate, and how the debt is to be paid. The note may be sold (*negotiated*) from lender to lender, in which case the person or business to whom payments are made will change. If the sale is *owner financed,* the note is payable to the seller, and the seller receives the note rather than the full price immediately. If the sale is financed by a third party, the third party immediately pays the seller that part of the price in excess of the down payment, and the note is payable to the financer.

Cedrick Squire sells Ava Ricious a house for $30,000,

14   Buying, Renting & Borrowing in Texas

with $5,000 down. Squire does not owe anything on the house. If the sale is to be owner financed, Ricious will pay Squire $5,000 cash, pay her share of the closing costs, and sign a note payable to Squire for $25,000 plus interest. If the sale is to be financed by Lender Savings & Loan, Ricious will pay Squire $5,000 cash, pay her share of closing costs, and sign a note payable to Lender in the amount of $25,000 plus interest. Lender will then pay Squire $25,000. The total amount of the note (regardless of who finances) will be much greater than $25,000 because future interest on the note will have to be paid.

In addition to the papers mentioned above, the buyer will sign a *deed of trust*. The purpose of this paper is to give the financer (whether owner or third party) an easily enforceable lien on the property.

A *lien* is essentially the same as a *mortgage;* a third word for the same thing is *security interest.* Traditionally, liens on real estate are more commonly called mortgages, while liens on moveable property (*goods*) are called security interests. What these words all refer to is the right of a creditor to take specific property of a debtor to pay off the debt in the event of default. It is therefore said that the debt is *secured by* the property.

A deed of trust works as follows: The debtor (*grantor* on the deed of trust, who is the buyer in a real estate purchase) conveys *legal title* to the property to someone designated by the financer (whether seller or third party) as the financer's *trustee*. The debtor retains *equitable title*. The trustee is given the power to sell the property and use the proceeds to apply against the debt in the event that the debtor should default. The deed of trust also contains a long list of acts that would constitute default. The most important such act, of course, is failure to pay an installment on time; but there are others, such as failure to pay taxes and insurance, etc.

What happens to the legal papers in a real estate sale after they are signed?

The buyer records the deed. The financer (seller or third party) records the deed of trust, but not the note. After recording, each party receives back from the county clerk the paper that he or she recorded.

Buying and Selling Homes   15

Even without recording, the papers are effective between buyer and seller after each delivers papers signed by him or her to the other. Recording is important, however, because it puts the whole world on notice, legally, of the transaction. Otherwise, the seller could later sell the property to someone else, and if that person agreed to pay for it and bought it in good faith without notice of the prior sale, that person would then have title. The first buyer could sue the seller only for monetary damages.

How is real property sold when the seller still owes money on it?

The seller may not have finished paying the purchase price, may have given a lien on the property to a lending institution for a home improvement loan, or may have engaged in any number of other activities which have encumbered the title to the land. Ordinarily, this does not pose a serious problem in selling the property. Such a sale is handled in one of several standard ways. The seller may, of course, pay off the debt before the closing. Other standard options include *refinancing, assumption,* and the buyer's purchasing the property *subject* to the debt.

Refinancing is simply a matter of the third-party financer's lending the buyer the money to pay off the debt immediately. Refinancing is, in effect, a consolidation of the existing debt secured by the property with the new debt for the purchase price.

Assumption is an agreement by the buyer (usually in the deed) to pay the existing debt. It is said that the buyer *assumes* the debt. The buyer is then *personally* indebted to the creditor. This means that if the buyer defaults, and if that property sells at the foreclosure sale for less than the amount of the debt, the creditor may have other property of the buyer sold to pay off the remaining part of the debt (the *deficiency*). Also, if the buyer cannot or will not pay the deficiency, the creditor can still sue the seller, who remains liable as a *surety*.

> Cedrick Squire still owes $10,000 to Charlotte O'Hara on a house that Ava Ricious finally agreed to purchase for $30,000, with $5,000 down. This sale is to be owner financed. If Ava Ricious assumes the $10,000 debt to Charlotte O'Hara, then Ricious will pay Squire $5,000 cash and give him a $15,000 note. If Ricious defaults on

the debt to O'Hara, O'Hara can have the land sold. If this does not pay off the debt, O'Hara can also have other property that Ricious owns sold. If this still does not pay off the debt, O'Hara can then have Squire's property sold until she recovers the amount owed to her.

A sale *subject to* a debt is like an assumption, except that the buyer does not become *personally* indebted to the original creditor. The original creditor may have the property sold in the event of default and may cause the property of the seller to be sold, but the buyer can lose no more than the property bought. *Subject-to* agreements are rare in sales of homes.

Buying and Selling Homes

Does a refinancing or assumption require the approval of the seller's creditor?

Under certain conditions, a refinancing or assumption does require the creditor's approval. Some deeds of trust have a *call clause* which provides that, if the property is sold without the creditor's permission, the entire unpaid balance of the loan may be *called due*. Then, there will be a default if the entire loan is not paid off immediately.

If the deed of trust securing the existing debt has a call clause, then usually the only alternative is to arrange refinancing of the debt with the same creditor, in return for the creditor's approving the sale. The buyer must go to the same creditor to add the balance (if any) of the purchase price onto the same loan in which the buyer agrees to pay the existing debt. That is, of course, exactly what the creditor wants and is the main purpose for which the call clause was invented.

The only safe way to get around the call clause is to refinance with another lender. This is often not economically feasible, however, as the same deed of trust will usually provide for a substantial penalty for prepayment (including prepayment by refinancing). The call clause/prepayment penalty arrangement is obviously anti-competitive and is possibly unconscionable in the legal sense. Some day this practice may be invalidated by the courts or the Legislature, but until then the lending institutions will maintain a firm grip on their existing accounts.

Is a formal closing always necessary in real estate sales?

A formal closing is not legally required. It is a procedure that has been devised to minimize misunderstandings and later legal problems in ordinary transactions, and some title companies require it for this reason. A closing, however, is unnecessary in many transactions, such as cash sales and transfers within a family without payment.

THE CONTRACT FOR DEED ALTERNATIVE

In the real estate procedure discussed above, a deed is made out to the buyer only a short time (usually from a week to a month) after signing of the earnest money contract. An alternative to this procedure, where the owner finances the sale, is for the buyer and seller to sign a contract calling for installment payments over a long period of time, with a deed signed only after all payments have been made. This is called a *contract for deed, contract of sale, executory contract for conveyance, installment land contract* and other similar names.

How does a contract for deed differ in result from a sale involving a deed, note and deed of trust?

As long as each party complies with the contract, the end result is the same. In practice, however, both parties seldom comply with these contracts (for reasons suggested below), so the contracts often end up being long-term rental agreements.

What advantages does a contract for deed have for the buyer?

The contract for deed allows the buyer to move into the house without paying closing costs or a substantial down payment. For this reason, it is used primarily for selling to low-income persons. Such an arrangement has the advantage, in comparison with a rental agreement, of allowing the occupant to stay indefinitely, without an increase in monthly payments, as long as no default occurs.

What disadvantages does a contract for deed have for the buyer, and what can the buyer do to minimize the disadvantages?

A contract for deed makes it much easier for the seller to take back the property (see next question). The buyer should read very carefully the terms of the contract, which usually requires the buyer to pay taxes and insurance, to keep the house in good condition, etc. The contract for deed provides that the seller may take back the property if the buyer fails to do any of these things.

Usually no provision is made for an "escrow fund" requiring part of the monthly payments to be set aside to cover taxes and insurance. Most institutional lenders provide for such funds in their deeds of trust, so the buyer automatically takes care of taxes and insurance through the monthly payments. Some contracts for deed

Buying and Selling Homes   19

provide that the seller may pay taxes and insurance, but a separate fund is seldom set up. As a result, when the seller does pay, these payments are added to the principal of the debt. Thus, some buyers may find that, after paying for years, they owe more than they did at the beginning. *A buyer who seriously intends to own the property some day should pay all taxes and insurance as they come due.*

At the end of the payment period (often 20 years or more), the seller may be unable or unwilling to sign a deed. The seller may have died, leaving heirs who are too young or too obstinate to sign, in which case the buyer must file a lawsuit. The buyer can obtain some protection by asking the seller to sign a deed immediately, then leave it in trust with a third party who will deliver it after the contract has been paid off.

Another problem that may arise during the payment period is that the seller may lose all or part of the title to the property. The seller may sell or mortgage the property to someone else, or liens may be imposed because of the seller's bankruptcy or failure to pay federal taxes. The buyer can prevent some of these calamities by *acknowledging* the contract before a notary public and recording it in the county deed records.[6] Some contracts, however, prohibit such recording (thus allowing the seller to keep the record clear regarding his or her title), and provide that the seller may take the property back if such recording is done. The validity of such forfeiture provisions is legally questionable.[7]

A second protection for the buyer is that as long as he or she is occupying the property, other potential buyers and lenders are probably on *notice* of the occupant's interest in the property. Under the law, a person who has received such notice cannot acquire a valid title or mortgage.

Title problems may also arise regarding the condition of the seller's title even at the time of the sale. For example, a developer of a low-income subdivision may sell lots on contracts for deed out of a tract of land that is heavily mortgaged. If the development then fails to make money, the developer will default, and the bank will foreclose on all of the land. *The buyer should have an attorney check the seller's title before signing a contract for deed.*

Finally, upon default the buyer may lose his or her *equity* in the property. Equity is simply the difference between the *present* market value of the property and the amount the buyer still owes on it. The buyer will have equity if he or she has paid a large part of the debt, if the property's value has increased substantially since the purchase, or both. Although one court case has established that the seller should pay the buyer's equity upon taking back the property,[8] a recent statute may indirectly have changed that rule.[9] A defaulting buyer with substantial equity should always consult an attorney.

What happens when the buyer defaults on a contract for deed?

The statute just mentioned above requires, at least in some cases, that the defaulting buyer be given notice and an opportunity to catch up on payments within certain specified time limits, with length of time dependent upon how much of the debt has been paid. This rule applies only where the property is used or is to be used as the purchaser's residence. It is further limited to cases in which the seller is seeking forfeiture of future interest and *acceleration* of the debt. Several courts have held that the notice requirement exists only where forfeiture of *equity* is sought and where the seller also seeks to make the debtor liable for future installments by *accelerating* the debt (calling it due immediately).[10] Thus, if the seller wants only to take the property back, and the buyer has no equity, the notice statute may not apply. The last word may not have been spoken by the courts on this, however. Consult an attorney to determine what notice is required in any particular case.

Once the required notice (if any) is given, the seller usually treats the buyer as a "tenant" and brings a *forcible detainer* (eviction) suit in a justice of the peace court. See *Chapter 2, Renting Homes and Apartments* for more information on this procedure. Herein lies the main advantage to the seller of the contract for deed, since an eviction action (which can be done easily without an attorney) is the cheapest and quickest lawful way to remove someone from a house. A *deed of trust foreclosure* (see *Chapter 4, Foreclosure on Homes*) takes at least a month and requires an attorney, and a suit in district court is much more costly and time consuming.

An argument can be made that an eviction action is not proper here,[11] especially where there is no clause providing for it in the contract for deed.[12] If so, the seller's only remedy is a slow and expensive suit in district court. If you are a buyer on a contract for deed who is threatened with foreclosure and wants to hold onto the property, this is all the more reason to consult an attorney.

Chapter 2
Renting Homes and Apartments

Landlord-tenant law in Texas in a fascinating blend of centuries-old common law and very recent acts of the Texas Legislature. It is fascinating, that is, to those who are uncommonly interested in legal history. To the rest of us, too often, it can be just plain confusing.

This chapter will try to take some of the confusion out of Texas landlord-tenant law concerning *residential* houses and apartments. Some of the rules are different for property used commercially, such as offices, shops and factories.

THE RENTAL AGREEMENT

The rental agreement is the first source of "law" to look to in a landlord-tenant dispute. What it says will ordinarily be enforced by the courts, although some specific provisions (some of which are discussed in this chapter) are not enforceable.

We will use the term *rental agreement* to refer to every agreement that creates a landlord-tenant relationship, whether the agreement is written or oral. Although the term "lease" is popularly used to refer to a written rental agreement, we will use the latter term, because in technical legal language a *lease* can be either written or oral.

Oral rental agreements are usually much simpler than written rental agreements:

> "I'll rent you this apartment for $250 per month, including utilities."
>
> "Fine, I'll take it."

Because such an agreement itself provides few rules, the rules set out by the legislature and the courts will apply. Those rules will be discussed in the latter parts of this chapter. This first part will discuss the rules concerning interpretation and enforcement of rental agreements themselves.

How is an enforceable rental agreement made?

The rental agreement need not be in writing unless it is for a term longer than one year.[1] Even if it is for longer than a year, however, it is enforceable under some conditions after the tenant moves in and begins paying rent.[2]

Even if the rental agreement is written, you can change the terms in the printed form by agreement with the landlord:

> Will Rent wants to move into the Swinging Singles Arms apartment complex, whose written rental agreement prohibits pets. Will has a very small cat, Tiny Terror. The manager agrees that Tiny can stay if Will makes a "pet deposit" and pays to have the apartment fumigated when he leaves. Will crosses out the "no pets" clause in the rental agreement and writes in by hand his agreements with the manager. Both Will and the manager initial the changes and sign the rental agreement. The agreement about the cat is now part of the rental agreement.

Who usually benefits from a written rental agreement?

Because landlords' attorneys write most written rental agreements, tenants are usually better off without them. To a large extent, they are written for the purpose of altering the usual rules of law, to the landlord's advantage. For example, many written rental agreements provide that the landlord may terminate the tenancy if the tenant breaks any of the rules or fails to perform any promise contained in the lease. No such provision ever applies to the landlord's promises.

Another advantage to the tenant of an oral rental agreement is that the tenant may be able to persuade the landlord to make promises rarely found in a written agreement. Such promises, if made as part of the original oral agreement, are just as enforceable as if made in writing:

> While Lee Swell was looking over Agua Dulce Manor, the manager sang the praises of his apartments. When he told Lee the plumbing was in mint condition, Lee asked if the landlord would fix it if it broke down. "Oh sure, no sweat," the manager promised, and they agreed orally that Lee would rent an apartment. Six months later when the toilet began to run, the landlord was obliged to fix it at no cost to Lee.

What if the landlord sells the building before the rental agreement expires?

After the sale of a building, the new owner is bound by all rental agreements concerning the building.[3]

The rest of this chapter discusses the law that applies to situations not discussed directly in the rental agreement (whether it be oral or written). No agreement can cover all situations, so you must know these general rules to know your rights.

THE TENANT'S RIGHT TO "QUIET ENJOYMENT"

Under an ancient court-made rule called the *covenant of quiet enjoyment*, every rental agreement (oral or written) contains an implied promise by the landlord not to evict the tenant wrongfully or otherwise disturb the tenant's right to live in peace and quiet.

Can a landlord enter the premises without my permission?

Unless the rental agreement provides otherwise, the landlord cannot enter the premises without the tenant's permission.[4] However, most written rental agreements provide that the landlord may enter to make repairs, show the property to prospective tenants, etc.

Is the landlord responsible if someone else bothers me?

This covenant of quiet enjoyment is no guarantee by the landlord that someone else will not disturb the tenant. Therefore, if the neighborhood children storm through the house, disturb your sleep and break the Ming vase, you can't sue the landlord.

A tenant does have some protection under this "covenant" if the disturbance is caused by other tenants of the landlord, either in the same building or on adjoining property. The landlord, as well as the offending tenant, may be legally responsible if the landlord consents to the offensive conduct or has knowledge of it. Will Rent had this problem and here is how he solved it:

> After Will and his cat had lived at the Swinging Singles Arms for a few months, Will complained to the apartment manager that another tenant's dog was barking all night long. Although that tenant had not negotiated a clause in her rental agreement permitting the dog, the manager did nothing. Will moved out, and the landlord sued for breach of the lease. The court held that Will had a right to move out since the landlord's failure to enforce the rules was a "constructive eviction."[5]

In some cases in other states, landlords have been held liable for injuries resulting from crimes committed against tenants. The cases have usually involved landlords who were found to have agreed, expressly or impliedly, to take certain measures to protect tenants from such crimes. Although Texas courts may, in some cases, find that landlords have voluntarily assumed various duties to safeguard tenants, landlords do not generally have a duty to provide security measures.[6]

REPAIRS AND IMPROVEMENTS

Until very recently, landlords were under no obligation to make any repairs, except when the rental agreement specifically required them to do so. In a landmark case in 1978, however, the Texas Supreme Court held that a *warranty of habitability* is implied in every rental agreement.[7] Then, in 1979, the Texas Legislature replaced this court-made rule with a detailed statute regulating repairs of rented homes and apartments.[8]

The tenant's rights under that statute may, however, be *waived* (given up) in the rental agreement. Any such waiver is effective only if it appears in writing, is underlined or printed in bold-face type, and specifically and clearly defines what rights are being waived. Therefore, as with most questions about landlord-tenant law, the rental agreement often determines who is responsible for what repairs.

What repairs must the landlord make?

Unless a valid waiver has been written into the rental agreement, a landlord generally must repair or remedy *any condition which materially affects the physical health or safety of an ordinary tenant.* The only exception is for conditions *other than normal wear and tear* that are caused by the tenant. "Normal wear and tear" is defined by Texas law as that "deterioration which occurs, based upon the use for which the rental unit is intended, without negligence, carelessness, accident, or abuse of the premises or equipment or chattels [moveable things] by the tenant or members of his household, or his invitees or guests. Provided, however, 'accident' shall not include breakage or malfunction due to age or deteriorated condition."

> Lisa Castle, another tenant at the Swinging Singles Arms, noticed that the furnace in her apartment had developed a gas leak caused by normal deterioration of a valve. Although, in a way, Lisa had "caused" the leak by turning the valve many times, the landlord had to repair it because the leak was caused by "ordinary wear and tear" and because it affected Lisa's physical health and safety.

What repairs must I make?

You must repair any damage to the landlord's property that you (or someone on the premises with your permission) causes intentionally or negligently. *Negligence* means carelessness, in the sense of failing to exercise the ordinary care of a reasonably prudent person in the same or similar circumstances.

> While Will was cleaning his rifle in his apartment, the gun fired because Will had failed to check to see if it was loaded. The bullet broke a gas pipe. Since the damage resulted from Will's negligence in failing to unload the rifle, he had to pay for the damage.

Some rental agreements may also require a tenant to pay for accidental damages, even if the damage was not caused by negligence.[9] Whether such a clause would be enforceable is questionable.

In many cases, there may be honest disagreement as to whether a particular repair was caused by "normal wear and tear" or by "negligence." In such a case, the landlord and the tenant may resolve their disagreement by a compromise (each paying part of the cost of repair) or by going to court.

> A few months after the landlord replaced Lisa's leaky valve, the furnace in her apartment developed a gas leak at a joint in the pipe. The joint was rusty, but it was the place where Lisa customarily banged on the pipe with a wrench when Will's stereo disturbed her. The issue was whether the "cause" of the leak was the pipe's rust or Lisa's banging, and reasonable people might disagree on the answer. Lisa and the landlord could agree to share the cost of the repairs, or they could each take their chances in court.

Notice that *nobody* is *required* to repair conditions that result from ordinary wear and tear but which would not materially affect the physical health or safety of an ordinary tenant. This is the case, for example, with a carpet that has developed holes from ordinary use. Since the worn carpet does not affect physical health or safety, the landlord is not required to replace it; but since it was damaged by ordinary wear and tear, the tenant is not required to replace it either. The tenant must live with the problem if it is not repaired, but, if the tenant moves out, the landlord will probably have to repair it to attract another tenant.

Ordinarily, an understanding develops between landlord and tenant about these non-essential repairs. Either the tenant ordinarily makes them because the rent is low enough to justify the cost, or the landlord makes them because the rent is high enough to cover them. Ultimately, if the cost of these repairs becomes unbearable, the tenant will move out and leave them to the landlord. Therefore, most landlords do make these "optional" repairs to a reasonable extent and simply pass the costs on to the tenants through the rent. Many written rental agreements spell out in detail what repairs the landlord will make.

What can I do to require a landlord to make repairs?

The procedure you *must* follow to require a landlord to make repairs is set out in detail in the Texas statute. Follow these steps *very* carefully:

1. **Tell the landlord exactly what needs to be repaired.** Your rental agreement may require this notice to be in writing, and it is in your best interest to put it in writing anyway. Deliver it personally or send it by certified mail, return receipt requested. See the sample notice labeled "First Notice of Need for Repair."

FIRST NOTICE OF NEED FOR REPAIR

June 1, 1980
T. Tim Tenant
1001 Hardknocks Lane, Apt. 103
Houston, Texas 77025

Mr. U. Scrooge
U. Scrooge Properties, Inc.
501 Depreciation Blvd.
Fat City, Texas 77001

Dear Mr. Scrooge:

This is to let you know that there is a gas leak in the kitchen stove in my apartment at the above address. I can smell the gas when the house is closed up.

Please have this fixed as soon as possible.

Sincerely yours,
T. Tim Tenant

Certified No. _____
Return Receipt Requested

2. **If repairs are not made within a reasonable time, send a second written notice.** You should decide at this point whether you want to move out or not, because you must give the landlord seven days' notice before leaving. Also, be sure to ask for a written explanation of reasons for the delay in making the repairs. If the landlord fails to provide it and you file a lawsuit, the court will presume the delay was unreasonable unless the landlord proves otherwise. See the sample notice labeled "Second Notice of Need for Repair."

SECOND NOTICE OF NEED FOR REPAIR

June 15, 1980
T. Tim Tenant
1001 Hardknocks Lane, Apt. 103
Houston, Texas 77025

Mr. U. Scrooge
U. Scrooge Properties, Inc.
501 Depreciation Blvd.
Fat City, Texas 77001

Dear Mr. Scrooge:

 This is in reference to the request in my letter of June 1, which you received on June 3, that you fix the gas leak in my apartment at the above address.

 The leak still has not been fixed, nor have I heard from you about it. Unless it is fixed within seven days from your receipt of this letter, I intend to (file a lawsuit) (terminate my rental agreement and file a lawsuit) under Art. 5236f of the Texas statutes.

 If you are unable to fix it within that seven days, please send me a written explanation of the reasons for the delay.

      Sincerely yours,
      T. Tim Tenant

Certified No. _____
Return Receipt Requested

Renting Homes and Apartments   29

3. **If repairs are not made within seven days of the landlord's receipt of your second notice, see a lawyer.** At this point, you can file suit for one month's rent, plus $100, plus actual damages (if any) resulting from the delay, plus court costs and your attorney fees. You can recover all of this regardless of whether you move out and regardless of whether the landlord makes the repairs before a judgment is entered in your favor, if you have given the notices explained above. In addition, if you choose not to move out you can obtain a court order requiring the landlord to make the required repairs and reducing your rent to account for the bad condition of the rental unit.

So far, the discussion has focused on requiring a landlord to make *repairs*. Actually, the landlord's duty is to *"repair or remedy any condition* which materially affects the physical health or safety of an ordinary tenant." Therefore, if the tenant is *affected* by a *condition*, such as being overrun with rats or roaches, then the landlord's duty is the same as when *repairs* are needed. The landlord must remedy the condition by exterminating the rats or roaches.

Can a landlord evict a tenant for demanding that repairs be made?

It is against the law for a landlord to evict a tenant in order to retaliate for demands that the landlord make legally required repairs. This is enforced by the following law: if a landlord files a suit for eviction within six months of the tenant's repair notice, the tenant can have the suit thrown out of court by proving as follows: that the purpose of the eviction was to retaliate for the repair notice; that the repair notice complained of conditions that would, in fact, materially affect the health and safety of the ordinary tenant; and that the repair notice was received by the landlord *before* the landlord filed the eviction suit.

Such retaliation by a landlord gives you the right to sue for one month's rent, plus $100, plus moving costs (if any), plus court costs and attorney fees. You may also bring suit if the landlord, within six months of your repair notice, retaliates by unlawfully interfering with your use of the premises, decreasing services, terminating the rental agreement, or increasing the rent.

However, you lose your right to sue the landlord for such retaliation *and* are subject to being evicted in the following situations:

- if you are behind in paying the rent at the time of a written notice to vacate *or* at the time of filing the eviction lawsuit;
- if property damage to the rental unit was *intentionally* caused by you or your family or guests;
- if you, your family or your guests have threatened, by word or conduct, the personal safety of the landlord, the landlord's employees or other tenants;
- if you have materially breached the rental agreement (but if you have merely stayed beyond the end of the rental agreement [*held over*], then there are no grounds for eviction, except as indicated below);
- if you have stayed after giving notice of termination of the rental agreement at the end of the rental term, *and* if the landlord's termination notice was prior to receipt of your repair notice;
- if you held over, and the landlord's notice of termination was motivated by a good faith belief that you or your family or guests may (a) adversely affect the quiet enjoyment of other tenants or neighbors, (b) materially affect the health or safety of the landlord,

other tenants, or neighbors, or (c) cause damage to the property of the landlord, other tenants, or neighbors.

Can I withhold rent if the landlord has failed to make repairs?

Even if the landlord has wrongfully failed to make needed repairs, you cannot lawfully retaliate by withholding rent. Your only lawful response is to go through the notice procedure explained above and, if necessary, to court. If you withhold rent in retaliation for the landlord's alleged failure to repair *and* the landlord has given written notice of the possible penalties, the landlord may then sue you for one month's rent, plus $100, plus court costs and the landlord's attorney fees.

What are my rights and the landlord's rights if the rental unit is damaged by fire or storm?

In addition to the rules regarding repairs, several special rules govern damage caused by fire, smoke, hail, explosion, etc. For one thing, if the landlord is insured against such a loss, then the time period within which repairs must be made does not begin until the landlord receives the insurance money.

If such a casualty loss makes the rental unit totally unusable, and if the loss was not caused by your negligence or that of your family or guests, then either you or the landlord may terminate the rental agreement at any time before repairs are completed. In that case, you are entitled to recover any rent paid for a period of time after moving out, plus whatever amount of security deposit may be due.

If such a casualty loss makes the rental unit only partially unusable, and if the loss was not caused by your negligence or that of your family or your guests, then you have the right to a rent reduction in relation to the extent of unusability of the unit. The catch here is that unless you and the landlord can agree on the proper amount of rent reduction, you must obtain a court order before withholding any part of the rent. Otherwise, you will be subject to eviction and a lawsuit for retaliatory rent withholding as discussed above.

May I be evicted for reporting housing code violations?

Most cities have housing codes requiring that buildings meet minimal standards of safety, sanitation, etc. Requiring the landlord to meet these standards is one way of obtaining needed repairs. The only Texas appellate court to consider this question has held that a retaliatory eviction for reporting housing code violations is illegal.[10] Therefore, even if you rent on a month-to-month basis, you can probably defend against an eviction if you can prove that the reason the landlord did not renew your tenancy was to retaliate against you for reporting a housing code violation. If the condition you complained of is one that materially affects the physical health or safety of an ordinary tenant, then you are entitled to the retaliation defense and civil penalties discussed above. Since any condition that violates a housing code will probably also affect one's physical health or safety, you should be on firm ground with such a defense. Remember, however, that you must give the notices described above before the landlord files the eviction suit in order to raise this defense.

Can I remove an improvement I have made on the premises?

The general rule is that permanent improvements may not be removed from the property unless the landlord agrees before construction that they may be removed.[11] Therefore, before installing or building anything that might possibly be considered permanent, be sure to get the landlord's agreement that you can take it with you when you move.

If the tenant has already erected an improvement without such an agreement, the situation calls for some judgement. For example, the tenant may have installed a new hot water heater. The tenant may decide to ask the landlord's permission to take it, hoping the landlord will give his consent. Or, the tenant may decide to take it without further discussion, leaving it to the landlord to pursue any legal remedies. Or, the tenant may want to avoid a dispute by leaving it. An attorney's advice may be worth seeking in dealing with disputes concerning very valuable improvements.

TERMINATION OF TENANCY:
WHEN THE TENANT MAY — AND MUST — MOVE OUT

A Texas statute determines what notice must be given to terminate certain rental agreements.[12] For simplicity, the agreements covered by this statute will be called *periodic tenancies*; all other tenancies will be referred to as *fixed-term tenancies*. The following questions and answers explain the rules applying to both periodic and fixed-term tenancies.

Periodic Tenancies

If the rental agreement, whether oral or written, does not specify that the tenant will stay for a certain time longer than one month, the tenant has a *periodic tenancy*.[13] Every time the rent is paid, the tenancy is automatically renewed for the length of the period between payments. For example, if the rent is paid monthly, each payment of rent extends the tenancy until the date rent is due the next month. If rent is paid weekly, of course, the period of renewal is only one week.

> Lisa Castle and the manager of the Swinging Singles Arms agreed that she would rent a one-bedroom apartment for $250 a month. Nothing was said about how long Lisa would stay, so Lisa's contract was for a periodic tenancy. Will Rent, however, wanted to make sure the rent wasn't raised on him in the coming months so he asked the manager for a six-month lease. The manager agreed, so Will got a fixed-term tenancy.

How much notice is required to terminate a periodic tenancy?

Either tenant or landlord can terminate a periodic tenancy with notice equal to the period between payments.[14] Thus, if rent is paid by the month, either party can cancel the rental agreement with one month's notice. The following example illustrates how this works with a periodic tenancy:

> Lisa Castle paid her $250 monthly rent on July 1, the date it was due. On July 15, her apartment manager told her he wanted her out within a week so he could rent to a relative. Lisa could lawfully stay until August 15 because she had a right to one month's notice.

Of course, if landlord and tenant agree that the tenancy will terminate earlier or later than the date set by these rules, their agreement will be effective. Therefore, Lisa may agree to leave voluntarily on July 22, in which case the landlord should refund the rent for the last week in July.

How is the rent adjusted if the tenancy is terminated in the middle of the month?

As shown in the example above, a periodic tenancy with rent payable monthly will terminate 30 days after notice of termination is given. On the date the rent is due after the date notice is given, you will owe rent only for that part of the month up to the date of termination. Therefore, if Lisa decided to stay as long as she lawfully could (until August 15), she would owe only one half the monthly rent on August 1.

Must the landlord give the required notice even if I am behind in the rent?

The notice requirements do *not* apply if there is *any* breach of the rental agreement, including being behind on the rent. When a landlord has the right to terminate the tenancy and evict you for nonpayment of rent, you have the right to only 3 days' notice:[15]

> In Lisa's case, if she had missed the July 1 rent payment and the landlord told her on July 15 to leave, she would have had only three days to pack up and move before the tenancy expired. Of course, she would be legally liable for the rent from July 1 through the day she actually left.

Fixed-Term Tenancies

If a rental agreement, whether written or oral, specifies that you will stay for a certain time longer than one month, you have a *fixed-term tenancy*. The notice provisions (discussed above) that apply to a periodic tenancy do not apply to a fixed-term tenancy. The tenancy simply terminates on the date agreed upon unless you and your landlord agree (expressly or by implication) to extend or shorten it.

What happens if I stay past the end of a fixed-term tenancy?

If you are nearing the end of your lease, it is time to talk to the landlord. If you stay after the original term expires without reaching an agreement with the landlord, the landlord has two choices. The landlord may treat you as a trespasser or may assume you have

Renting Homes and Apartments

agreed to extend the rental agreement for the same fixed term as before, except that if the lease was for longer than one year, the new tenancy will be for only one year.[16]

> Will Rent's original lease was for a fixed term of one year, beginning September 1, 1977, with rent due the first of each month. Will graduated from college in August 1978 and intended to stay only through September before moving to Houston to take his first job. Will paid the rent as usual on September 1, 1978 and stayed in the apartment. The landlord was within his legal rights when he considered Will's lease renewed for another twelve months.

Many written rental agreements for fixed-term tenancies have provisions that apply to termination of the tenancy. For example, some require notice by the tenant at least 30 days before the termination date in order for the tenancy actually to terminate on that date. Others provide that if the tenant stays after the termination date, the tenancy is converted to a month-to-month periodic tenancy. Such provisions in the rental agreement will control over the general rules discussed above.

Cancellation for Breach of the Rental Agreement

This section is important primarily to tenants with a rental agreement for a fixed term. Since a month-to-month tenancy can be terminated by either party on 30-days' notice, neither party ordinarily has to look for a breach by the other in order to end the tenancy.

If the landlord breaches the agreement, can I terminate the tenancy?

In the absence of an *agreement* by landlord and tenant that a breach by one allows cancellation by the other, such cancellation is generally not permissible.[17] If, for example, Will Rent agreed not to have pets but kept his cat at the apartment anyway, the landlord would have to let Will stay. The landlord's only remedy would be to recover damages from the property deposit or by suit. However, most written rental agreements provide that the landlord may cancel for any breach by the tenant. Unless you insist that similar provisions covering breaches by the landlord are added to the lease, the landlord's lease will not include such a breach of agreement clause for you.

The law probably does require the landlord to give notice that you are breaching the agreement and to allow you an opportunity to stop doing it before the landlord cancels.[18] However, it is possible that even this protection can be taken away by a clause in the lease.[19]

> Will's rental agreement at the Swinging Singles Arms prohibits making loud sounds or disturbing the tenants in any other fashion after 10 p.m. Despite this restriction, Will threw a party to celebrate the end of final exams and played and sang falsetto to old Beach Boys albums. Several of the tenants complained to the landlord, who warned Will he would be evicted if there were any more loud parties. The landlord probably could not terminate the tenancy for this incident alone, unless a clause in the lease so provided.

Termination of the Tenancy By Eviction

By evicting the tenant, the landlord terminates the tenancy, thus releasing the tenant from the duty to pay further rent.[20] Although some rental agreements contain clauses to the contrary, they are probably unenforceable.[21]

Under what circumstances can I correctly claim to have been evicted?

There are two types of evictions: *actual* and *constructive*. In an *actual eviction*, the landlord either tells you to move out or actually removes you bodily. Actual removal may be done by a court-ordered eviction (or threat of one), or forcefully (and unlawfully) without a court order. Either telling you to move out or actually removing you constitutes an eviction and releases you from further obligations to the landlord.

In a *constructive eviction*, the landlord materially and permanently interferes with your use of the premises. As a result, you may leave and not be held responsible for any more rent.[22]

The landlord, who lived next door to Will Rent, frequently had loud, all-night parties that made it impossible for Will to study or sleep. As a result, he moved out before the end of the term. Will properly terminated his tenancy and does not owe any future rent.

HOW TO RECOVER A SECURITY DEPOSIT

Many landlords require their tenants to pay a certain sum (usually a month's rent) when they move in to guarantee that they will pay rent before moving and pay for any repairs for which they are responsible. It is proper for a landlord to withhold part or all of the security deposit when the tenant moves, if the tenant actually owes the landlord the amount withheld. Some landlords, however, have made a practice of refusing ever to return security deposits. In response to this problem, the Texas Legislature has set out some important rules to help tenants recover security deposits that ought to be returned.

How soon must a landlord return a security deposit?

The basic rule is that security deposits must be refunded within thirty days after the tenant leaves. This rule is subject to several provisions:

- If the rental agreement contains a requirement that you give advance notice of surrender (moving out) as a condition of return of the security deposit — and if this requirement is underlined or printed in conspicuous, bold print — then you must comply with this notice requirement in order to have the security deposit refunded.

- The landlord is not obligated to return the security deposit until you furnish a *written* notice of your forwarding address. The same applies to the written description of damages and charges the landlord is required to send you if the whole security deposit is not being returned. The best way to send the forwarding address is by certified mail, return receipt requested, so you will have proof the landlord received it.

- If the landlord intends to withhold all or part of the security deposit, you must be furnished with a written description and itemized list of all deductions. However, if any rentals are due at the time you leave and there is no dispute about the amount, the landlord need not furnish an itemized list of deductions.

What kinds of expenses can a landlord deduct from a security deposit?

The landlord cannot deduct from the security deposit for "normal wear and tear." Just what deterioration constitutes normal wear and tear is frequently debated by landlords and tenants, but the legal definition in Texas is "that deterioration which occurs, based upon the use for which the rental unit is intended, without negligence, carelessness, accident, or abuse of the premises or equipment or chattels (moveable property) by the tenant or members of his household, or his invitees or guests."

> When Will Rent moved into his apartment, the carpet was nearly new, but the drapes were worn and faded. During the year he was there, the carpet became slightly frayed from normal traffic, and Tiny Terror, Will's cat, shredded the drapes. The landlord can charge Will only for damage to the drapes, because the carpet suffered no more than normal wear and tear.

What can I do if the landlord fails to return the security deposit?

A landlord who in *bad faith* retains a security deposit in violation of the rules outlined above is liable for $100, plus three times the amount of the security deposit wrongfully withheld, plus your reasonable attorney fees. If the landlord keeps a security deposit for thirty days after you have left and given a forwarding address, the landlord will then be presumed to have acted in bad faith unless he or she proves otherwise.

> Will's lease ended on August 31. Before that date, he gave notice that he was moving out, as required by the lease, along with written notice of the forwarding address to which his $150 security deposit was to be sent. His rent was paid through August 31, and he had caused no damage other than normal wear and tear. Will left on August 31, but by October 1 he still had not received any part of his security deposit. Will can sue for $100,

plus $450, plus a reasonable attorney fee. Unless the landlord can prove that he did not act in "bad faith," Will should win the suit. If the landlord proves he did not act in "bad faith," Will can expect to recover only his $150 deposit.

What can I do if the landlord withholds money for damages but fails to provide a written list of charges?

If the landlord, in *bad faith,* fails to provide the required written, itemized list of charges, you can sue for the entire security deposit plus reasonable attorney fees. Again, the landlord's bad faith is presumed simply from the failure to furnish a list of charges. It is then up to the landlord to prove otherwise.

What can the landlord do if I withhold the last month's rent?

Before the Texas landlord-tenant statute was revised in 1973, some landlords routinely kept security deposits. Knowing this, some tenants routinely withheld the last month's rent to be sure they would come out even. *Don't do it!* You will be liable, if the withholding was done in bad faith, for three times the amount of the rent withheld, plus the landlord's reasonable attorney fees. Bad faith will be presumed simply from the fact that the last month's rent was withheld.

THE LANDLORD'S CLAIM FOR RENT: WHAT HAPPENS IF THE TENANT "BREACHES THE LEASE"

Earlier in this chapter, Will Rent found himself obligated to another full year's lease when he had intended to stay only an extra month. The problems he may face in that situation, which are the same as those of a tenant who must move for any reason before a rental agreement expires, are discussed below.

What can a landlord do if I leave before the rental agreement expires?

The landlord has three options if you leave before the tenancy expires. The landlord can leave the place vacant and sue at the end of the term for all the unpaid rent. The landlord can sue immediately for damages equaling the difference between the rent you agreed to pay for the rest of the term and the reasonable rental value of the premises for the rest of the term (if higher than the agreed price). Finally, the landlord can rent to someone else if and when possible (or use the place in some other manner) and sue you for any loss of rent due to your moving out.

Landlords, however, rarely sue tenants who leave early. To do so would require paying an attorney, and the landlord would not be able to collect a judgment unless the tenant had some non-exempt property. (See *Chapter 15, The Homestead and Other Judgment Exemptions*.) Therefore, although there is no obligation to find another tenant, most landlords will try to do so. Then, even if the landlord does sue, the damages will be reduced by the amount of any rent collected from the new tenant(s) during the remainder of the former tenant's term.

Many rental agreements contain clauses allowing the landlord to recover *liquidated damages,* a specified amount of money awarded without regard to the facts of a particular case. Some of these clauses may be enforceable, but many are not.[23] You should never pay liquidated damages without consulting an attorney.

The usual effect of moving before the lease expires is that you lose the security deposit. Some landlords also send indignant letters or turn the matter over to a collection agency. In matters such as these, see *Chapter 16, Debt Collection Practices*.

How can I leave before the lease expires and not lose money?

One way of avoiding this problem is to *sublet,* that is, to find someone to "take over the lease" for the rest of the term. However, this cannot legally be done without the consent of the landlord.[24] Therefore, you should obtain the landlord's consent to the subletting, if at all possible. It is better still, for reasons discussed below, to try to get the landlord to agree to end your tenancy and have the new tenant enter into a separate agreement.

Even without the prior consent of the landlord, however, a subletting arrangement can be established if the new tenant simply moves in and the landlord accepts the rent without objection.[25] The landlord, however, does have the option of treating the new occupant as a trespasser and obtaining a court order to have him or her removed. Since this procedure is expensive and usually unprofitable for the landlord, most subtenants are allowed to stay.

One problem with a subletting arrangement is that the original tenant is still personally responsible for the rent if the subtenant fails to pay. The rental agreement between the original tenant and the landlord remains in force until the rental term expires.

> One month into a one-year rental agreement, Will Rent moves from his apartment in Austin to Carrizo Springs, where he has been transferred by his employer. Will's friend, Skip Lightly, agrees to "take over the lease" and moves in without talking to the landlord about it. The landlord accepts the rent from Skip without complaint. Three months later Skip moves out, and the apartment stays vacant for the rest of the year. Will owes eight months' rent.

The best way to have someone "take over your lease" is to ask the landlord to release you and to enter into a separate agreement with the new tenant. Since the landlord loses no money on such a deal, this method is acceptable to most landlords.

EVICTION PROCEDURES

Now we'll talk about what happens at the end of the line, when the landlord wants the tenant out but the tenant refuses to leave. Sometimes this happens because the tenant has fallen hopelessly behind in the rent, but cannot or will not find another place to live. Sometimes it happens because a real dispute exists between landlord and tenant as to whether the tenant has breached the rental agreement in some other way. Whatever the reason, the landlord wants to accomplish — and the tenant wants to prevent — an *eviction*.

"Self-Help" Eviction Procedures

Although legal procedures exist to evict a tenant who violates the rental agreement and refuses to leave voluntarily, some landlords prefer their own methods. "Self-help" evictions are not legal, so landlords who engage in such practices expose themselves to law-

suits and monetary damages. The following questions and answers describe several common but illegal eviction techniques.

May the landlord physically throw me out if I'm behind on the rent?

A landlord may not use force to remove a tenant, nor even threaten to use force. Furthermore, unless you have abandoned the rental unit, the landlord cannot remove your property. Your remedies, if the landlord violates this law, are the same as those for interrupting utilities paid directly to the utility company (as discussed below). [26]

If you are actually behind on the rent, the landlord may change the locks on the doors. However, after doing this, the landlord must leave a written notice on the front door saying where the new key may be obtained at any hour and giving the name of the individual

OAKLAND
UNIVERSITY
4957 0005 4750 9446
09/03 VISA

KLING P T V

DATE	QUAN.	CLASS	RATE	DESCRIPTION	AMOUNT	PRICE	AMOUNT
9/1/01	3		04			6.75	6.75
						12.95	12.95
						9.50	9.50
							SUB TOTAL 35.40
							SALES TAX 1.77
							TOTAL 37.17

SSBA

L 37.17 CA BL/DU

TX 034378437 5452715

AUTH. NO. 37760

X SIGNATURE Ben S Toll

THE ISSUER OF THE CARD IDENTIFIED ON THIS ITEM IS AUTHORIZED TO PAY THE AMOUNT SHOWN AS TOTAL UPON PROPER PRESENTATION. I PROMISE TO PAY SUCH TOTAL (TOGETHER WITH ANY OTHER CHARGES DUE THEREON) SUBJECT TO AND IN ACCORDANCE WITH THE AGREEMENT GOVERNING THE USE OF SUCH CARD.

PLEASE RETAIN THIS COPY FOR YOUR RECORDS

Thank You For Using Your Bank Card

SALES SLIP   CUSTOMER COPY

VISITOR TX
CO OP
UNIVERSITY
1592350

KHANG P TAK

T4H4 0520 5000 4T54

0610/81 VISA
25 3E-1   L   37.17 CARD

STSTZSTS 33FSFSEO T YOSTEPTS

who will give you the key. The new key must be given to you regardless of whether or not the delinquent rent is paid. This allows the landlord to get your attention and have a little chat about the delinquent rent, without allowing the landlord to throw you out into the street. Under Texas law, only a justice of the peace, not the landlord, can lawfully evict a tenant by physical force. (The justice of the peace does this by ordering the constable to use force if necessary.) Nevertheless, many landlords prefer to judge their own cases and unlawfully force tenants out.

> Lisa Castle skipped the October 1 rent payment. On October 20 the landlord appeared at the door with a pistol in his hand and told Lisa to get out immediately. Lisa left. That night he changed the locks on the doors and left a note saying Lisa owed him $166.66 in rent.
>
> The landlord violated the law, both by threatening the use of force and by failing to offer Lisa the new key. She may sue him for the same remedies as in the example below, in which the landlord cut off her utilities.

May the landlord cut off the utilities if I'm behind in the rent?

The landlord may not cut off the utilities (electricity, water, gas, etc.) if you pay for them directly to the utility company.[27] If your utilities are cut off anyway, you have the right to stay until the landlord follows the proper procedures for eviction, even if you are behind in rent payments at the time of the utility cutoff. Alternatively, you may legally terminate the rental agreement and move out without being liable for breaching the rental agreement. In this case, you will owe rent only up to the date you move out. In addition, whether you stay or move out, you may sue the landlord for actual damages, plus one month's rent, plus reasonable attorney fees, less any delinquent rentals or other sums owed to the landlord.

> Lisa Castle paid $250 per month in rent, due on the first of the month. She paid her electric bill directly to the electric company. Lisa skipped the July 1 rent payment. On July 20, the landlord cut off her electricity while she was at work, thus causing $50 worth of food to spoil. Lisa moved out.
>
> Lisa has the option of moving back in or terminating

the lease. In either case, she can recover in court $50, plus $250, plus reasonable attorney fees, less $166.66 (2/3 of a month) in delinquent rent.

If you pay the landlord for the utilities, however, the landlord does have the right to cut them off when the rent payments are delinquent. Otherwise, the landlord would have to continue paying for utilities used during the eviction process.

Judicial Eviction Procedures

Landlords need not resort to illegal eviction tactics. Effective procedures are available through the courts. Although judicial procedures take longer than the "self-help" measures described above, they are less likely to lead to violence. They also have the advantage of providing a third party — the justice of the peace — to make the decision, thus improving the chances that the rights of both parties will be considered fairly.

How long does an eviction take?

At a bare minimum, if the landlord files a bond (explained below), the constable can remove you on the seventh day after the landlord files the complaint in court. If the landlord does not file a bond and you do not appear in court — and the landlord, justice of the peace and constable are all in a hurry — you can be removed on the thirteenth day. Eviction will almost always take longer than these minimum times, however, because the landlord, justice of the peace, and constable are seldom so diligent. In addition, if you decide to contest the eviction, it may take weeks to get to trial. If the case is appealed, several more months may pass before you can be evicted.

Is it necessary to have an attorney to contest an eviction?

Retaining an attorney for full representation is often unnecessary, but it is a good idea at least to consult an attorney for advice. The attorney may be able to determine if one of the laws have been violated that will make the landlord liable for your attorney fees.

Renting Homes and Apartments 45

What are the procedures in an eviction suit?

Evictions (called "forcible entry and detainer" suits) are governed by certain Texas statutes and court rules.[28] If you expect to be involved in an eviction, it would be a good idea to look these up at a law office, law library, or the office of your justice of the peace. On questions of local procedure not covered in the rules we have cited, ask your justice of the peace or his or her secretary. The following is a summary only.

The first written notice you will receive from the landlord, if the landlord is represented by an attorney, is likely to order you to leave within ten days or be sued for the landlord's attorney fees and other claims. The landlord is correct in saying attorney fees can be recovered, *if* the landlord recovers possession and *if* the landlord can collect the judgment.[29] See the section on *The Landlord's Lien* in this chapter and *Chapter 15, The Homestead and Other Judgment Exemptions.* At a minimum, the landlord must give three days' written notice to vacate before filing suit if the suit is based on nonpayment of rent.[30]

When the landlord files the formal complaint with the justice of the peace, the justice will prepare a citation ordering you to appear in court and setting out the date, time, and place at which you are to *appear,* either personally or by filing a written answer. Sometime after the complaint is filed, the constable will deliver (serve) a copy of the complaint and citation to you. Call the justice's office to determine whether the *appearance* date is a trial date or only a deadline for filing a written answer.

If the landlord has filed a *possession bond,* you will be served with notice that the bond has been filed, along with the complaint and the citation. This notice will warn that you will be ordered to leave after six days from receipt of the citation, unless, within that time, you post a counterbond or demand and win a trial (which must be held within the six days). If the landlord has not filed a bond, the hearing will be six to ten days after service of the complaint and citation.

Each party has a right to trial by jury, upon filing a request and paying the $3.00 fee. A jury demand may result in considerable delay. The main problem is that a jury trial is much more complex, and an attorney on the other side may put the unrepresented party at an extreme disadvantage. Each party also has the right to have the justice of the peace, who presides at such trials, subpoena witnesses to testify.

If you lose at trial and the landlord has not filed a possession bond, you will have five days from entry of judgment before the judge can issue a document called a *writ of restitution* which instructs the constable to order you to leave. If necessary, the constable can legally throw you off the premises after the writ has been issued. During those five days before the writ is issued, you can either file an appeal to the county court or pack up and leave.

THE LANDLORD'S LIEN

If a landlord has a lien on a particular piece of your property, that property can be sold to satisfy the landlord's claim for delinquent rent. In such a case, you cannot claim a judgment exemption (see Chapter 15, *The Homestead and Other Judgment Exemptions*) for the property. In some cases, the landlord may have the right to take your property without a court order.

On what property does a landlord have a lien?

A landlord has a lien for delinquent rent on *all* the tenant's property found within the rental unit, if it is a residence, and on all property in a storage room — with the following important exceptions:

- all wearing apparel
- all tools, apparatus and books belonging to any trade or profession
- school books
- one automobile and one truck
- family library and all family portraits and pictures
- household furniture to the extent of one couch, two living room chairs, dining table and chairs
- all beds and bedding
- all kitchen furniture and utensils
- all food and foodstuffs
- all medicine and other medical supplies
- all goods known by the landlord or his agent to belong to

Renting Homes and Apartments 47

persons other than the tenant or other occupants of such dwelling
- all goods known by the landlord or his agent to be subject to a recorded lien
- all agricultural implements

Note especially that everything is exempt that does not belong to you as well as everything that already has a recorded lien on it. If you are still making payments on something, then it may have a recorded lien on it.

Can the landlord take property under a landlord's lien without going to court?

If a clause in the rental agreement allows the landlord to take property subject to the lien, and if the clause is underlined or printed in conspicuous bold print, then the landlord need not go to court before taking the property to collect delinquent rent. However, the landlord even then may take the property only "peaceably and without force or violence."[31] The landlord should be very careful not to take any of the exempt property listed above.

If there is no such clause in the rental agreement, the landlord may *not* take any of your property *without a court order*. Although a lien exists, it must be *foreclosed* in court before the property can lawfully be seized.

What can a landlord do with a tenant's property after taking it to enforce a lien?

Property taken by a landlord to enforce a valid lien may be sold by the sheriff after a court has entered a judgment for the landlord. As a practical matter, however, this is rarely necessary. If the landlord has not heard from you in weeks, then the landlord may reasonably assume that you have either abandoned the property or given it up in satisfaction of the rent. After a reasonable time has passed, it is probably proper for the landlord to sell the property or otherwise dispose of it. If the property is worth more than the amount of rent owed, the landlord should, of course, return the difference. You will probably have to seek the landlord out to recover the difference, however.

What may I do if the landlord takes my property wrongfully?

If the landlord *willfully* takes exempt property, or *willfully* takes property without a court order when there is no clause in the rental agreement allowing it, you may sue the landlord for one month's rent, plus actual damages, plus reasonable attorney fees, less any delinquent rentals or other sums owed.

> Lisa Castle's rent is $250 per month, due on the first of each month. She does not have a written rental agreement. At a time when she was one month behind in rent payments, her landlord seized her only couch, which was worth $200.
>
> The landlord violated the law in two respects: by acting without either a court order or a written authorization in the rental agreement; and by taking property exempt from the landlord's lien. Lisa may sue for $250, plus $200 (or the return of the couch), plus her reasonable attorney fees, less the delinquent rent.

In order for the landlord to be liable for all these damages, the seizure of property must have been *willful*. Exactly what this means has not yet been decided by the courts. It may mean only that the landlord (or the landlord's agent) must know the facts — in Lisa's case, that the landlord knew there was no written provision for a lien. Landlords may argue, however, that the tenant must prove the landlord knew the seizure was *illegal* because they knew the property was on the exemption list.

Landlords who seize their tenants' property should proceed with caution. Many do not do so, and they frequently violate the laws discussed above. Such conduct is occasionally so oppressive as to be legally "unconscionable" and expose them to damages under the Texas Deceptive Trade Practices-Consumer Protection Act (see *Chapter 6, Deceptive Trade Practices*). In this way, landlords sometimes hand their tenants powerful legal weapons to use against them.

Chapter 3
Buying Home Improvements

In these days of tight credit and runaway inflation, it makes sense to consider fixing up an older home instead of buying a new one. Today, however, remodeling is so expensive that most homeowners must borrow money to pay for it. Some of the saddest cases the authors have seen have involved families in danger of losing their homes because they tried to fix them up. In some instances, the families were cheated by shady or incompetent contractors. In others, the families just did not understand that when they signed the papers that they were putting liens on their homes.

This chapter will explain the legal procedures for financing home improvements and the papers that must be signed. With this information, the reader should be able to arrange for home improvements knowledgeably and to obtain the best possible price and quality on the work performed.

Does home improvement financing require putting a lien on my home?

Deeply imbedded in Texas law is a policy of encouraging ownership of homes by their occupants. That is why the homestead is judgment exempt; and even voluntary liens on a homestead are invalid except for financing the purchase price, securing property taxes, and financing home improvements.[1] See Chapter 15, The Homestead and Other Judgment Exemptions. The law permits voluntary liens to finance improvements to a homestead on the theory that the home will eventually be worthless if it cannot be repaired, there will be few repairs if they cannot be financed, and there will be little financing if lenders cannot obtain liens. Although there is no legal requirement that a home improvement financer *must* take a lien on the home being repaired, as a practical matter a lien is almost always required.

The requirement of a written lien applies only to *owner-occupied* homes. If improvements are made on property not occupied by its owner (for example, a rent home), the contractor obtains an *automatic* lien and has only to record an affidavit to that effect. A lien is created automatically whenever work or materials are furnished on credit to improve any real estate *other than* an owner-occupied home.[2]

A *mechanic's and materialman's lien* may be created in financing any type of home improvement or construction, from small paint jobs to hurricane fences to construction of entire homes. Much agony has resulted from homeowners failing to understand when they signed the papers that they would lose their homes if they failed to pay.

> Borden Naille was so impressed with the qualities of "Sta-Put Permalum Siding," as described by its salesperson, that he decided to have the siding installed on his rent house as well as his own home. Immediately after he made the final arrangements with the salesperson on the phone, the work began. Later, while the siding was being installed on both houses, Mr. Naille signed the papers. Within a month after the siding was installed, it began to warp and rust.
>
> Mr. Naille's attorney advised him that he would probably not have to pay for the shoddy work on either house, but that it might take a long court battle to clear the matter up. Meanwhile, he advised Mr. Naille not to pay on the contract on his home. Since the papers had been signed after the work began, the lien was invalid, so the siding contractor could not foreclose. However, he advised that Mr. Naille pay on the rent house contract.

Since the rent house was not a homestead, a lien had been placed on it automatically by the contractor's performing the work and filing lien papers with the county clerk, as well as by the voluntary lien Mr. Naille signed. With this strategy, Mr. Naille's attorney could easily prevent foreclosure on either house during the court battle in which it would be determined how much, if anything, Mr. Naille would have to pay the contractor.

Can I finance home improvements even if there is already a lien on my home?

Most homeowners owe money on their homes. When this is the case, the financer of home improvements will either refinance the existing debt, adding the home improvement loan to it, or will obtain a *second lien* on the home.

As holder of the second lien, the financer can foreclose if you fail to pay. The advantage enjoyed by the holder of the first lien is that the proceeds of the foreclosure sale go first to that financer. Any remaining proceeds then go to the holder of the second lien. Because the second lien, therefore, provides less security, a financer with a second or subsequent lien (if a licensed lender such as a bank or savings and loan) may charge higher interest than can the holder of the first lien.[3]

> Harvey Wallbanger signed a home improvement contract financed by Second Savings & Loan. Since he still owed money to First Bank & Trust on the purchase price of his home, Second Savings took a second lien. Five years later, Harvey lost his job and was unable to make the payments on either loan. At that time, he still owed $20,000 on the first (purchase money) lien and $10,000 on the second (home improvement) lien. At the foreclosure sale, the house sold for only $25,000. Of this, First Bank got $20,000 and Second Savings got $5,000. Second Savings also had the right to sue Harvey for the additional $5,000 he owed them. This would allow Second Savings to collect a judgment if Harvey ever got on his feet financially again.

What are the usual methods of financing home improvements?

As in any other financing, there are basically three options. First, the contractor may finance the job by accepting installment payments (carrying the paper) until the debt is paid. This is similar to owner financing of a sale. It is rare except on very small jobs, because contractors usually need their money right away. Under the second method, the contractor may agree initially to accept the installment payments, then sell the right to receive them to a financer (such as a savings and loan or a bank) for a lump-sum payment from the financer. The homeowner will then pay installments to the financer. Third, the homeowner may obtain a direct loan from a financer without ever signing an installment agreement with the contractor.

As in any other financing situation, you should shop for credit in order to obtain the best interest rate on a home improvement loan. Usually, the best interest rate will be found on a direct loan from a bank or savings and loan.

What papers are signed in a home improvement sale?

In a home improvement sale involving financing, you will ordinarily sign a *credit application,* a *contract,* a *mechanic's and materialman's lien,* a *note,* a *disclosure statement,* and a *completion certificate.* Some of the papers signed will combine two or more of these items, and additional incidental papers may be signed, but these are the basic home improvement papers.

The first thing signed is usually the *credit application.* This assists the potential financer in determining whether to extend credit to the homeowner. If the homeowner does not personally arrange with the lending institiution for the loan, the contractor will usually take the credit application to a lending insititution with which the contractor does business regularly.

The *contract* describing the work to be done and a *mechanic's and materialman's lien* (discussed above) will always be signed. The mechanic's and materialman's lien is usually drawn up in the form of a deed of trust, which allows the lien-holder to foreclose without going to court. See *Chapter 1, Buying and Selling Homes.* The lien is granted to the contractor, who assigns (sells) it to a third-party financer, if one is involved.

In addition, a *note* setting out precisely the terms of payment is usually included. In the note, you will promise to pay either the contractor or the third-party financer, depending on the method of financing used.

Another paper, the *disclosure statement,* contains the terms of the credit being extended, in compliance with the Federal Truth-in-Lending Act. See *Chapter 10, Understanding the Language of Credit.* In order to comply with the Truth-In-Lending Act, a *notice of rescission* is drawn up, enabling you to cancel the agreement within three days of the date of signing. This procedure is explained below.

The last paper to be signed is a *completion certificate,* in which you agree after completion that the work was completed properly. Since most financers will not release the bulk of the funds to the contractor until this has been signed, you have considerable power over the contractor as long as you have not signed this form. By signing the completion certificate, you do not give up the right to sue later for bad or incomplete work.[4] However, you do give up the power to keep the contractor from being paid until you have been satisfied.

What is the three-day "cooling-off period" and how does it work?

The Federal Truth-in-Lending Act provides that whenever a lien is taken on real property used or to be used as a residence — except for a first lien for the purchase of the residence — you have three days within which to cancel the agreement.[5] Cancellation may be accomplished by delivering or mailing a written notice to the creditor at any time before midnight of the third business day after the lien is signed. The Texas Home Solicitation Sales Act and a Federal Trade Commission rule also apply to many sales of home improvements, whether financed or not, and provide for a similar three-day cooling-off period. See *Chapter 7, Door-to-Door Sales and Mail Orders.*

How can I avoid being cheated in a home improvement deal?

Even after years of public outcry and legislation, the home improvement industry is still plagued by sharp operators and incompetent contractors. The smart consumer should watch out for several shady practices.

"Fly-by-night" contractors: Some contractors will disappear without finishing the work or after doing a very bad job. They may receive all or part of the payment in advance, then vanish. They may disappear after tricking you into signing a completion certificate before the work is finished. Or, they may leave town before hidden defects can be discovered. After the contractor performs this disappearing act, you are left with a debt to a financing institution and little or nothing to show for it. Although financers are increasingly being held responsible for the work of the contractors they support, they will usually try to collect on such debts anyway. See *Chapter 17, Financers' Responsibilities.*

Corporate-shell abusers: Most people engaged in business limit their personal responsibility for commercial activities by forming corporations through which they do business. Then, if the corporation fails, the owners will lose only the value of their stock in the corporation. By minimizing the corporation's assets, the owner(s) minimize their own responsibility. Then, for example, if the corporation hires bad workers and is sued by angry homeowners, the homeowners may win judgments that are worth little or nothing if the corporation is a shell with very minimal assets.

Some people abuse this protection by repeatedly forming corporations to operate risky and badly managed businesses, then pass on any losses to their customers while protecting their own profits and assets. It is sometimes possible to "pierce the corporate veil" and hold such owners responsible, but this usually requires more legal expenses than the average homeowner can afford. The best way to protect yourself from such operations, then, is to know something about the contractor *before* signing the contract. If you do not know the contractor's reputation, at least ask for several references (people for whom the contractor has worked). Require references going back several years, and check them out.

Incompetent workers: Some contractors have been known literally to round up youngsters off the streets of Matamoros to perform home improvement work, then assign a "supervisor" who could not even speak the same language as the "workers." This is an extreme example, to be sure, but it illustrates a problem which plagues the home improvement contracting business. Even some of the major home improvement and construction companies will sometimes try to cut costs and increase profits by hiring unskilled workers to do skilled work. Therefore, besides knowing the contractor's reputation, it is a good idea to check the work as it progresses.

Side loans: Some contractors will make a cash loan to a customer and include the loan in the price of the home improvement contract. In this way, they "sweeten" the deal for the customer while apparently obtaining a lien on the homestead. This deal does not seem so sweet later, however, if you are unable to repay the loan. The apparent lien obtained this way is invalid, and the contractor may be liable for a civil penalty, but this makes no difference if you do not have an attorney to resist the foreclosure.[6] This scheme primarily affects low-income homeowners who have difficulty obtaining financing in lawful ways.

Hidden finance charges: The contractor may have two prices: a cash price, and a higher "credit price" to which interest is added at the highest legal rate. This practice is clearly a violation of the usury laws, since the extra amount included in the "credit price" amounts to a hidden interest charge. Nevertheless, such tactics are widely practiced in various types of sales. The extra interest may either be shared with a financer or kept by the contractor. Either way, the homeowner is the loser.

All the schemes described above would disappear immediately if consumers would follow two simple precautions: *know the reputation of the contractor, and shop around for the best price.*

What is the responsibility of the financer if the contractor does bad work?

Whether or not the financer (usually a bank or savings and loan) has any responsibility for bad work depends upon the facts of the case. Often the situation is very unclear. Therefore, you should take with more than a grain of salt the financer's claim that only the contractor is responsible for the work. Complain loud and long, even if you have already signed a completion certificate. The contractor could not do business without financing, so legalities aside, the contractor and the financer are in the home improvement business together. For a discussion of financing legalities, see *Chapter 17, Financers' Responsibilities.*

This is not to say, however, that you should quit making payments on your home improvement loan. The law is unclear in this area, and the facts are often complicated. *Never quit making payments on a home improvement loan without first consulting an attorney.*

Don't let the problems discussed above discourage you from negotiating a home improvement contract. Just be aware of the problems that can arise if you are not careful in selecting a contractor with whom to do business. Just as with marriages, lawyers tend to get involved only in the home improvement deals that go bad. We remain convinced, however, that marriage is a useful institution, and we think the home improvement business is also here to stay.

Chapter 4
Foreclosure on Homes

Foreclosure is an ugly word. Those who recall the Great Depression remember how many lost their homes and farms when they were unable to keep up the payments. Unfortunately, the threat of foreclosure is still with us, and we may again be facing an economically unstable time.

Foreclosure is the sale of real property by a creditor to satisfy a debt secured by that property. Although a foreclosure may be ordered by a court and the sale carried out by the sheriff, most Texas foreclosures involve no court procedure at all. Creditors in Texas usually obtain a *deed of trust* which allows them to have the property sold by a *trustee* in the event of default. This *deed of trust sale* is the type of foreclosure sale to be discussed here, since it is the ordinary procedure in Texas.

What is a deed of trust?

In the *deed of trust,* you convey *legal title* to certain property to someone designated by your creditor as his or her *trustee.* The trustee is usually the creditor's attorney or another agent responsible to the creditor. Under the terms of the deed of trust, you must give the trustee the power to sell the property in the event you default on the debt. The deed of trust sets out at length the terms that constitute a default and allow foreclosure, and stipulates exactly what is to be done with the proceeds of the sale.

Brent Byer is buying a home for $40,000 from Sam

Sellers to be financed by a $35,000 note to Hoard Savings and Loan. At the closing, Sellers will sign a deed giving Byer title to the property. At the same time, Byer will sign a $35,000 note to Hoard Savings along with a deed of trust. In the deed of trust, Byer will grant legal title to the property to an officer or attorney of Hoard Savings, who is designated the *trustee* (Byer's grantee). Byer will agree that if he defaults, the trustee may sell the property and apply the proceeds of the sale to the debt.

Under what conditions may a creditor declare a default?

Those conditions that constitute a default are spelled out precisely and at length in the deed of trust. Although the exact terms vary from one deed of trust to another, some provisions are common to almost all of them.

First and most important, the failure to make a payment on time may always be considered a default if the creditor so chooses. It is very rare, however, for a creditor to initiate foreclosure proceedings before a payment is at least two or three months late. Usually, the only penalty for an overdue payment is a late-payment charge (which should be disclosed in the note or in a separate disclosure statement). These charges do add up, however, and making a payment late always means running a risk that the creditor will declare a default.

Second, most deeds of trust allow the creditor to declare a default, even while payments are up to date, if the creditor reasonably feels "insecure" about the prospect for future payments. The creditor's feeling of insecurity must be "reasonable" and not simply a subjective feeling. Although this clause has real potential for abuse, we have not seen abuse of it in practice. It is unlikely to be used except where bankruptcy has occurred or appears likely.

Failure to pay taxes and insurance may also constitute a default. Additionally, many deeds of trust require that the property be kept in "good" condition. By these and similar clauses, the creditor tries to protect the property in case the creditor may need to foreclose some day to recover the debt.

Foreclosure on Homes

After the creditor has declared a default, how much notice must I be given of the foreclosure sale?

At least 21 days before the date of the foreclosure sale, the trustee must mail you a notice of the time and place of the sale and must post a notice in the courthouse of the county in which the land is located. The sale must be held at this same courthouse, on the first Tuesday of the month, between 10:00 a.m. and 4:00 p.m.[1]

After the creditor declares a default, how may I prevent a foreclosure sale?

At any time before the sale, you may *redeem* the property and prevent the sale, by paying off the debt.[2] At this time, the amount of the debt to be paid will usually include the attorney fees incurred by the creditor in preparing for the sale.

If there has been no *acceleration* of the debt (calling it due immediately), then the amount owed will only total the amount of payments due and unpaid, plus attorney fees (if any). If, however, there has been an acceleration, you must pay the entire unpaid principal of the debt plus attorney fees. See *Chapter 11, Calculating the Costs of Credit,* to find out how to figure the amount due at any time by rebating unearned interest and insurance charges.

What must a creditor do to accelerate a debt?

The creditor's options depend on whether the *acceleration clause* in the note provides for automatic acceleration or acceleration at the option of the creditor. If the note says acceleration will be automatic in the event of default, then no advance notice need be given.[3] If the note provides for optional acceleration, then the creditor must at least notify you that one or more payments are overdue and must give you an opportunity to pay them before accelerating the debt.[4] Although most consumer notes still contain acceleration clauses of the optional type, many of those drafted recently provide for automatic acceleration.

Remember that even after acceleration, the property may still be redeemed by paying off the entire debt. This is often accomplished by refinancing, either with the same creditor or with another lending institution, or with a loan from a friend or family member.

Who may buy at a foreclosure sale?

Anyone may buy at a foreclosure, including the creditor. Sometimes, someone other than the creditor will bid on the property, but truly competitive bidding is more the exception than the rule.

What may the creditor do with the funds received at the foreclosure sale?

The sale price is applied first to attorney fees and expenses of the sale; then to the debt; then — in the rare case in which there is a surplus — the surplus goes to the debtor. More commonly, there is a deficiency, and the creditor may then sue the debtor for the amount of the debt not covered by proceeds from the sale.

What routinely happens, in practice, is that the creditor is the only one who bids at the sale. The creditor always bids the amount of the debt or less, to avoid having to pay any surplus to the debtor, no matter how valuable the property nor how small the debt. Some creditors routinely bid substantially less than the amount of the debt, so there will be a deficiency. Then, if the debtor threatens to attack the legality of the sale, the creditor can sue for the deficiency.

> Brent Byer defaults on a debt owed to Hoard Savings & Loan and secured by Byer's home. At the time of the foreclosure sale, the accelerated balance of the debt, plus attorney fees and expenses, is $5,000; the fair market value of the home is $30,000. Hoard Savings is the only bidder and bids $4,000. Byer now owes Hoard Savings $1,000, and Hoard Savings is free to sell the house for a clear $25,000 profit.

In practice, it is fairly rare for a debtor to default after paying such a large part of the debt. It happens, however, and can cost a family its most valuable asset.

How may I avoid or minimize loss from a foreclosure sale?

We emphasize again the importance of avoiding a foreclosure sale by redemption, if at all possible. Catch up on the payments immediately. If the creditor insists that acceleration has occurred, hire an attorney to argue about what constitutes proper notice of acceleration. Another option may be to refinance the debt through the same lender or another one and thus pay off the debt. A more risky option, but in some cases the only one available, is to advertise the foreclosure sale in the hope of driving up the price. In the example above, Mr. Byer lost a $25,000 equity ($30,000 value less $5,000 debt) in part because there was no competition in the bidding.

What must I prove to make a successful legal attack on a foreclosure sale?

To fight a foreclosure sale, you must prove two basic elements: that the price paid at the sale was "grossly inadequate"; *and* that there was some legal irregularity in the sale which contributed to the grossly inadequate price.[5] Thus, the grossly inadequate $4,000 price paid by Hoard Savings is not a sufficient reason, in itself, to invalidate the sale. Hoard Savings can keep its $25,000 rip-off unless Mr. Byer can prove that the notice of acceleration, notice of sale, or some other required step was improperly carried out.

A foreclosure sale may sometimes be prevented or attacked by use of the right of rescission under the Federal Truth-in-Lending Act. This option is generally available only where the deed of trust was signed as part of a home improvement transaction. Rescission is discussed in *Chapter 3, Buying Home Improvements,* and *Chapter 11, Calculating the Costs of Credit.*

Attacks on foreclosure sales are usually costly and uncertain, especially where the debtor has waited until after the sale to consult an attorney. At the very least, you should consult an attorney no later than ten days before the date of the foreclosure sale.

There is no substitute for careful financial planning for preventing a foreclosure. The discussion of legal procedures in this chapter should suggest why such planning is important. Even when foreclosure is threatened, however, it can often be avoided at the last minute by negotiation or refinancing. Too many families have lost their homes because they did not understand the basic principles outlined above.

PART TWO
BUYING GOODS AND SERVICES

Chapter 5
Warranties

Everyone is likely to be stuck with a "lemon" sooner or later. In the past, the only legal protection available to the consumer was the common law warning "buyer beware." Since the mid-1960's, however, new laws providing strong remedies for irate buyers have placed the consumer in a much better position. Some of these laws, including those concerning warranties, now provide incentives for the *seller* to beware.

HOW TO RECOGNIZE A WARRANTY

A warranty is a promise, made as part of a sale or rental agreement, that a product or service meets a certain standard of quality. The term *guarantee* means that same thing. A warranty may be very general, such as "free from all defects," or very specific, such as "hand woven from 100% Uvalde County mohair."

A warranty may be *express* or *implied*. An express warranty is one in which a statement of quality is actually made. It may be either written or oral. An implied warranty is created by law, even in the absence of an oral or written statement of quality.

Do all statements about quality create warranties?

Very general or vague statements, often referred to as "puffing," do not create warranties.[1] The statement "this is the best radio you can buy for the money" is puffing and is therefore legally meaningless. But the statement "this radio will play well for at least a year" constitutes a warranty.

Must I hear or read a statement for it to constitute a warranty?

An express warranty exists only if it is part of the *basis of the bargain*. If you overhear a salesman tell someone else that a certain radio will play for a year, that does not give you a warranty. It becomes part of someone else's bargain. On the other hand, a statement you hear on a television commerical does become part of your bargain because it is directed to everyone.

Nevertheless, it is not necessary for you to read a *written* warranty for it to become part of your bargain. Just as you are stuck with the bad things in a written contract, regardless of whether or not you read them, you can also take advantage of the good things without reading them. Anything in writing that pertains to the bargain and could have been read before the bargain was closed is considered a part of that bargain.

Can an oral warranty be part of a written bargain?

You may have heard that oral statements cannot form part of a written agreement. This rule, known as the *parole evidence rule,* is discussed in *Chapter 8, Automobiles and Other Goods*. This rule does not apply, however, where the agreement is entirely oral. Furthermore, even where this rule does apply, you still have a legal right to sue for damages resulting from a false oral statement. You can argue that the statement itself, even if not such a part of the bargain as to constitute a warranty, still constitutes fraud and a deceptive trade practice. The legal result is generally the same. Even so, it is always best to get in writing any statement on which you rely. This will help you to prove later that the statement actually was made and exactly what was promised.

When does the law imply a warranty?

The Uniform Commercial Code in Texas creates several types of warranties which automatically apply when a product is sold. These are called *implied warranties*.

For consumers, the most important implied warranty is the *im-

plied warranty of merchantability.[2] At first glance, this warranty looks like a true "anti-lemon law." It provides that, when a product is placed on the market, the consumer can expect the product to be of at least *merchantable* quality. The law implies a promise by the seller or manufacturer that the product meets these standards, among others:

- the product will pass without objection in trade or commerce;
- the product is fit for the ordinary purpose for which such goods are used; and
- the product is of average or fair quality within the contract description.

This theory of merchantability sounds great, but there are several practicalities which discourage consumers from pursuing their rights under implied warranties. First, many consumers don't know such warranties exist. Second, several legal technicalities can cause the consumer to lose a suit based on an implied warranty. For example, several Texas cases have held that the implied warranty of merchantability does not apply to sales of used goods, but this is not clearly established yet in cases in which an individual, rather than a business, is buying a used product.[3] Despite these limitations, however, the implied warranty of merchantability can be a powerful weapon for a consumer stuck with a lemon.

Can the implied warranty of merchantability be disclaimed or limited by a seller?

The implied warranty of merchantability may be disclaimed in writing.[4] Such a disclaimer must be conspicuous and must use the words *merchantability, as is, with all faults,* or other clear terms. As a result, sales contracts will sometimes include such statements as the following:

> Buyer understands and agrees that the described [product] is purchased AS IS without warranty of merchantability or fitness . . .

> or

> No representation, promise or warranty, express or implied, has been made with respect to the merchantability, suitability, or fitness for any purpose.

Under the Magnuson-Moss Warranty Act, discussed later in this chapter, implied warranties may not be disclaimed or limited in a product carrying a *full warranty*. In addition, even a *limited warranty* may restrict implied warranties only to the time within which the written *limited warranty* is effective. For that reason, you will often see warranty clauses similar to the following:

> WARRANTY DISCLAIMERS: Any implied warranties arising out of this sale, including but not limited to the implied warranties of merchantability and fitness for a particular purpose, are limited in duration to the above one (1) year period. Dealer shall not be liable for loss of use of the product or other incidental or consequential costs, expenses, or damages incurred by the purchaser.

What warranties are required in the sale of mobile homes?

Texas law makes a special provision for the sale of mobile homes. The Texas Manufactured Housing Standards Act requires that all mobile homes sold in Texas comply with certain minimum standards of quality.[5] The seller and manufacturer must then provide a one-year warranty that the mobile home complies with these standards.

HOW TO READ A WARRANTY

The warranty has become an important part of the modern sales pitch. This trend became apparent in the early 1960s when Chrysler offered the first long-term "power train" warranty on its automobiles, which proved to be a very successful sales device. Unfortunately, some sales personnel use pitches that obscure or misrepresent the actual coverage of the warranties being offered. Some written warranties are even worse than worthless:

> Tella Hollic purchased a new 1980 Pinnacle TV. It carried a 3-year written warranty. Soon after she bought the set, the picture completely died. Tella brought the TV in for repair or exchange. Later, a Pinnacle representative told her that they discovered the problem was in the picture tube. They would be happy to replace it for $850. "But I have a warranty," complained Tella. The representative calmly referred her to the written warranty. The fine print said "covers all parts except those specified on page 184 of the dealer's sales and service

catalog." Of course, the picture tube was one of those excluded from coverage.

Tella's story illustrates how a written warranty can be worse than no warranty at all. Written warranties often promise less quality than you would expect from a good product. This may be done in several ways:

- The written agreement may be so long and complicated that no one will read and understand it.
- The buyer may be required to fill out and mail a warranty registration card in order to receive warranty coverage.
- The buyer may have to pay transportation and shipping costs if the product needs to be repaired or replaced.
- Certain parts may be excluded from the warranty coverage.
- The warrantor may reserve the right to decide if a defect exists.
- The use of certain products may be required during routine servicing of the product.

Worst of all, the warrantor may use the express warranty to limit or eliminate more extensive implied warranties which have been created by law.

Are there any laws designed to discourage deceptive warranties?

A new federal law, the Magnuson-Moss Warranty Act, is designed to solve such problems concerning written warranties on consumer goods.[6] The Magnuson-Moss Warranty Act is primarily a disclosure law. This is means that the consumer must be given certain specified information about the terms and conditions of the warranty in language that an average customer can read. The warranty must also be contained in a single document.

What is the difference between a "full warranty" and a "limited warranty"?

Every written warranty must be designated either as a *full warranty* or as a *limited warranty*. This designation must be clearly written on the warranty as a title. The title may also specify how long the warranty will be effective. Consequently, you will see titles such as FULL ONE YEAR WARRANTY or ONE YEAR LIMITED WARRANTY.

The Magnuson-Moss Warranty Act creates certain minimum requirements for all written warranties. If it meets only these minimum requirements, a written warranty must be designated a *limited* warranty. In order to be designated as *full*, a warranty must comply with the following additional requirements:

- It must provide for repair or replacement of a defective or malfunctioning product *without charge* and *within a reasonable time*.
- It may not limit or disclaim any implied warranty covering the product.
- It may not require the consumer to do anything other than give notification of the defect in order to receive satisfaction under the warranty.
- It may not limit the warranty's protection to the original buyer alone.

WHAT TO DO IF A WARRANTY HAS BEEN BREACHED

The following suggestions apply to all complaints about purchases of goods, whether a warranty is involved or not. Your complaint may be that fewer items were delivered than were promised, or that the color was not what you ordered. The procedures to follow for pursuing these complaints are the same as those for breach of warranty.

What are my basic options when a warranty is breached?

Most warranty claims are resolved through informal negotiations. The seller usually agrees to repair or replace a clearly defective product under warranty. However, it is helpful in negotiations to know the legal options you will have if the seller refuses to do what you think is fair. These legal options include rejecting the goods, revoking acceptance, and suing for damages.

Option A: Rejecting the Goods

If you make your complaint immediately after your first reason-

Warranties 71

able opportunity to inspect the goods, you may reject them even for fairly minor defects:[7]

> Dan Divan wanted some new furniture for his bachelor pad. He went down to Fantasy Furniture and picked out a 12-foot couch. It was made of rare tundra pine, suede and leather, and was designed by Lion d'Own. The couch that was delivered to Dan's home, however, was made of rare tropical pine instead of rare tundra pine.

Dan was within his rights to return the couch and recover his money.

However, this right can be limited by the *terms of the contract*. The contract may require the purchaser to accept substitutions. If a written contract exists, the written description of the goods is what counts. Be sure the written description is clear, accurate and complete.

Option B: Revoking Acceptance

Even after a product has been accepted, a buyer may return it and demand his or her money back under certain conditions, as in the following case:[8]

> Otto Gasser purchased a new car. After driving it for several weeks, he noticed that the transmission failed to work properly. He brought it back to the dealer and complained. The dealer assured him that a minor adjustment would take care of the problem. After several return trips to the dealer, Otto finally took the car to an expert mechanic who discovered the transmission had an inherent and serious production defect.

Because of this defect, Otto has the right to revoke his contract with the dealer, return the car, and demand his money back. The buyer may revoke acceptance of a product if *all* of the following conditions exist:

• The product does not conform to the contract. Numerous cases have held that a grossly defective product does not conform.

• The nonconformity *substantially impairs the value* of the product to the buyer. A recent Texas case held that a defective battery did not substantially impair the value of a new car.

• The purchaser accepted the product without knowledge of the defect, or upon the seller's promise that the defect would be repaired.

• The revocation takes place within a reasonable time after the consumer discovered or should have discovered the defect. What is a "reasonable time" depends on the circumstances, but the closer the revocation is to the date of purchase, the more likely that it will be legally effective.

• Revocation is made before there are any changes in the condition of the product which are not caused by the defect. If Otto had a wreck not caused by the bad transmission, he would not be able to revoke.

Theoretically, revocation provides a great remedy for the consumer stuck with a lemon, and this remedy should not be overlooked. But a consumer who chooses to revoke should be aware of the following legal and practical effects of revocation:

• The product must be returned, and you take the chance that

Warranties

the seller may refuse to honor the demand for reimbursement. In that case, all you can do is take legal action.

- If a consumer loan has been arranged with a bank or credit union to finance the purchase of the item being returned, that loan will not be cancelled by the revocation, in most cases. You will still have to pay it.

Despite these limitations, it often makes sense to revoke when all the conditions listed above are present. Revocation may save legal expenses and a long, drawn-out court battle. In cases involving substantial amounts of money, it will frequently be worthwhile to seek an attorney's advice on whether to revoke.

Option C: Suing for Damages for Breach of Warranty

You may prefer to keep the defective product because there is something about it you like. In this case, you will want the seller to pay you money to make up for the defect if the seller cannot or will not repair it. The following suggestions will help you preserve your right to recover the money in court if the seller will not pay it without a lawsuit.

Even if you have rejected the goods or revoked acceptance, you can still sue for damages in some cases. If, for example, a breakdown of your new car has caused you to lose your job, you can sue for your loss of income (if this remedy is not expressly excluded in the warranty) even if the seller has given you your money back on the car.

> P. K. Uptruck decided to buy a 4-wheel-drive truck. He went down to AA-OK Used Cars and picked one out. It carried an AA-OK three-month warranty. P. K. drove it around Central Park the week after he bought it. The 4-wheel-drive wouldn't work. He called AA-OK and was told, "Bring it by. We'll fix it when we get around to it." That made P. K. mad, so he took it to Jethro's Jeep Garage instead. The new 4-wheel-drive cost P. K. $500. He sued AA-OK for breach of warranty.

P. K. is very likely to lose his suit. One requirement in a suit for breach of warranty is that you give the warrantor a *reasonable opportunity* to cure the defect.[9] This means you must inform the warrantor of the defect and give the warrantor a chance to repair or replace the product. Always keep records of your efforts to have the product repaired or replaced.

Several factors must be considered in deciding when you have given the seller a "reasonable opportunity." One factor is time. In the example above, P. K. would almost certainly have to return the jeep to AA-OK Used Cars at least once. If they kept it for three weeks without working on it, or if they tried unsuccessfully to fix it half a dozen times in a three-week period, they would ordinarily be found to have had their "reasonable opportunity." Just how much time they must be given depends on other factors, such as difficulty of repair, availability of parts, and whether they appear to be making a good-faith effort to do the repairs. If, for example, AA-OK Used Cars merely added transmission lubricant to a transmission that obviously had broken parts, P. K. could reasonably assume they were just playing games and could take the jeep to Jethro's for proper repairs!

What are the usual stages of a warranty dispute?

First stage: *Immediately* notify the seller that there seems to be something wrong with the product. Also, if you know immediately that you want your money back, tell the seller right away and return the product or tell the seller to pick it up. Most disputes are resolved at this stage by the seller's repairing or replacing the product or making a refund.

Second stage: Put your complaint in writing and send it to everyone who may be responsible for helping you, such as the general manager of the company that sold the product and the person in charge of their customer services. The letters should explain exactly what you have done, what you want done, and what you intend to do next. It may be appropriate to send copies to organizations such as the Better Business Bureau, the Attorney General of Texas, the Federal Trade Commission in Washington, D.C., etc. If you do this, note at the foot of the letter the distribution of such copies to show the company that you intend to pursue the claim.

At this stage, also, you may want to have the product examined by a mechanic or other expert who will give you an unbiased opinion as to exactly what is wrong with the product. This information will add clout to your complaint letters and help guide your bargaining strategy. Whether it is worthwhile to obtain an expert's opinion depends on the cost of obtaining the opinion and the value of the product.

Third stage: You may decide to skip the second stage, or your complaints may achieve no results. The next step, then, is to take "self-help" steps such as these:

• Cancel the agreement. Demand your money back and stop making payments if you arranged credit through the seller.

• Repair the product and demand that the warrantor reimburse you. Be sure, first, that you have given the seller notice and a reasonable opportunity to cure the defect.

• Repair the product and notify the seller that you are deducting the cost of repair from your balance, if you arranged credit through the seller.

All of these self-help actions should be put in writing and sent to the seller. Be sure to keep copies of what you send and everything you receive from the seller for use in court later, if necessary.

Notice the suggestion to stop paying or deduct the cost of repairs from payments only if the seller has arranged your credit. Even in such cases, however, this is not *always* the best strategy. The advice of an attorney is especially helpful here since complicated legal principles are involved, and stopping payment can affect your credit rating and lead to repossession or foreclosure. For more discussion of this problem, see *Chapter 17, Financers' Responsibilities*.

Fourth stage: The warrantor may fail to respond favorably to your self-help action. Your only alternative, in that case, is to file a lawsuit. At this point, you will need the advice of an attorney unless your loss is less than $500. If you are claiming less than $500, you can sue in a justice of the peace court without an attorney. See *Chapter 18, Self Help*.

The great majority of warranty claims are resolved to everyone's satisfaction without the use of any formal legal procedures. This is because both parties usually act reasonably and in good faith. It helps to know your legal rights, though, to be sure you are not being too easily "satisfied" and to protect yourself if the other party does not act in good faith.

Chapter 6
Deceptive Trade Practices

Deceptive trade practices have become a major problem in today's marketplace. Each year billions of dollars are lost by consumers who are victimized by fraudulent practices. Therefore, in 1973 the Texas Legislature passed the Deceptive Trade Practices-Consumer Protection Act to protect consumers from such practices. This law was somewhat weakened by amendments added in 1979, but it still provides some protection for consumers. The purpose of this chapter is to explain the meaning and importance of the Consumer Protection Act, as this law is generally called.[1]

What does the Consumer Protection Act do?

The Consumer Protection Act was designed "to protect consumers against false, misleading, and deceptive business practices, unconscionable actions, and breaches of warranty and to provide efficient and economical procedures to secure such protection."[2] Here's how it works:

Evan T. Guard saw this ad in a magazine:

TOO GOOD TO BE TRUE!
Now you can decrease your gas bill by 50 percent. Powercoast, a new fuel additive developed by the space program, is

now available for only $99.99 a case during this special offer.

Evan bought a case, put the additive in his tank, and got absolutely no results. Later analysis proved that Powercoast was made of 2 parts Mad Dog wine and one part pickling vinegar. NASA, of course, had never heard of it.

Prior to 1973, the law primarily used for protection from deceptive trade practices like this was the law of *fraud*. It may seem that the sale in the example above was obviously fraudulent; but the fact is that, given the difficulty and expense of getting a case through court, Evan would have no effective remedy in a suit for fraud.

The main problem is that obtaining a judgment would cost more than the amount of the award Evan could expect to receive. All he could hope to recover would be his *actual damages* of $99.99 (assuming the mixture did not damage his engine), but Evan would probably have to pay $500 to $1,000 in attorney fees to obtain that judgment. In addition, this case would not be as "open and shut" as it might at first appear, because some Texas courts would require proof that the Powercoast pushers *intended* to defraud their customers by *knowing* the advertised facts were untrue. Powercoast might come into court with dubious "scientific" testimony and bogus test results to convince a jury that they reasonably believed, when they placed the ad, that the Mad Dog wine and pickling vinegar mixture could really do what they claimed. Until the Consumer Protection Act was passed, the rule of the marketplace had been "buyer beware or be ripped off." The major problem was this: who has time to test every product before buying it?

The Consumer Protection Act eliminates many of these barriers to the enforcement of a consumer's rights. For one thing, it confronts the problem of legal fees by providing that a consumer who prevails in court can recover his or her own attorney fees from the offending merchant. In addition, the Act provides for more than actual damages (discussed below) to give consumers an incentive to complain about relatively small fraudulent practices. Finally, the Act in many cases does not require a consumer who has been deceived to prove that the merchant knew about the deception. Therefore, the burden is now on merchants to know about their products, to make only truthful claims about their products, and to engage only in lawful practices.

Deceptive Trade Practices

What is a deceptive trade practice?

The Consumer Protection Act lists 23 trade practices which it declares unlawful.[3] These are often referred to as the "laundry list." Some of the more important deceptive trade practices include the following:

- *Passing off goods as being those of another.* This refers to switching or substituting brands, or implying that a product is a well-known brand.
- *Causing confusion or misunderstanding about the source, sponsorship or approval of a good.* In the example above the seller implied that NASA had developed the Powercoast additive.
- *Causing confusion or misunderstanding about the seller's affiliation or certification.* A home insulation salesperson who falsely implies that he or she is with the Department of Energy violates this prohibition.
- *Representing goods as new when they are not.*

- *False advertising, advertising goods with intent not to sell them as advertised, or advertising specials with intent not to meet the expected public demand.* This provision outlaws "bait-and-switch" tactics, fraudulent "going-out-of-business" sales, and misrepresenting the reasons for or the amount of price reductions.
- *Making false or misleading statements about another seller in an attempt to influence the consumer not to buy from that person or business.*
- *Misrepresenting the rights which a contract confers on either seller or buyer.*
- *Disconnecting or resetting an odometer.* Federal law also requires that a written odometer statement be provided to every purchaser of a motor vehicle.
- *Chain-referral sales and multi-level distributorships known as pyramid and ponzi schemes.*[4]
- *Falsely representing that work has been done or parts replaced.*

What about deceptive acts which aren't on the list?

Prior to the 1979 amendments, consumers could take advantage of a general provision which declared all false, misleading and deceptive acts to be unlawful. The 1979 amendments made this general provision unavailable to private consumers.[5] However, several of the "laundry list" provisions are so broad as to cover most forms of deception or fraud:

- Representing that goods or services have sponsorship, approval, characteristics, ingredients, uses, benefits, or quantities which they do not have;
- Representing a person has sponsorship, approval, status, affiliation, or connection which he or she does not have;
- Representing that goods or services are of a particular standard, quality, or grade, or that goods are of a particular style or model, if they are of another.

In addition, the Consumer Protection Act provides a remedy for what are called "unconscionable" acts.[6] An act is unconscionable if it does either of the following:

- takes advantage of a person's lack of knowledge or experience to a grossly unfair degree; or

• results in a gross difference between the amount paid and the value of the product or service received.

Breaches of warranty are also covered by the Act.[7] Of course, you would have a claim for breach of warranty anyway. See *Chapter 5, Warranties*. However, the usual remedy for breach of warranty does not include multiple damages awards and attorney fees, which are provided for in the Act. A "laundry list" provision also makes it illegal to misrepresent the consumer's rights under a warranty.

How much money can I recover under the Consumer Protection Act?

If you win a suit under the Act, you will recover actual damages, plus twice that portion of actual damages not exceeding $1,000. In addition, if you show that the seller *knowingly* practiced the deception, you *may* recover (at the discretion of the judge or jury) an amount up to three times the actual damages in excess of $1,000. For example, if actual damages are $3,000, then

$3,000 + (2 x $1,000) = $5,000 automatic
$2,000 x 3 = $6,000 potential
                          $11,000 maximum damages

What defenses are there to a claim under the Consumer Protection Act?

A merchant can defend against a claim under the Consumer Protection Act by showing that the false statements were made in reliance upon any of the following:
• official government records;
• written information provided by another source;
• written information concerning a test required or authorized by a governmental agency.

To establish such a defense, the merchant must also show that, before the transaction took place, you (the consumer) received written notice of the merchant's reliance on this information.

What kinds of cases concerning deceptive trade practices will an attorney handle?

The Consumer Protection Act is designed to encourage attorneys

to handle relatively small consumer disputes. For the average person, this means that the attorney must be willing to accept a case on a contingent fee basis, that is, the attorney will be paid only if the case is won. Several factors affect an attorney's decision to accept a particular case:
- likelihood of winning;
- amount of work involved;
- amount of potential recovery;
- likelihood of collecting the judgment from the particular defendant (the defendant's solvency).

Therefore, no hard and fast rule can be made regarding what types of cases a particular attorney will handle. An attorney's interest in a given case or a particular client will also be a factor in the decision whether or not to accept a case.

In general, if you are uncertain whether or not to consult a lawyer, the best advice is to go ahead and do so. The initial consultation fee is generally fairly low, usually ranging from $15 to $25, or is free. One visit may, in fact, be all you need to understand your rights and your options. See *Chapter 19, Lawyers* for suggestions on how to find a knowledgeable, reputable attorney.

What can I do for myself before hiring an attorney?

Several suggestions on what you can do for yourself are given in *Chapter 18, Self Help*. Whatever else you do, however, you must give *written notice* to the person or business against whom the complaint is being made at least 30 days before filing.[8] This notice must include the following:
- a statement that the letter is intended as notice prior to filing suit under the Consumer Protection Act;
- the specific complaint of the consumer;
- the expenses claimed, including attorney fees, if any.

Remember that if the complaint is for breach of warranty, you must give the seller a "reasonable opportunity to cure" the defect before making a demand for damages. See *Chapter 5, Warranties*.

The seller may choose to respond by sending a written promise to pay the amount of actual damages and expenses. In that case, the issue is settled. If the seller sends what you demanded within 30 days, you are barred from suing again for the same claim. This fact should be considered carefully when deciding what to demand. You shouldn't sell short your claim for damages, but an inflated claim can reduce the chance of settlement and make you look greedy at trial.

The seller may, instead, make a settlement offer that is less than the amount of damages you claimed. This offer must be made within 30 days of receipt of your written notice. You then have 30 days after receiving the settlement offer to accept it. If you take no action within that time, the seller and the courts will consider the offer to have been rejected.

The law creates an incentive to consider seriously a reasonable settlement offer. If you reject the offer and the dispute goes to trial, the judge may find that the amount *offered in settlement* and the amount *awarded by the jury or judge* are substantially the same. If this occurs, you will not receive more than the lesser of the two amounts.

What relief from deceptive trade practices can I expect from public agencies?

The Attorney General of Texas and local district and county attorneys have authority to enforce the Consumer Protection Act. The Attorney General's office has a Consumer Protection Division that maintains several offices around the state for this purpose. For addresses and phone numbers of these local offices, see *Chapter 20, Consumer Assistance Agencies.*

One serious limitation of the Consumer Protection Division is that it will prosecute only cases involving practices that affect large numbers of people. Cases that do not appear to affect more than a few people are referred to the local Better Business Bureau, if there is one. Nevertheless, it may be worthwhile to discuss your complaint with the Consumer Protection Division. Others may have complained about the same practices before or may complain later.

What legal rights protect consumers from deceptive auto repair practices?

Several studies have found that a high percentage of automobile repairs are unnecessary to begin with or are improperly performed.

Good parts are replaced, needless work is performed, and consumers are charged for parts and work they have not received. Costs are deliberately underestimated, then inflated after the car is dismantled. Work is often performed by poorly skilled workers without proper supervision.

Texas courts have held that every repair agreement includes an implied warranty that repair work will be done in a "skillful and workmanlike manner."[9] In addition, the Consumer Protection Act prohibits knowingly making false or misleading statements of fact concerning the need for parts, replacement or repair service. However, these rules are very vague, and it is seldom obvious when they have been violated. For the most part, protection from false, misleading and deceptive auto repair practices constitutes a missing link in Texas' consumer protection statutes.

What are the rights of mechanics who do auto repairs?

Mechanics also have protection from unreasonable behavior by consumers. A mechanic who performs work on a car has a *possessory lien,* which allows the mechanic to keep the car until the bill is paid. After 60 days, the mechanic may even sell the car.[10] This right to keep a car until the repairs are paid for gives a mechanic considerable leverage, which may force the consumer to pay a disputed amount. If this happens to you, tell the mechanic that this payment is being made "under protest"; then, sue to recover any unfair charges.

Would new legislation solve these auto repair problems?

Reform legislation on auto repairs has been introduced in several sessions of the Texas Legislature with little success. Such proposals have included bonding of auto repair shops, licensing of shops and/or mechanics, and requiring written estimates on all work. At least two states, Colorado and California, now require written estimates. Certain recurring deceptive activities in auto repairs should be added to the list of acts specifically prohibited by the Consumer Protection Act. In addition, a statutory implied warranty which could not be waived would provide more definite protection than the current court-made (case) law. Also, a mechanic's violation of the consumer's rights should result in the loss of any lien the mechanic would otherwise have had on the car. These laws, however, won't be passed unless Texas consumers encourage their state legislators to pass them.

What can I do to protect myself from deceptive auto repair practices?

Perhaps the most obvious and effective protection from deceptive auto repair practices is to find a mechanic whom you can trust, and deal with that mechanic as much as possible. Second, don't sign a blank work order. Even though there is no law requiring written estimates, you can request one. Ask that the estimate be made in writing on the work order or another piece of paper; then request that the mechanic call you for authorization if the cost will go more than 10 percent over that estimate. Third, if you feel that excessive work has been done, ask to have all the old parts returned. You may need them if you decide to pursue a complaint under the Consumer Protection Act.

Even if you believe you have a claim, it's probably not a good idea to give the mechanic a check to get possession of your car and then stop payment on the check. Under the current law, the mechanic would still have a right to possession of the car. It is questionable whether the mechanic could repossess the car without going to court once you took the car into your possession. However, you would risk criminal prosecution for "theft of services."[11] You would not be guilty if you acted in "good faith," but the legal proceedings could be expensive and embarrassing.

The Legislature intended for the Consumer Protection Act to make a profound change in business practices in Texas. Under traditional legal principles, consumers had been practically powerless to obtain relief from shady business practices. Except in cases involving thousands of dollars in damages, the expense and inconvenience of going to court made such suits prohibitive.

When it passed the Consumer Protection Act in 1973, the Legislature confronted this problem in the same way the federal antitrust statutes dealt with monopolistic business practices — by allowing consumers who win lawsuits under the Act to collect three times their actual damages plus attorney fees. This gave consumers more incentive to take their complaints to court, and it gave those in business more incentive to eliminate deceptive practices and deal fairly with consumers. The Consumer Protection Act, therefore, has had a regulatory effect on business practices far beyond the scope of the individual cases that have been taken to court.

Furthermore, the Consumer Protection Act has accomplished all this at little expense to the taxpayer, since the Act did not require a new and costly enforcement agency. Although the Attorney General of Texas exercises some enforcement powers, the Consumer Protection Act is enforced primarily by consumers acting in their own self interest and filing lawsuits as "private attorneys general." In fact, the Consumer Protection Act has been so effective that some business interests spent millions of dollars in 1979 lobbying the Texas Legislature to throttle the Act with amendments. They succeeded in having the treble damages provision replaced with the complicated formula explained in this chapter, and in adding a number of procedural barriers to hinder consumer lawsuits.

We have seen that Texas consumers, together with business people who understand that fair dealing is good business, can have an effective voice in the Legislature. However, we have also seen that the dollars of well-financed special interests make a more persuasive argument to some of our elected officials. Since representatives of the public interest will never have the dollars with which to answer back, they must depend upon their constituents, the consumers and voters of Texas, to speak clearly. Just by letting their representatives know they are aware of the issues being debated, individual Texans can have real influence.

Chapter 7
Door-to-Door Sales and Mail Orders

In his classic study *The Poor Pay More*, sociologist David Caplovitz concluded that door-to-door credit merchants were responsible for some of the more outrageous incidents of exploitation reported by the families surveyed.[1] Poor people, however, are not the only victims of shady door-to-door sales.

The door-to-door sales technique is not in itself deceptive or unfair, but its success does depend on impulse buying. The appeal is usually the promise of a low down payment and easy terms. This is a high-pressure sales technique that lends itself to shady practices. Such practices are also encouraged by laws requiring the consumer to pay the installments whether satisfied with the product or not. Although these laws have been changed substantially in recent years, few consumers are aware of their rights in this area. See *Chapter 17, Financers' Responsibilities*

Because door-to-door sales have proven to be a special problem, these sales are now regulated by both a Texas statute and a Federal Trade Commission (FTC) regulation.[2] Both these laws provide for a *three-day "cooling off period"* in door-to-door sales. This means the buyer has an absolute right to cancel the agreement until midnight of the third business day after the contract is signed. You can cancel simply by mailing a notice of cancellation (described below) at any time within that three-day period. In addition, both laws require that all contracts and notices used in a door-to-door sale be in the same language as that principally used in the oral sales presentation.

In what types of sales am I protected by the three-day cooling off period?

The FTC rule provides for a three-day cooling off period in any sale, lease or rental of consumer goods or services costing a total of $25 or more, whenever the sales pitch *and* the consumer's agreement to buy are both made at any place other than the seller's place of business. Therefore, you are protected if the sales pitch and purchase agreement are made at a neighbor's home, or on a sidewalk, or in your own home. You are protected even if the sale is made in response to your invitation, as long as the sales pitch and purchase agreement are both made outside the seller's place of business. The

FTC rule has common-sense exceptions for immediate personal emergencies, sales entirely by mail or telephone, and repair of moveable things.

Although the FTC rule does not apply to real estate, the Texas three-day cooling off period does apply to purchases of real estate for more than $100 as long as the sales pitch and purchase agreement are both made at the buyer's residence.[3] Even the Texas law does not apply, however, if the buyer of real estate is represented by an attorney or if the deal is negotiated by a real estate broker.

What do I have to do to cancel a door-to-door sale?

Any contract that results from a door-to-door sale (as defined above) is required to contain the following notice:

> You, the buyer, may cancel this transaction at any time prior to midnight of the third business day after the date of this transaction. See the attached notice of cancellation form for an explanation of this right.

You must also be given a separate "Notice of Cancellation" form that looks like this:

NOTICE OF CANCELLATION

_____
(date of transaction)

You may cancel this transaction, without any penalty or obligation, within three business days from the above date.

If you cancel, any property traded in, any payments made by you under the contract or sale, and any negotiable instrument executed by you will be returned within 10 business days following receipt by the seller of your cancellation notice, and any security interest arising out of the transaction will be cancelled.

If you cancel, you must make available to the seller at your residence, in substantially as good condition as when received, any goods delivered to you under this contract or sale; or you may, if you wish, comply with the instructions of the seller regarding the return shipment of the goods at the seller's expense and risk.

If you do make the goods available to the seller and the seller does not pick them up within 20 days of the date of your notice of cancellation, you may retain or dispose of the goods without any further obligation. If you fail to make the goods available to the seller, or if you agree to return the goods to the seller and fail to do so, then you remain liable for performance of all obligations under the contract.

To cancel this transaction, mail or deliver a signed and dated copy of this cancellation notice or any other written notice, or send a telegram, to

_____ at _____
     Name of seller   Address of seller's place of business

_____ not later than midnight of _____
                                                                                         date

I hereby cancel this transaction.

_____ _____
     date   Buyer's signature

The form must include the date of the sale, the date by which the agreement may be cancelled, and the address to which the notice of cancellation must be sent.

To cancel, the buyer simply dates and signs the form and mails it. It would be wise to send it by certified mail, return receipt requested. Make sure it is postmarked before midnight of the third business day following the sale.

What are my rights if the door-to-door seller does not provide a cancellation form?

Even if the seller does not provide a cancellation form or does not give notice of the right to cancel, you still have that right. Cancellation may be done in any reasonable manner, but, to simplify matters, it *should be in writing.* A certified letter to the seller's place of business identifying the transaction and stating the buyer's desire to cancel is sufficient. You should also be sure to keep your copy of the contract.

The seller's failure to provide the required notice and form is a violation of the Texas statute.[4] One consequence of such a violation is that the buyer may cancel at any time, even after the three-day period.[5]

Do I have any further obligations after cancelling a door-to-door contract?

You have several obligations even after a contract has been cancelled. If you have already received goods and the seller demands their return, you must comply. However, you are required to do nothing more than make the goods available to the seller at his or her residence. If the seller fails to demand return of the goods within 20 days, you become the owner without further obligation. A seller who performs services after a contract is properly cancelled is entitled to no compensation, but you have a duty to take reasonably good care of property after giving notice of cancellation.

What must the seller do when a door-to-door contract is cancelled?

The intent of the Texas Home Solicitation Sales Act is to put the buyer who has cancelled back in the same position as before the agreement was made. Therefore, within 10 days from the date of cancellation, the seller must do the following:
- refund all money you have paid;
- return any trade-in or offer you cash equal to the trade-in allowance if the seller cannot return the item undamaged;
- cancel all security interests and negotiable instruments;
- restore all buildings to their original condition (in home repair sales) unless you request otherwise;
- notify you as to whether the seller intends to take possession of property which has been delivered or to abandon it.

What is the consequence of a seller's violating the Texas Home Solicitation Sales Act?

You may sue any seller who violates the Home Solicitation Sales Act for actual damages, attorney fees and court costs. Violation of the Act is considered in itself to be a deceptive trade practice.[6] Therefore, the multiple damages rules of the Deceptive Trade Practices-Consumer Protection Act may apply. See *Chapter 6, Deceptive Trade Practices.* Most important, violation of any of the requirements of the Act make the contract *void* and unenforceable.[7]

Buying, Renting & Borrowing in Texas

What laws protect those who shop by mail?

Federal law gives the consumer certain rights when shopping by mail.[8] You can cancel a mail order if the item ordered does not arrive within a reasonable time. If a time is advertised by the seller, that time is what is considered "reasonable" under this law. Otherwise, 30 days is considered to be a "reasonable" time. The seller must notify you of any shipping delay and provide a free means for you to reply. When you cancel, the seller must make a refund within seven business days. If the sale is on credit, the seller has one billing cycle to make a refund and adjust the account. If you receive *unordered* merchandise in the mail, *you may keep it without paying for it*. This federal law, however, does not apply to C.O.D. (cash on delivery) orders, to negative check-off plans (such as Book-of-the-Month Club), or to certain specific businesses, including photo finishing and magazine subscriptions.

The laws discussed in this chapter have probably helped to curb deceptive practices in door-to-door sales and mail orders. However, no law will ever reach the root of the problem, which is that many of us frequently buy on impulse in response to clever sales pitches and alluring advertisements. Perhaps some of this is inevitable in a fast paced, affluent society. Perhaps we are all too easily convinced that happiness can be bought. Whatever our motives, impulse buying causes problems which can best be resolved by applying common sense and a little financial discipline.

Chapter 8
Automobiles and Other Goods

The law distinguishes between two general types of tangible property: *real estate* (land and improvements attached to it); and *goods* (everything that is moveable). Part One of this book, *Buying and Renting Homes,* dealt with real estate. This chapter will discuss the special legal rules concerning sales of automobiles, plus some other rules that apply to sales of goods generally.

AUTOMOBILE TITLES

A *certificate of title* describes the vehicle and states the names of the owner and lienholder (if any). Certificates of title are issued on all "motor vehicles" in Texas, including automobiles, trailers, house trailers, motorcycles, etc.

What is the purpose of a certificate of title?

The certificate of title provides reliable identification of the owner of a vehicle and of the lienholder, if any. It also provides a reliable and simple procedure for transferring ownership. This procedure is simpler than transfers of real estate, in which title is evidenced by many documents prepared over a long period of time.

94   Buying, Renting & Borrowing in Texas

See *Chapter 1, Buying and Selling Homes*. The certificate of title method is more reliable than procedures for transferring ownership of goods other than motor vehicles, because such transfers generally do not require any documents.

What are the mechanics of transferring a certificate of title?

In a sale in which the seller is not an automobile dealer, the buyer and seller often go together to the county tax collector's office to do all the paperwork at once. This simplifies things greatly, but is not necessary as long as the following steps are taken:

1. The buyer pays the seller (or signs a credit contract), and the seller signs on the back of the certificate of title before a notary.

2. The seller and buyer sign before a notary a "Seller, Donor or Trader's Affidavit" describing the sale and amount of sales tax to be paid.

3. The seller gives the buyer the following: (a) Certificate of Title, (b) Seller, Donor or Trader's Affidavit, and (c) receipt for payment of current registration (license plate) fees. The buyer then takes these documents, with cash or other acceptable means of paying sales tax and fees, to the office of the county tax collector.

4. There, the buyer (a) turns in the above three documents, (b) signs an "Application for Original Title," and (c) pays the sales tax and title fee. This should be done within 20 days of the seller's signing the title to avoid a late fee.

5. As an alternative to steps 3 and 4, the seller (usually a dealer when this method is used) may collect all the necessary papers described above, plus the sales tax and title fee, and submit them all to the county tax collector.

6. The tax collector gives the buyer a receipt, which serves as a temporary "title." The tax collector then mails the papers and funds to the State Department of Highways and Public Transportation. If everything is in order, the Department will mail the buyer a new certificate of title, which the buyer then signs on the front.

If there is no lien (that is, if the buyer paid cash rather than purchasing the car on credit), the buyer's certificate of title is marked "Original." If there is a lien, the buyer's certificate of title is marked "Duplicate Original," and the "Original" goes to the creditor who owns the lien. The "Duplicate Original" is printed in red

Automobiles and Other Goods 95

The Comptroller of Public Accounts
Form 2C00-2.09
(Rev. 8-77)

SELLER, DONOR, OR TRADER'S AFFIDAVIT

Assessor-Collector's Tax Receipt No. _____

Texas Dealer License No. _____

IN COMPLETING FORM, CHECK APPROPRIATE SECTION BLOCK:

The motor vehicle and all accessories attached thereto was disposed of as set out below:

Make of Vehicle	Motor or Vehicle Identification No.	
Year Model	Body Style	License Number

☐ (1) was **SOLD** to _____

For a total sales price of.............	$ _____
Less trade-in...................	$ _____
Taxable Value	$ _____
Amount of 4% Sales or Use Tax	$ _____
Less Sales or Use Tax paid to the State of _____	$ _____

AMOUNT OF TAX COLLECTED $ _____

↳ The following described vehicle was traded in:

Make of Vehicle	Motor or Vehicle Identification No.	
Year Model	Body Style	License Number

☐ (2) **GIFT** — was transferred to _____
without any consideration paid or to be paid for said motor vehicle, nor assumption of Lien. **AMOUNT OF TAX COLLECTED** $ __10.00__

☐ (3) Was **TRADED EVEN** for the motor vehicle described as follows:

Make of Vehicle	Motor or Vehicle Identification No.	
Year Model	Body Style	License Number

AMOUNT OF TAX COLLECTED $ 5.00 each party

Before me this day personally appeared the person(s) whose signature(s) appears below who by me being duly sworn upon oath says the above statements are true and correct.

sign here ▶ Seller, Donor, or Trader _____ by _____

Address _____

SEAL — Subscribed and sworn to before me this _____ day of _____, 19 _____
   Notary Public | County | State

PURCHASER, DONEE, OR TRADER'S AFFIDAVIT

The above statements are true and correct.

sign here ▶ Purchaser, Donee, or Trader _____ by _____

Address _____

SEAL — Subscribed and sworn to before me this _____ day of _____, 19 _____
   Notary Public | County | State

WARNING: TEX. TAX.-GEN. ANN. art. 6.05(1)(Supp. 1977)

Any person who knowingly signs a false joint affidavit is guilty of a <u>felony</u> punishable by imprisonment for not more than five(5) years nor less than two(2) years or by a fine of not more than One Thousand Dollars ($1,000) or by both fine and imprisonment.

Form 2C00-2.09(Back)(Rev. 8-77)

(4) NEW RESIDENT MOTOR VEHICLE USE TAX AFFIDAVIT

THE STATE OF TEXAS

Collector's Receipt No. _____

COUNTY OF _____

AMOUNT OF TAX COLLECTED $ <u>15.00</u>

Before me, the undersigned authority, on this day personally appeared the person whose signature appears below, who by me being sworn, says that he is a new resident of Texas, that he is making application for certificate of title and registration in this State on a motor vehicle purchased in the state of _____ and that said motor vehicle is

Year	Make	Body	VIN	License No.

sign here ▶ New Resident _____ by _____

Address _____

Subscribed and sworn to before me this _____ day of _____, 19 _____

Notary Public | County | State

SEAL

(5) REGISTRATION OR TRANSFER OF MOTOR VEHICLE ON WHICH NO SALES, USE, OR TRANSFER TAX IS DUE – AFFIDAVIT OF FACTS

THE STATE OF TEXAS

Collector's Receipt No. _____

COUNTY OF _____

Before me, the undersigned authority, on this day personally appeared (name) _____ and after being duly sworn, deposes, and upon oath says; that on the _____ day of _____, 19 _____, he acquired the following described motor vehicle:

Year	Make	Body	VIN	License No.

on which the undersigned claims exemption from payment of taxes under the Motor Vehicle Retail Sales and Use Tax Law, TEX. TAX.-GEN. ANN. Ch. 6 (1969), for the following reasons:

_____
_____
_____
_____
_____
_____
_____

sign here ▶ Person or Organization _____ by _____

Address _____

Subscribed and sworn to before me this _____ day of _____, 19 _____

Notary Public | County | State

SEAL

TAX ASSESSOR–COLLECTOR MUST NOT ACCEPT THE AFFIDAVIT UNLESS IT HAS BEEN COMPLETED IN EVERY DETAIL.

Automobiles and Other Goods

STAPLE HERE

APPLICATION FOR TEXAS CERTIFICATE OF TITLE
(FOR ALL VEHICLE CLASSIFICATIONS)

MAKE OF VEHICLE	VEHICLE IDENTIFICATION NO
YEAR MODEL	BODY STYLE

TEXAS LICENSE NUMBER	MFG RATED CARRYING CAPACITY TON	EMPTY WEIGHT

PREVIOUS OWNER	CITY	STATE

NAME AND LOCAL RESIDENT ADDRESS OF OWNER

ZIP CODE

THE SAID MOTOR VEHICLE IS SUBJECT TO THE FOLLOWING LIENS AND NONE OTHER

1ST LIEN DATE	NAME AND ADDRESS OF FIRST LIEN HOLDER

ZIP CODE

2ND LIEN DATE	NAME AND ADDRESS OF SECOND LIEN HOLDER

IF APPLICATION IS FOR CORRECTED TITLE, CHECK REASON(S) BELOW

MARK "X" FOR CORRECTION
☐ Make in Error ☐ Body Style in Error ☐ Year Model in Error
☐ VIN in Error ☐ Other

SIGNATURE OF OWNER OR AGENT

ALL ABOVE INFORMATION (EXCEPT SIGNATURE) TO BE TYPED OR PRINTED

Before me this day personally appeared the applicant(s) whose signature(s) appear above who by me being duly sworn upon oath says that the statements set forth above are true and correct

NOTARY SEAL

Subscribed and sworn to before me this _____ day of _____ 19 ___

_____ _____ TEXAS
NOTARY PUBLIC   COUNTY

**APPLICATION MUST BE FILED WITH COUNTY TAX ASSESSOR-COLLECTOR
FEE $3.00**

TAX COLLECTOR'S RECEIPT
FOR TITLE APPLICATION NO. _____ (FORM 31)
(SHOW COMPLETE NO —INCLUDING PREFIX OR SUFFIX IF ANY)

TAX COLLECTOR _____ COUNTY _____

DATE OF RECEIPT _____ BY _____ DEPUTY _____

STATE DEPARTMENT OF HIGHWAYS
AND PUBLIC TRANSPORTATION
MOTOR VEHICLE DIVISION   40th and JACKSON AVE.
AUSTIN, TEXAS 78779

Form 30U

98   Buying, Renting & Borrowing in Texas

STAPLE HERE	**TAX COLLECTOR'S RECEIPT FOR TITLE APPLICATION** Receipt is hereby acknowledged of fee of $3.00 and application for ORIGINAL - CORRECTED Certificate of Title			No. E 658128	
	By Owner		Address		Zip Code
	Betty Cunningham		456 Oak Ave.	Blank TEX	77777
	Year	Make	Body Style	Motor or Vehicle Identification No	
	79	Ford	4 Dr	9U92H156542	
	Surrendered Title No		License No		
		New		ABC 123	
	1st Lien Date	Name and Address of First Lien Holder			
	None				
	2nd Lien Date	Name and Address of Second Lien Holder			
	None				
	Date Issued	County	Tax Assessor Collector		Deputy
	9-15-79	Blank	R. L. Gorham		AR
	DUPLICATE To State Department of Highways and Public Transportation		STATE DEPARTMENT OF HIGHWAYS AND PUBLIC TRANSPORTATION		
	Form 31 Rev. 5-78				

TEXAS CERTIFICATE OF TITLE

CHEV   1L69H4C134676   00000000
1974 4DR
XXX000   4400   0000000   SAMPLE   03/2/74

QUALITY MOTOR CO   CENTER CITY, TEX   ORIGINAL

JOHN DOE   12/20/73 ABC FINANCE CO
123 COLLEGE AVENUE   321 MAIN
CENTER CITY, TEX 78700   CENTER CITY, TEX 78700

B. L. DEBERRY, ENGINEER-DIRECTOR
R. W. TOWNSLEY, DIRECTOR MOTOR VEHICLE DIVISION

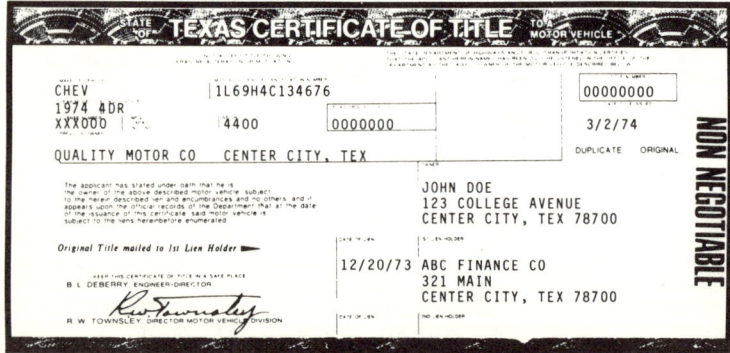

STATE OF TEXAS CERTIFICATE OF TITLE TO A MOTOR VEHICLE

CHEV   1L69H4C134676   00000000
1974 4DR
XXX000   4400   0000000   3/2/74
                                                 DUPLICATE   ORIGINAL
QUALITY MOTOR CO   CENTER CITY, TEX

The applicant has stated under oath that he is the owner of the above described motor vehicle subject to the herein described lien and encumbrances and no others and it appears upon the official records of the Department that at the date of the issuance of this certificate, said motor vehicle is subject to the liens hereinbefore enumerated.

Original Title mailed to 1st Lien Holder ➤

JOHN DOE
123 COLLEGE AVENUE
CENTER CITY, TEX 78700

12/20/73 ABC FINANCE CO
          321 MAIN
          CENTER CITY, TEX 78700

B. L. DEBERRY, ENGINEER-DIRECTOR
R. W. TOWNSLEY, DIRECTOR MOTOR VEHICLE DIVISION

NON NEGOTIABLE

Automobiles and Other Goods 99

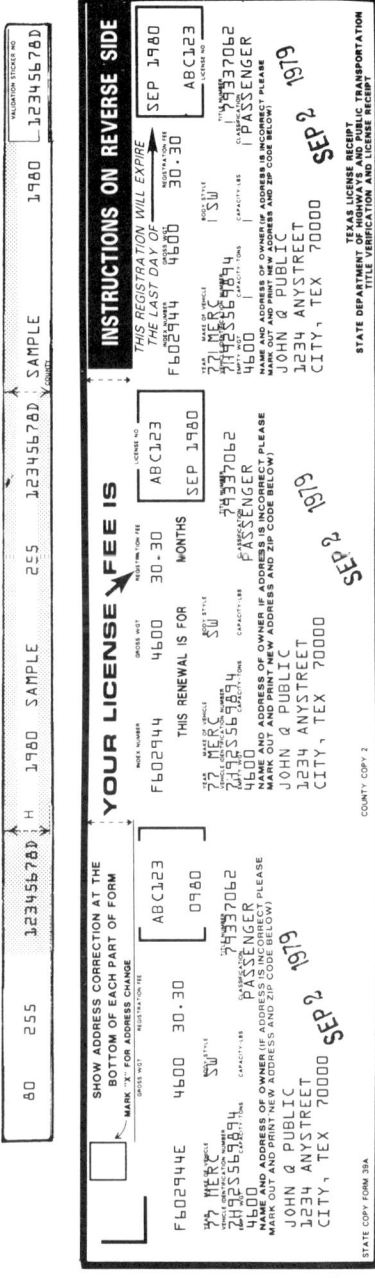

and has the word "non-negotiable" on its face; the "Original" is blue and can be negotiated (sold, traded, etc.). Until the lien is removed, the buyer cannot sell the vehicle, since a "Duplicate Original" cannot be used for a sale. When the debt is paid, the creditor signs the release of lien form on the "Original" and gives the "Original" to the buyer. The buyer then submits the "Original" to the tax collector, fills out Form 3011, pays a title fee, and is issued an "Original Certificate of Title" showing that there is no longer any lien.

What is the legal effect of "selling" a motor vehicle without transferring the certificate of title?

Some sellers, including some automobile dealers, "sell" motor vehicles on credit without transferring the title. Instead of obtaining a non-negotiable duplicate original certificate of title, the buyer obtains the seller's promise to transfer the title after full payment has been made. Presumably, the purpose is to cut down on the paper work necessary for a proper transfer of title with the seller receiving a lien.

This practice, however, is a criminal offense punishable by a $200 fine.[1] Of more practical importance, you run the risk of having purchased a car from someone who does not *have* a title. Similarly, even if the seller has a title at the time of the sale, the seller may be dead or otherwise unable to transfer the title when you have paid the debt. Without a certificate of title, you will not be able to renew the registration (license plates) nor sell the car. The vehicle, therefore, will be worthless within a year.

This means that, whether you are buying or selling, it is to your advantage to comply with the Certificate of Title Act. Failure to do so can lead to real nightmares. See your county tax collector to transfer certificates of title or for information about them.

How can a lost or stolen certificate of title be replaced?

The county tax collector can provide an affidavit form to be filled out. A certified copy of the certificate of title will then be provided by the State Department of Highways and Public Transportation.[2]

Automobiles and Other Goods 101

What can be done to require issuance of a certificate of title?

If you believe you own a motor vehicle but cannot obtain a certificate of title from the State Department of Highways and Public Transportation, or if your title has been suspended, follow these steps:

1. Make a formal application for a title with the county tax collector of the county of your residence, if you have not yet done so, even if you expect to be refused.

2. Apply with the county tax collector for a hearing.

3. At the hearing, present your evidence as to why you should be given a certificate of title. If you lose at this hearing, you may appeal to the county court in the same county by filing an appeal within five days of the date of the tax collector's decision.[3] This procedure may work if you have bought a car on credit without obtaining the certificate of title and then have been unable to obtain the certificate of title from the seller after paying off the debt.

102   Buying, Renting & Borrowing in Texas

What should new residents of Texas do to obtain Texas certificates of title for their motor vehicles?

Any motor vehicle owner who moves to Texas must obtain a Texas certificate of title and Texas license plates for each motor vehicle owned. This must be done within 30 days of establishing a residence in Texas or beginning gainful employment here.[4] The new resident should first have the vehicle inspected at any service station or garage designated as an official inspection station. For $5 the vehicle will be inspected and a certificate issued to the effect that it is the same vehicle as that described on the certificate of title from the former state. Then take the papers furnished by the inspection station and the certificate of title from the former state to the county tax collector of the county in which you live and do the following:

1. Fill out a "New Resident Motor Vehicle Use Tax Affidavit" and pay a $15 "use tax."

2. Fill out an "Application for Texas Certificate of Title" and pay a $3 filing fee.

3. Pay the fee for registration (license plates) applicable to the particular vehicle.

4. Obtain a Texas driver's license from the local Texas Department of Public Safety office.

How can I find out who owns a particular motor vehicle?

You can determine the current owner of any motor vehicle registered in Texas by calling the State Department of Highways and Public Transportation at 512/475-7611 and giving the current license plate number of the vehicle.

ODOMETERS AND THE LAW

When it comes time to sell a car, one with 25,000 miles on it will obviously bring a better price than the same car with 75,000 miles. It will also bring a higher profit to the used car dealer, especially if the car had a "mileage" of 75,000 miles when the dealer bought it.

The way some used car dealers make the additional miles vanish is by turning back the odometer (mileage indicator). Although odometer tampering has always been illegal, the laws against this practice have not been well enforced. To put some teeth into the laws against odometer tampering, Congress passed the Motor Vehicle Information and Cost Savings Act.[5]

What is the effect of federal odometer disclosure requirements?

Every person selling a motor vehicle, whether a dealer or individual owner, *should comply with the odometer requirements of the federal Motor Vehicle Information and Cost Savings Act.* This primarily provides that the seller (or other transferor) of a motor vehicle must sign a form disclosing to the buyer the mileage shown on the odometer, and whether or not the seller knows this mileage to be correct. The necessary form can be obtained from most auto dealers.

Most individuals and some dealers do not know they must do this. Although there is no automatic penalty for simply failing to provide the form, there is a risk involved for the seller. If you, as the buyer, can later prove that the seller failed to make the disclosure or made it incorrectly "with intent to defraud," you can recover $1500 (or three times the actual damages, whichever is greater), plus costs and attorney fees from the seller.

How can I tell whether an odometer has been rolled back?

If you find that a car had more miles on it when the dealer bought it than when it was later sold, you know there has been an odometer roll-back. One can often find this out by requesting a title search and contacting the former owner. Another way to detect an odometer roll-back is to look at the records of the inspection station where the car was last inspected. These records should show the car's odometer reading at that time, which may be higher than the present mileage. Other records of previous mileage may be on the car itself. An oil-change sticker on the car door, for example, may show a higher previous mileage.

An experienced mechanic can sometimes estimate that certain moving parts of a car have moved a lot more miles than the odometer shows. In addition, even an amateur can sometimes detect crude tampering with the odometer itself. Scratch marks are often left by tampering, or a whole column of numbers may be broken if, for example, the mileage has been knocked down from 89,000 to 29,000.

104 Buying, Renting & Borrowing in Texas

Odometer tampering is still so common that consumers' attorneys look for it as a matter of course in investigating any complaint about an automobile. Make your own odometer investigation *before* buying any motor vehicle.

How can I find out about the previous ownership of a motor vehicle?

You can find out about a motor vehicle's past by ordering a title history for a small fee. The history may disclose many facts of interest to you as the buyer. For example, the vehicle may once have been a rental car, or it may not be the "one-owner car" the seller said it was; and, as suggested above, a previous owner may disclose surprising information about the mileage and other features. To order a title history, send the $5 fee and the current license plate number (or title number or vehicle identification number) to this address: Motor Vehicle Division, State Department of Highways and Public Transportation, 40th and Jackson, Austin, TX 78779.

The title history will go back 10 years, or to the time the car was registered in Texas. The title history, then, will list only transfers within Texas. Therefore, if the vehicle is less than 10 years old and has never been registered outside Texas, this will be a complete title history. You may also be able to obtain title histories from other states by contacting the appropriate state agencies.

THE IMPORTANCE OF WRITTEN CONTRACTS

The rules discussed below apply not only to automobiles, but to sales of all kinds. This discussion will help you to know when you have a contract and when you do not. It will also discuss the effect of oral agreements on a written contract.

What contracts have to be in writing?

Under the *statute of frauds,* a contract to sell *real property* is generally not enforceable at all unless it is written down and signed by both parties. Contracts for the sale of real property are discussed in *Chapter 1, Buying and Selling Homes.*

Similarly, a contract for the sale of *goods* (moveable things) for

$500 or more is not enforceable unless it is in writing and signed by the person against whom enforcement is sought.[6] This rule is usually swallowed up, however, by an exception: such a contract *is* enforceable if the person against whom enforcement is sought admits that the contract was made. In such a case, it is enforceable to the extent of the quantity of goods admitted to be covered by the contract.

> Pasqual Parsimoni orally agreed to buy a used Bentley Bomber for $2,500. Before the certificate of title was transferred, he read an article claiming the Bomber was unsafe. Pasqual then refused to complete the purchase. The seller, Blaze Autos, filed suit, claiming that the bottom had dropped out of the Bomber market. Blaze said that the best it could get for the car was $2,000 at a later sale. It also claimed that Pasqual had agreed to buy a boat trailer for $600.
>
> At the trial, Pasqual admitted that he had agreed to pay $2,500 for the car but denied agreeing to buy the boat trailer. Pasqual is liable for the $500 in damages for breach of the Bomber contract, but he is not liable for refusing to buy the trailer.

A less important exception to the statute of frauds is that, where goods are to be specially manufactured, an oral contract to buy them will be enforced as soon as the manufacturer has started working on them or ordered materials for them.

If there is a written contract, do oral statements have any legal effect?

The general rule (known as the *parol evidence rule*) is that, where there is a written contract (whether required by the statute of frauds or not), neither party will be allowed to prove that oral statements made at or before the time of signing are part of the agreement.[7] This is one good reason that, when a salesperson makes a promise, the familiar advice to "get it in writing" should be followed.

This rule has several important exceptions, however. The "usual course of dealing" of the parties (how they have dealt with each other in similar transactions in the past) is legally admissible in court. Even terms that do not appear in the contract at all may be added, unless the written contract specifies that it is the complete agreement of all parties involved. Finally, the most important way around the parol evidence rule is to argue that the complaint being made is not based on violation of the contract.[8]

> Suppose in our example that Blaze Autos told Pasqual the Bentley Bomber had 20,000 miles on it. After signing the contract, Pasqual discovered that its actual mileage was 120,000. He could call the representation a "warranty" in the contract, but if he did he would lose. On the other hand, he could call it fraud, a violation of the federal odometer statute, and six varieties of deceptive trade practices. Then his complaint would not be "on the contract," and the fraudulent statement would be admissible.

In summary: Get it in writing, if possible. If the agreement is not in writing, though, make your complaint and pursue it anyway.

PART THREE
BORROWING MONEY

Chapter 9
Credit and Collateral

One of the authors once overheard a law professor lament that a first-year student had asked in class, "What is a mortgage?" "I thought," the professor sniffed, "that my students were starting law school with a somewhat firmer foundation." Whereupon, the author made a beeline for the law library to pore over a half dozen definitions of "mortgage."

We think the professor was out of touch with his students if he thought most of them knew about mortgages. However, we agree with him that the concept is fundamental to understanding our commercial system. The sad truth is that our educational system teaches very few of us the fundamentals of how the commercial system works.

This chapter will explain how and why debts are *secured* by *collateral,* and will briefly examine how consumer credit is funneled from financial institutions to retailers and consumers. This discussion should lay a foundation for subsequent chapters detailing what happens if the consumer fails to pay a debt *(Chapter 4, Foreclosure on Homes; Chapter 14, Repossession; Chapter 15, The Homestead and Other Judgment Exemptions; Chapter 16, Debt Collection Practices)* and when a financer is responsible for a consumer complaint *(Chapter 17, Financers' Responsibilities).*

THE IMPORTANCE OF COLLATERAL

What does it mean for a debt to be secured by collateral?

Collateral is specific property that a debtor agrees a creditor may take if the debtor fails to pay as agreed or otherwise defaults. The creditor's right to take the collateral is called a *security interest,* a *lien,* or a *mortgage.* All three terms mean exactly the same thing. *Security interest* is a more modern term and is ordinarily used in referring to the creditor's interest in collateral that is moveable (*goods*). The term *mortgage* is traditionally applied to the creditor's interest in real estate, while a *lien* commonly pertains to both goods and real estate.

A creditor who has not secured a debt with collateral may still be able to collect without the debtor's voluntary cooperation. However, collection of such an *unsecured* debt is more expensive and uncertain because a lawsuit must be filed to obtain a judgment. After a judgment has been obtained, the creditor may still not be able to collect because the debtor's property may be *judgment exempt,* that is, exempt from being taken to enforce a judgment. See *Chapter 15, The Homestead and Other Judgment Exemptions.* Thus, a creditor who does not have a security interest in collateral is literally less "secure" than one who does.

What legal documents are used to secure a debt?

When the collateral is moveable (goods), the document the debtor signs to give the creditor a security interest is called a *security agreement.* This document describes the collateral and stipulates that the debtor gives the creditor a security interest in the collateral to secure payment of a certain debt. The security agreement may be a separate document, but it is usually contained in the note or other credit contract.

When the collateral is real estate, the document the debtor signs to give the creditor a security interest (commonly called a mortgage) is called a *deed of trust.* This is a legal device used in Texas and some other states to allow the creditor to obtain title to the collateral without going to court if the debtor defaults.

Credit and Collateral   111

How does a creditor take collateral away from a defaulting debtor?

If the collateral consists of goods, the creditor may simply seize the goods in a "self-help" repossession. To accomplish this legally, the creditor must do so without "breaching the peace." See *Chapter 14, Repossession.*

If the collateral is real estate, the creditor may have the property sold at a *deed of trust sale* after giving notice of the sale to the debtor. See *Chapter 4, Foreclosure on Homes.*

How does a creditor protect the security interest in case the buyer should decide to sell the collateral or use it as collateral for another debt?

The method by which the security interest is protected is determined by the nature of the collateral. If the collateral consists of goods other than a motor vehicle, the creditor files a *financing statement* in the county courthouse and/or other appropriate place. This protects the creditor's security interest from a *good-faith purchaser.* That is, if the debtor then sells the collateral to someone else, the creditor can still repossess it if the debt is not paid. If the collateral is a motor vehicle, the notation of the lien on the certificate of title has the same effect as the filing of a financing statement. If the collateral is real estate, the creditor files the deed of trust in the real property records of the county in which the land is located. Like a financing statement, this is a public document that gives all the world legal notice of the creditor's interest in the collateral, so that a purchaser or later creditor will take the collateral only subject to the earlier creditor's interest. When the debt has been paid, the creditor signs a release form that is filed so that the earlier security agreement or deed of trust will no longer be in effect.

Can a security interest provide that the collateral secures future debts to the same creditor?

The *future indebtedness* security interest is taken routinely by many creditors. When the buyer later buys something else on credit before paying off the first debt, the second debt is secured by the first purchase as well as by the second. As long as the buyer stays in debt to the same seller, this can go on indefinitely. At some point,

112   Buying, Renting & Borrowing in Texas

default on a relatively small debt will allow the creditor to repossess many items of considerable value. Texas needs legislation to prevent abuse of this device. Meanwhile, consumers should protect themselves by paying off each installment contract before signing another one with the same creditor.

Look at the following example to see how this device can work to the creditor's advantage:

> Happy Homeowner bought an electric heater in January, 1979, for $50 and charged it to her credit account at E-Z Pay Department Store. In March, Happy charged a $100 lawn mower to the same account; in May, a $225 window cooler; and in September, a $150 table. On October 1, she lost her job and had to quit making the $50 minimum monthly payments. At that time she had paid $450 on a total debt of $525 (plus interest). On November 1, she was still out of work so offered to return the table to pay off her account. The

credit manager told her she would have to pay the full amount owed in cash, although it was less than $100, or the store would repossess the heater, the lawn mower, and the cooler, as well as the table.

At the time of the repossession, Happy would owe only $75 plus interest; but, after the repossession, she would also owe a repossession fee and, probably, attorney fees and fees for storage and resale of the collateral. Since repossession sales bring notoriously low prices, she might well be left with nothing.

HOW CREDIT IS EXTENDED BY SELLERS

All consumer credit is, logically, extended either by the seller or by someone else. If funds are obtained from someone else to pay for the items purchased the credit is called a *loan*. Even where credit is initially extended by the seller, the consumer usually ends up owing the money to a financial institution (bank, savings and loan, etc.) to which the seller *assigns* (sells) the right to receive payments.

Nevertheless, it frequently makes a great difference legally whether or not the credit was originally extended by the seller or the lender. The maximum finance charge that may be assessed is determined by who extends the credit. See *Chapter 11, Calculating the Costs of Credit*. This distinction may also determine whether or not the consumer has a right to quit paying if the product is defective or other complaints against the seller exist. See *Chapter 17, Financers' Responsibilities*.

What are the differences in the basic credit plans used by sellers?

There are two types of consumer credit contracts: charge accounts (*open-end* credit, including credit card accounts) and installment contracts (*closed-end* credit). With a charge account, buyer and seller agree initially on the terms and limits of credit; then, many items may be purchased later under that same agreement. In an installment contract, credit is extended only for the items listed in the contract.

Buying, Renting & Borrowing in Texas

How can a buyer end up making payments to a financing institution?

Most small businesses obtain funds to cover inventory and other costs by borrowing from a financial institution (usually a commercial bank). These loans are secured by the inventory and the debts owed (and to be owed) the business by its customers. Sometimes, especially when large items like automobiles are sold, the arrangement requires that the business assign its installment contracts to the financer. After assignment, the customer will then pay the financer rather than the dealer. See *Chapter 17, Financers' Responsibilities* for a discussion of the lender's obligation regarding breach of warranty, etc., in such a sale.

In effect, the dealer is arranging financing for the customer. This is very convenient, but it can also be very expensive. By arranging your own loan, you can often save several percentage points on the credit, which may mean hundreds of dollars on a major purchase like an automobile. Some dealers also give better prices on cash sales. See *Chapter 11, Calculating the Costs of Credit.*

HOW CREDIT IS EXTENDED BY LENDERS

Most of this discussion about credit extension in sales applies to direct loans as well. A deed of trust is used to create a mortgage on real estate, whether the creditor is the seller or a lending institution. Similarly, a security agreement is used to create a security interest in goods, no matter who the creditor is. However, several legal devices are especially relevant to direct loans and will be discussed below.

What is a note?

A credit contract with a seller *may* be in the form of a note, while a direct loan of money from a lender is almost always in that form. The note usually includes, or is signed at the same time as, a security agreement (if the collateral is goods) or a deed of trust (if the collateral is real estate).

The note is a formal written acknowledgment of a debt and of the promise to pay it. In the note, the debtor *(maker)* promises unconditionally to pay the creditor *(payee)* a specified sum of money on or before a given date; or, as in most consumer notes, in installments. Since the rules pertaining to the formalities of a valid note are complex, no attempt will be made to summarize them here.

A properly drafted note (as opposed to any other written promise to pay) has two advantages to a creditor: the maker, in event of default, may be sued by very simple procedures without proof as to how the promise to pay came about; and the note may be *negotiated* (sold) more easily because the buyer of the note can, in some cases, collect more easily than the original payee. See *Chapter 17, Financers' Responsibilities* for further explanation of what these rules mean to the consumer.

What is a signature loan?

A *signature* loan is simply an unsecured loan. Since there is no collateral, the creditor's only legal recourse if the debtor does not pay is to file a lawsuit. Unsecured loans are usually either very small loans at very high interest rates or are loans to borrowers with excellent credit records.

What is a cosigner?

The term *cosigner* usually applies to a *surety*, that is, one who agrees to pay the note if the principal maker defaults. If a surety pays, the surety can then sue the maker. Signing as a surety is a responsibility that should not be taken lightly, since a surety would not be required if the lender considered the maker to be a good credit risk.

If a person owing money to a bank defaults on the loan, can the bank take funds out of that person's account with that bank?

The bank is better protected if it takes a security interest in the account because the debtor is then unable to withdraw the funds until the debt is paid; but, if the funds happen to be there, the bank can reach them.[1] This happens frequently to cosigners, often to their surprise.

Must a loan be repaid if the goods purchased by the loan turn out to be worthless?

Sometimes, the lender may not be responsible for complaints about products purchased with the money lent. However, if the lender is affiliated with the seller or if the seller refers the consumer to the lender, the lender may then be held responsible. *Chapter 17, Financers' Responsibilities* explains these responsibilities in detail. You should consult an attorney before intentionally withholding payment on a direct loan if you value the collateral or your credit rating.

What can it cost me if my credit card is lost or stolen?

If your credit card is lost, stolen or for some other reason used without your authorization, you cannot be billed for more than $50 of the unauthorized charges on each card.[2] You may be able to hold your loss to less than this amount by reporting the problem immediately to the card issuer. You cannot be billed for any items charged after you make this report, which may be made either orally or in writing.

The card issuer is supposed to provide a notice with the name and address to which this report should be made. Some card issuers put this information on the credit card, while others provide it in a separate statement. If you do not have this information available, you will have to use common sense in locating the card issuer and making the report. An immediate phone call, followed by a letter confirming the call, is the safest method of making this report. Such a call could easily save you $50.

Although this chapter is only a thumbnail sketch of consumer finance, it contains some essential concepts. Rereading this discussion of collateral after you finish the rest of the book may be even more helpful.

Chapter 10
Understanding the Language of Credit

In the period of rapid economic expansion after World War II, credit became central to the standard of living of most Americans. With credit we buy homes, cars, vacations, and sometimes, unfortunately, groceries. Even so, most of us do not shop for credit as shrewdly as we do for the things we buy on credit. As consumers, we can easily become confused or misled about the true cost of a credit purchase.

Much of this confusion results from the fact that the cost of credit may be expressed in two ways: by the *add-on* method; and by the *simple interest* method. Both these methods will be discussed in *Chapter 11, Calculating the Costs of Credit*. Further confusion results from deliberate deception, such as the hiding of finance charges in bogus "fees." To resolve both confusion and deception, Congress passed the Federal Truth-in-Lending Act, which became effective in 1968.[1]

The Texas Credit Code also has provisions requiring meaningful disclosure of credit terms.[2] Since its major disclosure provisions are satisfied by compliance with the Truth-in-Lending Act, only Truth-in-Lending will be discussed here. The Real Estate Settlement Procedures Act, which is beyond the scope of this book, requires certain disclosures in the sale of real estate.[3]

118   Buying, Renting & Borrowing in Texas

How can the Truth-in-Lending Act help me?

The Truth-in-Lending Act clarifies the terms of a credit transaction by requiring the lender to give you certain information.

First, the Truth-in-Lending Act requires that creditors disclose the basic cost of credit by the *simple interest* method rather than (or in addition to) the *add-on* method. Truth-in-Lending calls this simple interest rate the *annual percentage rate* and requires creditors to use that term in their contracts. Disclosure of the annual percentage rate (or simple interest rate) is important because it allows the consumer to shop around and compare the credit prices of various lenders. The annual percentage rate is, after all, the price you pay either to use the money or to use the goods while paying for them. Assuming that all other terms are equal, the credit shopper can take advantage of the best credit deal simply by choosing the one with the lowest annual percentage rate.

Second, the Truth-in-Lending Act requires that certain words be used in disclosing credit terms. This allows the customer who is

Understanding the Language of Credit 119

comparing annual percentage rates to determine whether other credit terms really are equal. For example, the term *finance charge* is supposed to refer to one clearly defined credit term. The credit shopper thus needs only to compare two *finance charges* rather than comparing "total interest charged" on one contract with "time-price differential" on another contract with "credit service charge" on another. A recent amendment to the Truth-in-Lending Act also requires disclosure of certain terms of consumer leases.

What are the most important credit terms to compare when shopping for credit?

The best way to become familiar with basic credit terms is to study the sample disclosure form on page 000, which is worded in unusually clear language. Because of Truth-in-Lending requirements, most consumer contracts use the following basic terms:

Annual percentage rate: This is what has been traditionally called the *simple interest* rate. It expresses accurately the basic cost of credit. *Shopping around for credit means asking several creditors what their annual percentage rates would be to extend credit to you for a given purchase.* In doing this, read each contract carefully to be sure the basic purchase is really the same in each case. You want to be sure to compare financing on the same amount of credit insurance, official fees, etc. as well as the same cash price or loan.

Finance charge: This is the basic dollar charge for the extension of credit, which in Texas has traditionally been called "interest" in loans and "time-price differential" in sales. It includes all charges that would not be made if the customer were paying cash; except that it does not include premiums for various types of credit insurance and official fees, if these items are separately itemized. Since most creditors do itemize these items in their disclosures, they are usually included in the amount financed rather than in the finance charge.

Amount financed: This is the sum of the unpaid cash price (or loan) and, ordinarily, all the insurance premiums and official fees being financed.

Total of payments: This is the total of the amount financed plus the finance charge. Thus, it is the total of all the payments (in addition to the down payment) that you will make.

RETAIL INSTALMENT CONTRACT
Automobiles

Buyer's name: J. P. Consumer
Address: 1403½ E. 3rd, Austin, Texas
Seller's name: R. Q. Seller
Address: 600 N. Lamar, Austin, Texas

This agreement covers my instalment purchase from you of the motor vehicle described below. In this agreement, the words **I, me** and **my** mean the buyer. **You** and **your** refer to the seller.

I understand that you will assign this agreement to First Texas Bank. (Address: 400 N. Congress) and I will make my instalment payments directly to them. I also understand that anyone else who signs this agreement will be responsible individually and together to the same extent that I am.

About my purchase. The vehicle I am buying is described below:
- **Make:** Chevrolet
- **Key number:** 1346-U
- **Body type:** 2-door
- **Model (if truck, give its tonnage):** Monte Carlo
- **Color:** Burgundy
- **Number of cylinders:**
- **Year:** 1980
- **Serial number:** 137564890
- ☒ New ☐ Used

Equipment: ☒ Auto transmission ☒ Radio ☒ Heater ☒ Air Conditioner ☐ Power Steering ☐ Power Brakes ☐ Other

Promise to pay. After deducting my downpayment in cash and trade-ins, I will make a **total of payments** of $7993.44. This represents an **ANNUAL PERCENTAGE RATE** of 13.18% and includes the cost of any insurance and any other charges we have agreed on.

I will pay this amount described below in item 9 in 48 equal monthly instalments of $166.53 each. (And a final unequal instalment of $ N/A). My instalments will be due the same day every month starting on 2/2/80.

The **finance charge** will begin when you assign this contract to 1st Tx. Bank. You estimate that this will be approximately 5 days after I sign this contract.

Here is a breakdown of my obligation:
1. Cash price: $6373.00
2. Sales tax: 219.49
3. Total cash price (1+2): $6592.49
4. Downpayment: 885.85
   - (a) Trade-in:
     - Less unpaid balance on an open lien: N/A
     - Net allowance: N/A
   - (b) Cash downpayment: 885.85
   - Total downpayment: 885.85
5. Unpaid balance of cash price (3-4): 5706.64
6. Charges: 185.45
   - (a) Credit life insurance: N/A
   - (b) Joint credit life insurance: N/A
   - (c) Credit accident and health insurance: 283.77
   - (d) Other charges: License $11.30
7. Unpaid balance/Amount financed (5+6): 480.52 / 6187.16
8. **FINANCE CHARGE**: 1805.85 / $7993.44
9. Total of payments (7+8): $8878.86
10. Deferred payment price (3+6+8): $8878.86

ANNUAL PERCENTAGE RATE: 13.18%

Charge for late payments. If I have not paid any instalment within 10 days of the date it is due I will pay late charge of 5% of the unpaid instalment but not more than **$5**.

Prepaid and refinanced amounts. I can prepay any amounts due under this agreement anytime. If I do, you will refund the unearned **finance charge** figured by the Rule of 78's a legally acceptable method used to figure refunds. If you refinance my debt you will figure my **finance charge** refund in the same way.

In any case I must pay a minimum **finance charge** of $15 and this will be deducted before you figure any refund due.

Entire balance due. You can require that the entire balance of debt be paid at once without prior notice or demand if
1. I do not pay an instalment on time, or
2. I break one of my promises under this agreement, or
3. I have made any false or misleading statement on my application, or
4. I become unemployed or insolvent, or
5. I do not keep the purchased vehicle properly insured, or
6. I die, or
anything else happens that you feel endangers the vehicle or my ability to repay.

Collection costs. I agree to pay any necessary court costs if you take collection action, plus an attorney's fee of 15% of the amount due if the attorney is not a salaried employee of the holder of this agreement.

Delay in enforcement. You can waive or delay enforcing any of your rights without losing them. You can waive or delay enforcing a right as to one borrower without waiving it as to the other. Also you can release one borrower from his or her responsibilities under this agreement without releasing the other. You need not give anyone notice of your waiver, delay or release.

Security interest. I agree to give you a security interest under the Uniform Commercial Code in the purchased vehicle and any equipment added to it. I give you permission to file a financing statement covering your security interest without my signature on it.

Risk of loss. If the purchased vehicle is lost, damaged or destroyed, I will still have to pay you all amounts due under this agreement.

Trade-ins. I promise that any vehicle I give as a trade-in is free of any lien or other claim.

Repossession. You can repossess the purchased vehicle if the entire balance of what I owe becomes due at once. If you decide to do this, I will deliver the vehicle to you. If I do not, you have the right to enter the premises where it is kept and take it yourself. You need not notify me before you do this and you can use my license plates for transporting the vehicle.

You can sell the vehicle and apply the proceeds to the balance of what I owe. Before you do, you can deduct the costs of repossession, storage, preparation for sale, sale and legal expenses plus an attorney's fee of 15% of the amount due if the attorney is not a salaried employee of the holder of this agreement. If the sale doesn't cover all that I owe, I will still be responsible for the difference. But I can still recover the vehicle before you sell it by paying any amounts due under this agreement and any charges you are legally entitled to.

Assignment. You can assign any of your rights under this agreement without my consent.

Law that applies. This agreement will be governed by Texas law. If any part of the agreement is unenforcible, this will not make any other part unenforcible.

NOTICE TO THE BUYER
1. Do not sign this agreement before you read it or if it contains any blank space.
2. You are entitled to a completely filled-in copy of this agreement.
3. Under the law, you have the right to pay off in advance the full amount due and certain conditions to obtain a partial refund of the credit service charge.
4. According to law you have the privilege of purchasing the insurance on the motor vehicle provided for in this contract from an agent or broker of your own selection.

Understanding the Language of Credit

Insurance protection. If I want either credit life or credit accident and health insurance, you can provide me with this coverage through an insurance company you select. I understand that this insurance is not required.

I do ☒ do not ☐ want credit life insurance. The maximum coverage is **$20,000**, and the premium is $ __185.45__ for the term of the loan.

I do ☐ do not ☒ want joint credit life insurance with my spouse. (My spouse must also be a buyer.) The maximum coverage is **$20,000**, and the premium is $ _____ for the term of the loan.

I do ☒ do not ☐ want credit accident and health insurance. The maximum coverage is **$20,000**, but no more than **$500** a month. The premium is $ __283.77__ for the term of the loan.

__J. P. Consumer__   __1/2/80__
Buyer's signature   Date

_____   _____
Buyer's signature (Spouse)   Date

I understand you do not provide liability insurance for bodily injury and property damage caused to others.

I have read this agreement and received a completed copy. I understand that it contains all our rights and responsibilities and will be binding on my heirs and legal representatives. Our agreement cannot be changed without your written permission.

RETAIL INSTALMENT CONTRACT

Buyer 1   Date
__J. P. Consumer__   __1/2/80__
Buyer 2   Date

Insurance other than joint credit life insurance will cover the buyer signing on line 1 only.

Seller   Date
__R. Q. Seller__   __1/2/80__

NOTICE. ANY HOLDER OF THIS CONSUMER CREDIT CONTRACT IS SUBJECT TO ALL CLAIMS AND DEFENSES WHICH THE DEBTOR COULD ASSERT AGAINST THE SELLER OF GOODS OR SERVICES OBTAINED PURSUANT HERETO OR WITH THE PROCEEDS HEREOF. RECOVERY HEREUNDER BY THE DEBTOR SHALL BE LIMITED TO AMOUNTS PAID BY THE DEBTOR HEREUNDER.

Reprinted by permission from Carl Felsenfeld and Alan Siegel, *Simplified Consumer Credit Forms* (Boston: Warren, Gorham & Lamont, 1978).

Do creditors really comply with the Truth-in-Lending Act?

Most creditors do comply with the essential requirements of the Act. Therefore, comparison of annual percentage rates is a fairly reliable way to shop for credit — as long as all the other terms of credit (such as credit insurance, official fees, etc.) are equal. These terms are discussed more fully in *Chapter 11, Calculating the Costs of Credit.*

Many credit contracts, however, contain other violations of the Truth-in-Lending Act. The primary reason for such violations lies in the fact that many contracts are full of fine print containing "agreements" favorable to the creditor. These "agreements" are terms of credit that legally must be disclosed under the Truth-in-Lending Act. By squeezing in so many of these terms, many creditors protect their financial interests but leave themselves open to lawsuits for failing to define all of the terms. A second reason that creditors sometimes fail to comply with the Truth-in-Lending Act is that they fail to train sales personnel to fill out the forms properly. Another reason is that some creditors still try to take an extra bite by hiding undisclosed finance charges in inflated "fees."

If a creditor fails to comply with the Truth-in-Lending Act, what can I do about it?

If a creditor fails to comply with the Truth-in-Lending Act, you may file a civil suit for twice the finance charge (but not less than $100 nor more than $1,000), plus actual damages (if any), plus your reasonable attorney fees and court costs. In the case of a consumer lease, you may sue for 25 percent of payments under the lease rather than twice the finance charge. You must file suit within one year of the date of the violation, which is usually the date of signing of the contract.

> Nye Eve bought a 1970 Ford Filly from Slick's Used Cars for $1,000 on credit and agreed to pay a $400 finance charge. If Slick's credit papers contained a Truth-in-Lending violation, she could sue him for $800 plus reasonable attorney fees and court costs.

This manner of calculating damages is unusual in our legal system, in which damages are usually awarded only to compensate for *actual loss.* In a Truth-in-Lending suit, however, the consumer need not prove any actual loss at all. The purpose behind this part of the Truth-in-Lending Act is to encourage consumers to file suit in cases involving little or no actual injury. The Act protects not so much the private interest of the person filing suit as the interest of the public, which has an interest in requiring all creditors to comply with the Truth-in-Lending Act. Thus, instead of enforcing the Act solely through a federal agency, Congress created this system of "private attorneys general" (that is, attorneys retained by consumers) to serve the public interest with private lawsuits. This is similar to the policy behind the Texas Consumer Protection Act, described in *Chapter 6, Deceptive Trade Practices.*

How can I determine whether a credit contract contains Truth-in-Lending violations?

Determination of such violations is usually a complex legal decision requiring careful analysis by an attorney. If you regularly extend or arrange for credit, have an attorney check your contracts and monitor your salesperson's practices in filling out the forms. If you are a debtor and have a dispute with a creditor, an attorney may

Understanding the Language of Credit

be able to find Truth-in-Lending violations that will increase your bargaining power.

Who is required to comply with the Truth-in-Lending Act?

Only a person or business that regularly extends or arranges for *consumer* credit is required to comply with the Truth-in-Lending Act. *Consumer* credit is that which is primarily for personal, family, household or agricultural purposes. Thus, if you do not normally extend or arrange for consumer credit, you need not make Truth-in-Lending disclosures when making an isolated credit sale, such as the sale of your home. However, if you frequently extend or arrange for consumer credit for any purpose, you must make these disclosures in every such transaction, possibly even including the sale of your own home.

These are only the major rules regarding compliance with the Truth-in-Lending Act. Since the rules are considerably more detailed than this brief summary, anyone who thinks he or she may regularly extend or arrange for extensions of consumer credit should consult an attorney.

Chapter 11
Calculating the Costs of Credit

Frequently we, as attorneys, are asked to calculate how much someone owes right *now* on a debt. Simply adding up the pending payments won't do, because that would give your creditor a lot of free money in unearned interest and credit insurance premiums. You need a basic understanding of how interest is calculated to calculate the exact amount you owe. This procedure, known by the confusing name of "Rule of 78s," is complex but not impossible to understand. This chapter will provide all you need.

Besides detailing how to figure what you owe, this chapter will explain how to determine whether the rate of interest is legal under the usury laws, and how to determine whether the *annual percentage rate* (which must be disclosed under the Truth-in-Lending Act) is disclosed correctly. This chapter will also explain how to decide whether to buy on credit or to pay cash, enabling you to make inflation, taxes and interest rates work for you, rather than against you.

To be honest, this chapter is more complicated than the others. If you don't relate well to numbers, you may find this chapter rough going. If that is the case, skip it and read on, but remember the information is here if you need it later. These suggestions alone may save you the cost of this book many times over.

126 Buying, Renting & Borrowing in Texas

What items are usually included in the costs of credit?

The *finance charge* is the basic price we pay for buying on credit. In Texas, the finance charge is called *interest* when charged for a loan of money; it's called *time-price differential* when charged by a seller for extension of credit to a buyer. The Federal Truth-in-Lending Act, however, uses the term *finance charge*, whether the transaction is a loan or a sale. Since the math is the same either way, no distinction will be made in this chapter, and the term *finance charge* will be used here.[1]

Credit life insurance pays off the debt if the debtor dies before the loan or credit contract has been paid off. If, for example, the debt is secured by the family automobile and the insured breadwinner dies, the insurance will pay most or all the remaining debt, leaving the surviving family free of this obligation. The survivors, however,

Calculating the Costs of Credit 127

may have to pay part of the debt to make up for delinquent payments or to pay the cost of the insurance.

In most cases, credit life insurance is a needless expense. Real security for survivors can be assured only by a thorough estate plan. Such a plan ordinarily includes enough regular life insurance (usually at much lower cost than credit life) to pay debts and provide for the future. As with many types of insurance, a high proportion of credit life premiums goes to the insurance company and to the creditors who sell the insurance. Texas State Board of Insurance regulations require that the ratio between claims incurred and premiums charged be at least 50 percent.[2] Unless insurors are accepting a much lower profit margin than this regulation allows, nearly half the premium dollar is *not* returned to insurance claimants.

Most credit contracts provide that credit life insurance is optional and will be provided only if the debtor signs a separate statement asking for it. The Truth-in-Lending Act strongly encourages this optional provision for the very reason that credit life insurance is rarely a good buy. Creditors like to sell it, however, because they earn a commission on it. Since it is usually optional, think twice before allowing credit life insurance to be included in any credit contract you sign if you have other life insurance.

Credit accident and health insurance makes payments on the debt while the debtor is sick or otherwise disabled. Like credit life insurance, it is usually optional and requires a separate signature by the debtor. Also like credit life, it is a poor investment except for families without the assets or other types of insurance to see them through periods of disability.

Like other health insurance, credit accident and health coverage excludes conditions existing at the time of purchase of insurance. Many claims on credit accident and health insurance are denied by insurance companies because of pre-existing health conditions.

Physical damage insurance pays for damage to or destruction of the collateral. If, for example, a debt is secured by an automobile that is destroyed in an accident, the insurance company will pay the fair market value of the automobile as it was just before the accident. This payment will be made to the creditor to the extent of the balance due at the time of the accident. If the automobile is worth more at the time of the accident than the debt owed, the balance left over will be paid to the debtor. Unlike liability insurance, physical damage insurance is paid without regard to who was at fault in the accident. It differs also from liability insurance in that automobile owners are not required by law to have physical damage insurance. Like the other types of insurance discussed above, physical damage insurance is often a poor investment, especially when the collateral is of small value in relation to the debtor's resources. In such a case, replacing the damaged items would not constitute a particular hardship for the debtor, and the money saved by not investing in physical damage insurance could be better spent elsewhere.

Unlike credit life insurance, physical damage insurance is usually required by creditors. The buyer, however, always has the option of purchasing the insurance through an agent other than the creditor. Where substantial amounts of money are involved, this may easily be worth the effort of comparing prices. Even so, the insurance is often unnecessary, in which case its cost is a major reason to pay cash rather than to finance a consumer purchase.

Miscellaneous fees often include charges necessary only because credit is being extended. Fees for license plates and motor vehicle titles would be charged even in a cash sale, but some auto dealers take an extra and illegal "bite" by charging more than official fees and pocketing the difference.[3] Fees for credit investigations, appraisals, credit document preparation, and dozens of similar items dreamed up by clever creditors add to the total, and a finance charge is assessed on these fees as well as on the use of the money or property for which the debtor has contracted. Under heavy pressure from car dealers, the Texas Legislature, in 1979, legitimated the charging of a maximum of $25 in "documentary fees" for preparing papers involved in sales of motor vehicles. Fees are legal, in any case, if charged for items for which the creditor has actually paid, such as real estate appraisals and credit report fees. Whether legal or not, however, these miscellaneous fees should be considered when you are deciding whether to buy on credit, and when you are comparing credit options.

How can I save money when buying on credit?

The following money-saving tips include some suggestions we have made before:
 • Do not buy credit life insurance unless you are sure your survivors would need it if you died before paying the debt and that the same purpose cannot be served in cheaper ways.

Calculating the Costs of Credit 129

- Do not buy credit accident and health insurance unless you expect to need it to pay the particular debt if you become disabled.

- Do not maintain a balance on credit cards if you can avoid it. As explained further below, credit cards carry some of the highest interest rates of all sources of credit.

- Shop around for your credit. A loan from a bank or other lending institution will usually (but not always) carry a lower finance charge than credit extended by a seller, and credit costs can vary widely among lenders and sellers.

Assume, for example, that you are planning to buy a three-year-old car and will finance $3,000 of the price to be paid in monthly payments over three years. As of this writing, the law allows an auto dealer to charge a finance charge of $1,125 on this credit sale,[4] but allows a bank to charge only $720 for a loan to finance the car, a difference of $405.[5] Ironically, if you were to finance through the dealer, you would probably end up paying a bank or other lending institution anyway, since the dealer would probably assign (sell) the contract to a lending institution.

In researching this book, we discovered one instance in which this $405 saving could have been made by walking across the street. The first auto dealer with whom we talked financed auto sales by arranging direct loans with a bank. Therefore, the dealer could charge a maximum of $720. The second dealer, across the street, entered into credit contracts directly with customers, then sold the contracts to a bank. Therefore, on the same sale, that dealer could assess a finance charge of $1125. The latter dealer said the rate charged depended on the customer, but that the maximum amount was frequently charged. In new car sales, the position of the dealer and the bank are reversed — the dealer can charge only 7.5 add-on, while the bank can charge 8.0. The meaning of this *add-on rate* is explained below.

The experience noted above is not an isolated example of the importance of shopping for credit. Consider the following situations:

> You want to make home improvements costing $1,000, to be paid in monthly payments over 3 years and secured by a second lien on your home. A home improve-

Buying, Renting & Borrowing in Texas

ment contractor could charge you a finance charge of $330, while a bank could charge only $240.

AND

You want to buy furniture costing a total of $3,000, to be paid in monthly payments over three years and secured by the furniture. The furniture store could charge you a finance charge of $810, while a bank could charge only $720.

The twists and turns of the Texas usury laws have produced these differences in finance charges. Because interest rates and usury laws are changing rapidly as of this writing, the fine points of the law will not be discussed.[6] The important point is that, both for legal and market reasons, it pays to shop for credit.

How can I calculate how much of each payment is principal and how much is interest?

Whenever an installment payment is made, part of the payment goes to pay the finance charge and part to pay the amount financed.

You borrow $1,000 and agree to pay it back in 12 monthly payments of $90 per month at 14.45 percent annual percentage rate (explained below). When you make your first monthly payment of $90, the amount considered to be finance charge will be 14.45 percent of $1,000 divided by 12 (because 14.45 percent is the *annual* rate, and only one-twelfth of a year has passed). $1,000 × .1445 × $1/12$ = $12.04. Of the $90 payment, $12.04 is finance charge, and $77.96 is amount financed, so a balance of $922.04 remains on the amount financed. When you make your second $90 monthly payment, the finance charge is $922.04 × .1445 × $1/12$ = $11.10, and $78.90 is the amount financed, so a balance of $922.04 − $78.90 = $843.14 remains. Each month, the amount credited to finance charge is less, because the preceding monthly payment decreased the amount financed to which the finance charge is applied. The same calculation is made over and over, as follows:

Calculating the Costs of Credit

**Amortization Table for $1,000 Loan
Repaid in 12 Months at 14.45%
Annual Percentage Rate**

Payment Number	Payment	Finance Charge	Amount Financed	Balance
1	$ 90.00	$12.04	$ 77.96	$922.04
2	90.00	11.10	78.90	843.14
3	90.00	10.15	79.85	763.29
4	90.00	9.19	80.81	682.48
5	90.00	8.22	81.78	600.70
6	90.00	7.23	82.77	517.93
7	90.00	6.24	83.76	434.17
8	90.00	5.23	84.77	349.40
9	90.00	4.21	85.79	263.61
10	90.00	3.17	86.83	176.78
11	90.00	2.14	87.86	88.91
12	90.00	1.08	88.92	-0-
	$1,000.00	$80.00	$1,000.00	

If your bank or other lending institution will not provide you with a table like this, you can order one for $5.00 from Compustat Publishing Company, P.O. Box 1401, Canyon Lake, Texas 78130. Be sure to send them the amount of the loan, rate of interest, amount of monthly payments and length of the loan.

What is the difference between "simple" interest and "add-on" interest?

These two terms are simply different ways of expressing the finance charge as a percentage. In the table above, the *simple interest rate* (which is the same as the *annual percentage rate*) is 14.45 percent. The *add-on rate* is 8.0 ($8 per hundred dollars financed per year). The Truth-in-Lending Act uses the term *annual percentage rate* and requires that it be used by creditors in disclosing the cost of credit. This term will therefore be used here, but bear in mind that *annual percentage rate* ordinarily means the same as the traditional term *simple interest*.

The *add-on rate* is the simpler of the two terms to calculate. The add-on rate is equal to the number of dollars of finance charge per hundred dollars financed per year. In the example above, at an annual percentage rate of 14.45 percent per year, the finance charge is $80 for each $1,000 (ten $100 units) financed per year. The $80 represents an add-on rate of $8 per hundred per year, or 8.0.

In equation form, where A equals the add-on rate, the calculations look like this:

$$A \times 10 \text{ (hundreds)} \times 1 \text{ (year)} = 80$$
$$10A = 80$$
$$A = 8$$

On the other hand, the annual percentage rate on an installment loan is very difficult to calculate without the use of prepared tables or a computer. With the tables, however, it is relatively simple. You plug into the tables the number of payments, finance charge, and amount financed, and the table shows the annual percentage rate.

On an installment contract, the annual percentage rate is higher than the add-on rate because the annual percentage rate reflects the diminishing balance as each payment is made. The add-on rate does not take this into account. Thus, the add-on rate for a $1,000 loan with an $80 finance charge paid off over one year will always be 8.0, regardless of whether the payments are made in installments or in one lump sum. This accounting method is misleading, since the debtor who pays in monthly installments has "use" of less of the money each month. The annual percentage rate method takes this into account by expressing the ratio between the finance charge and the *average* unpaid balance of the amount financed per year.

Only on installment credit does the annual percentage rate differ from the add-on rate. If the loan in the example above were paid off by a single payment of $1,080 at the end of one year, both the annual percentage rate and the add-on rate would be 8.0.

How can I calculate how much I owe at any given time?

This question arises most often in two situations: when the consumer wants to pay off the remainder of a debt all at once *(prepayment)*, and when the creditor declares a default and *accelerates* the debt. Acceleration results in the entire debt being due at once. In either case, when a debt is paid early, you (as the debtor) owe substantially less than you would have paid by paying each installment as it came due. When a debt is paid early, only a portion of the finance charge and credit insurance have been earned by the creditor and insurance company. The creditor can now take these prepaid funds and can use them to extend credit to someone else, giving the insurance company a new risk to insure. In Texas, the courts have held that, in some cases, a creditor who computes the amount owed at the time of prepayment or acceleration by simply multiplying the monthly payment by the number of unpaid payments may be sued for charging unearned interest in violation of the usury laws.[7]

There are several ways to determine how much of the finance charge is unearned at a given time. You may, of course, ask the creditor how much is due. Where credit has been extended as part of a retail sale of a motor vehicle or other goods, the creditor must provide you with a written statement of payments made and the total amount still due under the contract.[8] Your request must be in writing. Such an accounting must be provided free to you once

134   Buying, Renting & Borrowing in Texas

every six months, and the charge for more frequent statements cannot be over $1 each. Be sure, however, to determine whether the creditor is merely giving the total of the unpaid payments or is performing the calculations necessary to rebate unearned finance charge and insurance. Chances are the creditor is giving you the total of the unpaid payments, and you will have to do the calculations yourself.

You can do the calculations for most transactions by using the *sum of the periodic balances* method of calculating how much is owed. Besides being faster (unless you have access to a computer), this method is legally required when a debt is to be prepaid, unless the debt is at 10 percent interest or less, or is secured by a first lien on real estate.[9] In the latter types of debts, in which the sum of the periodic balances method is not required, the *actuarial* method (preparing an amortization table as in the example above) should be used. The two methods of calculation produce almost the same results, with the sum of the periodic balances method favoring creditors slightly.

When the debt is payable in substantially equal periodic payments (for example, monthly, as in most consumer credit contracts), the sum of the periodic balances method can be applied by a formula known as the Rule of 78s, which is explained below. This rule takes into account the fact that less finance charge is earned each month as each payment reduces the unpaid balance.

> You purchase a car for $3,997.72, with a finance charge of $1,749.08, to be paid in 60 monthly payments of $95.78 each, with no insurance or other charges added. After paying for 12 months, you decide during the thirteenth month to prepay the rest from your savings account. You may determine how much you owe by making the following calculations:
>
> **Step One:** Determine the proportion of the total finance charge that is unearned. This is called the *rebate ratio* and is calculated as follows:
>
> X = number of full months remaining after prepayment date (47 here)
>
> Y = number of payments in the whole contract (60 here)

$$\text{Rebate Ratio} = \frac{X(X + 1)}{Y(Y + 1)}$$
$$\text{Rebate Ratio} = \frac{47(48)}{60(61)} = \frac{2256}{3660}$$
$$= .6163934$$

Step Two: Subtract the *acquisition charge* allowed by law from the finance charge. On motor vehicles, it is $25.00:[11]

$1,749.08 − $25.00 = $1,724.08

Step Three: Multiply the remaining finance charge by the rebate ratio to determine the amount of unearned finance charge:

$1,724.08 × .6163934 = $1,062.71

Step Four: Subtract the amount of unearned finance charge from the total of unpaid payments to determine the amount owed:

Unpaid payments = 48 × $95.78
= $4,597.44

$4,597.44 − $1,062.71 = $3,534.73 owed

Unearned premiums on credit life and credit accident and health insurance are rebated by the same formula, except that there is no acquisition charge to deduct.[11]

Unearned premiums on physical damage insurance, however, are rebated under entirely different rules. In general, if the insurance is cancelled at the request of the insurance company, the rebate is *pro rata*. This means that the rebate ratio is the ratio between the number of days left in the term of the policy and the number of days in the total term for which you originally contracted. If the insurance is cancelled at your request (as in prepayment), the rebate is *short rate*, which contains a small penalty for cancellation. The short rate can be computed only by the use of short rate tables available from the State Board of Insurance. Rebates resulting from the repossession of an automobile are pro rata.[12]

To tie all these rules together, look at the sample car purchase contract in *Chapter 10, Understanding the Language of Credit*. Suppose you bought a car on this contract and that after making five payments you lost your job and quit paying. After you had missed the next three payments, the creditor repossessed the car. You can determine how much it would cost to get the car back by making the following calculations:

A. *Charges due*
 1. Total of unpaid payments $7,160.79
    (43 × $166.53 = $7,160.79)
 2. Delinquency charges
    (item 13 on contract) 15.00
    (3 × $5.00 = $15.00)
 3. Expense of repossession 100.00
 4. TOTAL BALANCE DUE
    (1 + 2 + 3) $7,275.79

B. *Less credits due*
 5. Unearned finance charge $1,180.78
    $$\left(\frac{39(40)}{48(49)} = .6632653 \times (\$1,805.25 - \$25.00) = \$1,180.78\right)$$
 6. Unearned insurance 311.22
    (.6632653 × $469.22 = $311.22)
 7. TOTAL CREDITS DUE (5 + 6) $1,492.00

C. PAYMENT NECESSARY TO REDEEM
   (4 − 7) $5,783.79

Instead of paying the redemption amount and recovering the car, you may choose to allow the creditor to sell it. In this case, you should add the sale price to the "credits due" column. If the sale price is more than $5,783.79, you should receive the balance, less cost of the sale. If it is less than $5,783.79, you owe the deficiency plus cost of the sale.

The calculations would be exactly the same if you wanted to know the balance due so you could prepay — except there would be no costs of repossession and resale included in these calculations.

Do I always have a right to prepay without forfeiting the unearned finance charge?

A special statute allows savings and loan associations to charge

Calculating the Costs of Credit   137

penalties for prepayments.[13] This is why savings and loans have been able to develop the *prepayment penalty/call clause* device (discussed in *Chapter 1, Buying and Selling Homes*) to keep future buyers of the property from doing business with other lending institutions. On the other hand, there is an absolute right to prepay in full and receive a rebate according to the sum of the periodic balances method in all loans to individuals at more than 10 percent annual percentage rate (except those secured by residences) and in all credit sales other than sales of real estate. In loans at less than 10 percent annual percentage rate and those secured by residences, the rebate should be computed by the actuarial method. Prepayment penalties are not usually included in such loans (except those made by savings and loans), because such a penalty might make the loans usurious.

How can I decide whether to pay in cash or buy on credit?

People with savings must decide from time to time whether to buy an item on credit or to pay cash from the savings. Since many factors must be considered, it isn't possible to give general advice on such a decision. To help you decide, however, the following discussion will summarize some of the major considerations you may want to keep in mind.

Comparison of alternative uses for your money. Applying the math lessons in this chapter will give you some idea of how much you can gain (or lose) in dollars by paying cash rather than buying on credit.

> In the example above, assume that you made the first five payments on time, then started thinking about prepaying the rest of the debt on the car. With unpaid payments of $7,160.79 and a rebate of unearned finance charge and insurance of $1,492.00, you could prepay by withdrawing $5,668.79 from your savings account. At 5½ percent simple interest for the next 40 months, your $5,668.79 would have earned only $992.04 in your savings account. By prepaying, you would save $1,492.00 − 992.04 = $449.96 on your car purchase. Of this, $188.74 is a solid saving on the finance charge. The value of the remaining saving of $311.22 on the credit

insurance depends on the extent to which it was a good buy for you in the first place.

On the other hand, if you kept your $5,668.79 in a money market fund for 40 months at an average net yield of 12 percent, it would earn you $2,267.52 in interest.[14]

Income taxes. By prepaying a debt or buying on cash, you avoid paying taxes on the interest income you would otherwise have earned from your savings. However, if you itemize deductions, you lose the interest deduction you would otherwise have had for the interest you would have paid on the debt.

Assume you are in a 40 percent tax bracket, and you itemize deductions. After taxes, your $2,267.52 money market earnings would look more like $1,360.51 if you did not prepay the debt. However, because of its value as a deductible item, the $1,180.78 in finance charges you would pay if you did not prepay the debt would save $472.31 in taxes. This would constitute an after-tax cost of only $708.47. Therefore, by staying in debt, you would be ahead by $1,360.51 − 708.47 = $652.04 after taxes and before adjustment for inflation. The difference would be much less significant if you did not itemize deductions; and you would do better to pay off the debt if you were in a 30 percent tax bracket and did not itemize deductions.

Inflation. If inflation occurs between the time you contract a debt and the time you pay it off, you have the advantage of paying back the principal and interest with money that is worth less than what you borrowed. Assuming an average rate of inflation of 12 percent per year (1 percent per month) over 40 months, the money with which you make the first payment will be worth 1 percent less than it was worth when you borrowed it; and the money with which you make the last payment will be worth 40 percent less. On the average, your payments will be about 20 percent lower when adjusted for inflation than if inflation were disregarded. Therefore, after inflation adjustment, you are not paying back $7,160.79, but rather 80 percent of that amount, which is $5,728.63. You have "saved" $1,432.16, which is more than the finance charge.

However, if you invest the $5,668.79 from your savings account

Calculating the Costs of Credit 139

in money market funds at 12 percent, then inflation will also cost you in real income. With your after-tax interest of $1,360.51, this fund will be worth $7,029.30 after 40 months, in current dollars; but in inflation-adjusted dollars, it will be worth 40 percent less, that is, $4,217.58. Inflation will have cost you $2,811.72, while saving you only the $1,432.16 calculated above.

Here is a summary of what would happen to your $5,668.79 savings if you kept it on interest at 12 percent for 40 months, com-

How To Determine Whether To Use Savings To Avoid Debt

Savings Kept On Interest		Savings Used To Avoid Debt	
$5,668.79	(savings on hand)	$5,668.79	(debt avoided or prepaid)
+2,267.52	(interest at 12%)		
7,936.31			
− 907.01	(taxes on interest)		
7,029.30			
−1,180.78	(finance charge paid on debt)		
5,848.52			
+ 472.31	(value of tax deduction for interest paid on debt)		
5,376.21			
−2,811.72	(cost of inflation to savings)		
2,564.49			
+1,432.16	(effect of inflation on, i.e., cheapening of, money used to repay debt)	Balance:	
		$5,668.79	(debt avoided or prepaid)
$3,996.65	(value of savings on interest)	−3,996.65	(value of savings on interest)
		$1,672.14	(net value of using savings to pay debt)

pared to what would happen if you used it to buy in cash or to prepay a debt. These calculations are based on the assumption that the relevant interest income will be taxed at an average rate of 40 percent, that you itemize deductions, and that inflation occurs steadily at 12 percent per year over the 40 months involved.

Bear in mind that the result depends entirely on your tax situation, the relevant interest rates, and inflation. Plug in those assumptions that apply to you, and you may find you're better off keeping your money in savings. This example simply suggests some things to consider as you make your own decisions.

Need for liquid assets. The need to have some funds readily available for emergencies, opportunities, etc., will very often be the deciding factor on whether to use savings or to buy on credit. It rarely makes sense, for example, to use *all* your savings to avoid or reduce debt when you have a growing family to support and enough income to pay off the debt as it comes due. You may instead want to keep funds on hand to take advantage of an irresistible sale or to pay an unexpected bill. Only when you have more than a comfortable reserve of liquid assets does the type of calculation described above become helpful.

Chapter 12
Credit Bureaus

It's a fact of life that we live in a credit-oriented economy. Most people use credit to acquire their luxuries; some even use it for necessities. Credit records have therefore become important to most consumers.

Prior to the enactment of the federal Fair Credit Reporting Act in 1970, credit records were rather mysterious things. Credit reporting agencies refused to reveal the contents of their records to consumers, and there was no requirement that erroneous reports be corrected. The consumer, for the most part, was at the mercy of the credit bureaus. The Fair Credit Reporting Act represents an attempt to solve these problems and others connected with the business of maintaining credit records.[1]

What is a credit record and how is it created?

Your credit record reflects your history of borrowing money and buying on credit. It also reflects your habits regarding the repayment of debts. To illustrate how a credit record works, let's look at a fictitious borrower, Dell Inquent.

> Dell wanted to purchase a freezer from Shylock's Department Store and put it on Shylock's Retail Installment Plan. Dell had purchased on credit from Shylock's before. Shylock's own record of her account was therefore part of her credit record. Shylock's could rely totally on its own experience in determining whether or not to

extend credit to her, or it could have her fill out an application in which she would give credit references and identify her employer.

Many creditors will want to have more extensive information on your credit record. Therefore, they order a report of your credit history with various other creditors. This report is collected, stored and disseminated by one or more credit bureaus, which make the report available to potential creditors for a fee.

What is a credit bureau and how does it work?

Many people believe that there is a single credit bureau in each community. In fact, there are often many. These are not necessarily part of the same organization.[2] Each generally deals only with its own "members," which may be retail stores, credit unions, finance companies, etc. who pay for the credit bureau's services. Of course, some may be members of more than one credit bureau. Members provide information about their own customers to the credit bureau. The credit bureau compiles this information into a credit record for each consumer. It then disseminates the information to its members when a consumer applies for credit, a job or insurance.

The system described above is purely local. However, some credit bureaus do have the ability to obtain information from around the country. Most metropolitan areas have a major credit bureau which accounts for a substantial percentage of the area's business.

It is important to keep in mind that credit bureaus differ a lot. The types of creditors that make up their membership may be substantially different. Some firms have their records computerized, some do not. They also vary in the degree of enthusiasm with which they will comply with the Fair Credit Reporting Act.

How can my credit record affect me?

Credit records are used by businesses from which you seek credit. These businesses can include lending institutions, retailers who sell goods on installments, and organizations that issue credit cards. A poor credit record may result in your being denied credit or paying more for the credit you do obtain. Employers often use credit records, and these may be a factor in hiring, promotion and firing. Insurance companies also use credit records. However, they ordi-

Credit Bureaus   143

narily use a more specialized reporting service than that provided by regular credit bureaus.

What is a credit report?

We have been speaking generally of your credit *record,* which includes your entire credit history, wherever it may be recorded. The term credit *report* is used in the Fair Credit Reporting Act to refer to the information on a consumer which is in the hands of a particular credit reporting agency (such as a credit bureau). This is what a credit bureau actually reports to a prospective creditor, employer, etc.

Are there any limitations on who can see my credit report?

The Fair Credit Reporting Act includes a section which is intended to protect the confidentiality of credit reports.[3] However, the

language of that section is not very strong. Anyone showing a "legitimate business need" for the information in connection with business involving you may legally have access to that report. The Act does, however, provide valuable limitations to access by governmental agencies.[4]

Are there any limitations on what may be contained in a credit report?

Of course, credit reports must be true and accurate, and there are limitations on the length of time for which an unfavorable item may appear on credit reports. Credit reports may not include bad debts, accounts placed for collection, criminal records and other adverse information more than seven years old.[5] Bankruptcies and judgments against the debtor are an exception. They may appear for ten years.

"Snoop reports" are investigative reports which contain information about your character, reputation and lifestyle. They are created by means of interviews with friends, neighbors, acquaintances and co-workers. Prior to preparation of such a report, you must be informed of the following:

- that an investigative report may be requested;
- what an investigative report is;
- that you have the right to make a written request for a complete and accurate statement of the nature and scope of the report.

If you request such a statement, it must be provided within five days from the date the request was received.[6]

These rules apply only to investigative reports being prepared for use by third persons. Employers or lenders who are preparing their own reports are excluded from these rules.

How do I know if I have been affected by a credit report?

Suppose Shylock's refused to grant credit to Dell Inquent. It is very possible that their decision was based on information contained in a consumer credit report. If this is so, it is Shylock's legal duty to inform Dell of that fact. Furthermore, Shylock's must supply Dell with the name and address of the credit bureau which made the report.[7]

It is possible that a consumer credit report may not have been a factor in Shylock's decision. In that case, Dell must make a written request in order to receive information about the reasons for the denial. This request must be made within 60 days from the time she learns of the denial.[8]

Do I have a right to see my credit report?

A credit bureau must clearly and accurately disclose to you a summary of information it is reporting about you, including the following:

• the nature and substance of all information (except medical records) contained in the file at the time of your request;

• the sources of this information (except sources of investigative reports);

• identification of anyone who has received the report for employment purposes during the past two years;

• identification of anyone who has received the report for any other purpose during the past six months.[9]

This disclosure must be provided in person or by telephone after you have properly identified yourself. Credit bureaus have various methods of telephone identification. They may request that you send a letter to them and arrange for them to call you at a certain time. You are entitled to have one person accompany you when you receive the disclosures in person.

If you check your credit report within 30 days of having been denied credit, the credit bureau may not charge you a fee to review your file.[10] In other circumstances, there will be a small fee for checking your credit. Currently that fee is usually around $4.

How can I tell what the summary of my credit report means?

When you go to check your record, the credit bureau must provide trained personnel to explain the information to you. Let's consider Dell Inquent's situation again.

> Dell went down to Megalopolis Credit Bureau to see if she could determine why Shylock's had denied her credit. She filled out an application and was introduced to Farrah Praise, one of the bureau's counselors. Farrah explained that Dell's credit record reflected the terms of each credit agreement she had made. These included,

among other types of credit, retail installment agreements, revolving charge accounts, and open-end accounts or loans. All of this was coded, so Farrah had to interpret as she went through the record.

Dell wanted to know what her "credit rating" was. In response, Farrah took great pains to point out that the credit bureau *does not "score"* consumers. It simply provides the information in the record to its members on request. The creditors then use it in whatever way they see fit.

Obviously, there is some "rating" or "scoring" going on here. The credit bureau participates by providing the categories into which your present and former creditors have placed you. Potential creditors interpret this information and use it to decide whether to give you credit. While these methods may be efficient from the credit bureau's viewpoint, there is a lot of room for subjectivity and inaccuracy.

What can I do if my credit report is inaccurate?

Suppose that when Dell received the summary of her credit report, it reflected a bad debt with Benevolent Finance Company. She had never done business with that firm. If Dell were reviewing her record in person, an oral challenge would probably prompt the bureau to check out the information. The Fair Credit Reporting Act requires the reporting agency to reinvestigate disputed information.[11]

Despite this, it is best to challenge the information in writing to create a written record in case legal action may be necessary. Dell may simply send a letter to the credit bureau stating, "I've never had an account at Benevolent Finance Co. Please verify your information." The credit bureau must promptly remove the disputed information if it is found to be inaccurate or can no longer be verified. Checking this information shouldn't take more than three or four days.

The law also requires that the credit bureau send certain notices of the correction or deletion.[12] This notification will not happen automatically; you must request it. You have a right to have notices sent to all persons who, during the prior six months, have received reports containing the deleted information. If the reports have been used for employment purposes, the time limitation is two years. The credit bureau, however, is required to send notification only to those "specifically designated" by you. You should request that notices be sent to everyone who has received reports during the time limits mentioned above.

What if the credit bureau verifies the information but I still dispute it?

Some disputes are not so neat or easy to correct. To illustrate, let's look at Dell Inquent's credit report again.

> Dell's record shows Worth Less Appliance Center as reporting that it repossessed an item she purchased two years ago. In fact, she purchased an all-electric "Doggy Food Processor" from Worth Less. The machine never worked. After several attempts to have it fixed, she returned it, demanded her down payment back and quit paying on the account. Since that time, nothing else has happened.

Apparently Worth Less handled this account as repossessed and uncollectable. This may have been unfair. However, when the credit bureau reverifies, the report will still show "repossessed and uncollectable" and won't reflect the true picture.

In such a case, you are entitled to file a statement of dispute.[13] The credit bureau *must* include this statement of dispute in your credit report. They may limit your statement to 100 words, but they must provide you with assistance in writing a clear summary of the dispute. The credit bureau is required to send notices of the consumer's statement of dispute to certain prior recipients of the credit report. The same rules apply as for notice of corrected or deleted information.

It is difficult to say what effect statements of dispute may have. As pointed out before, each creditor has its own rating system, and these may be very subjective. Still, statements of dispute probably have some effect and should be filed when appropriate.

The law doesn't specifically give you the right to a free review of your file to make sure disputes are being handled properly. Some attorneys believe there is an implied right to do so. You should definitely request it. At a minimum, however, you always have a right to see the information in your file by paying a small fee, as explained above.

How are joint accounts reported?

Prior to the passage of the Equal Credit Opportunity Act (see *Chapter 13, Equal Credit Opportunity*), joint accounts were recorded in the husband's name with the wife's credit history as an addendum. Now credit bureaus must identify accounts which are used by both spouses. Each spouse is entitled to have such accounts listed in his or her own name. Once the record is listed under both names, it will be provided to anyone requesting it under either name.

A woman who has not previously had an individual credit record may have to take some action in order to get the joint record listed in her name. A request to the credit bureau should be sufficient.

To summarize: you have a right to be told when you are denied credit on the basis of a credit report; to be told what credit bureau has supplied information on your credit history; and to be told what information the credit bureau is giving out. Further, you may require the credit bureau to verify any information you dispute, and if they refuse to change it, you may require them to report your side of the story, too. Credit bureaus do make mistakes, and creditors do report wrong and biased information. Because your credit history is a valuable personal asset, you should use these rights to keep it working to your advantage.

Chapter 13
Equal Credit Opportunity

Overuse of credit can be disastrous to one's economic well-being. When used for proper purposes, however, access to credit is an important privilege in our society. Those who cannot obtain credit through conventional lenders may be forced to do without many possessions they consider necessities. When they are able to borrow money, they may have to turn to sources of credit that are less conventional, more expensive and, in some cases, illegal.

Access to credit should be, but too often is not, based on one factor only — the potential borrower's ability to repay. Of course, creditors would like to determine this before making a loan, and they have a right to do so. In doing so, however, they are prohibited by law from discriminating against potential borrowers because, for example, they are black, Mexican-American, female or elderly. This chapter will summarize the laws prohibiting such discrimination in extending credit.

In spite of these laws, credit discrimination persists in many forms. It may be obvious, as when all women are denied credit because the creditor expects that women will become pregnant, quit their jobs, and fail to repay. Discrimination may be more subtle, however. Statistical or actuarial analysis is sometimes used to justify actions that are in fact discriminatory. For example, if actuarial analysis revealed that women between ages 19 and 35 quit their jobs every three years on the average, a creditor might use that data to justify denying credit to all women of that age category, regardless of numerous other factors which should be considered. Discrimination of this sort is now illegal as a result of public demand for laws providing protection for minorities, women and the elderly.

What types of credit discrimination are illegal?

A federal law called the Equal Credit Opportunity Act represents one attempt to eliminate credit discrimination.[1] This law provides that a creditor may not discriminate on the basis of *race, color, religion, national origin, sex, marital status* or *age* in any aspect of a credit transaction. A creditor may not even discourage a person from applying for credit for any of these reasons. Furthermore, a creditor may not discriminate against an applicant because all or part of the applicant's income comes from a public assistance program, nor because the applicant has, in good faith, exercised any right under the Equal Credit Opportunity Act.

What rules apply to credit discrimination based on race, color, religion and national origin?

Generally, a creditor may not even ask about the race, color, religion or national origin of a credit applicant. However, if the credit is to be used to buy residential real estate, the applicant will be asked to reveal race and national origin as well as sex, marital status and age. This exception allows federal agencies to gather statistics on discrimination in housing.

What rules apply to credit discrimination on the basis of sex?

Elimination of credit discrimination against women is the most ambitious and difficult purpose of the Equal Credit Opportunity Act. Discrimination against women in matters of money and business is deeply imbedded in our culture and expresses itself in many of our property laws. This, in turn, affects creditors' perceptions of the ability of female applicants to repay.

The Equal Credit Opportunity Act specifically forbids consideration of the sex of the applicant in determining credit ratings. Technically, the creditor may not even ask what the applicant's sex is.[2]

Similarly, questions about birth control practices and the intention or ability to have children are prohibited.

Despite such restrictions, many credit applications still request applicants to identify themselves as Mr., Mrs., Miss or Ms. Checking one of these titles, however, is strictly optional. In most instances, the creditor will still be able to determine if the applicant is female. With this in mind, women should be alert to the possibility of unlawful credit discrimination.

What rules apply to credit discrimination on the basis of marital status?

According to federal law, a creditor may not inquire about the marital status of anyone seeking individual, unsecured credit unless that person lives in a community property state.[3] Since Texas is a community property state, a creditor may legitimately ask about marital status in all types of credit transactions in Texas. The reason for this exception is that a person whose spouse becomes hopelessly mired in debt may also suffer financial ruin, and this possibility is a legitimate concern of a creditor.

Here are some other regulations relating to marital status, especially that of women:

> A creditor cannot take into account the existence of a telephone listing in the name of the applicant (since family telephone listings are usually in a man's name only).
>
> A creditor cannot refuse to open an account in a person's birth-given name, a spouse's name, or a combined name.
>
> A creditor cannot require a co-signer unless the applicant relies on another's income. However, in a community property state such as Texas, the signature of a spouse can legally be required.

The Equal Credit Opportunity Act and the Fair Credit Reporting Act (see *Chapter 12, Credit Bureaus*) combine to give every married person the right to have a credit history in his or her own name. If both the husband and the wife are liable for or are permitted to use the account, a credit history must be kept in both names and must reflect the fact that both spouses may use the account. When considering such credit histories, the creditor must recognize this type of joint account.

Are there any special rules affecting those who are divorced and widowed?

In Texas, creditors may ask questions about the applicant's marital status but may use only the terms "married," "unmarried," and "separated." The term "unmarried" applies to single, divorced and widowed persons. Credit may not be denied on the basis of marital status. However, creditors can require a person to reapply or can change the terms of an existing account after a change of marital status.

A divorced applicant is not required to reveal alimony, child support or separate maintenance payments as a source of income if he or she does not want the creditor to consider these payments in determining the credit rating. Generally, however, the applicant will want to include these sources of income. If they are included, the creditor must take them into account to the extent that the payments are likely to be consistent. This regulation sets out a list of factors to be considered in determining probable consistency of payment.[4] Unless a credit applicant has a large, independent source of income and need not rely on payments from the former spouse, the creditor will soon learn that the applicant is divorced. However, creditors may not lawfully discriminate on this basis.

What rules apply to credit discrimination on the basis of age?

There is no prohibition against asking the age of a credit applicant. However, the Equal Credit Opportunity Act prohibits credit discrimination against the elderly. The general rule is that age may not be taken into account *except* to determine if the applicant is old enough to enter into a contract. In certain evaluating systems (see the discussion of "credit scoring" below), age may be taken into account, but only if the age of elderly applicants is not treated as a negative factor. When evaluating an application, a creditor may not discount or exclude income because it comes from an annuity, pension or other retirement benefit, nor may a creditor close a charge account when a person reaches a certain age. Age, however, may be a factor in determining the cost and availability of credit life

Equal Credit Opportunity 153

and credit health insurance; but *credit* may not be refused because such insurance is not available to an elderly person.

How can I tell if I have been discriminated against?

Credit discrimination produces one of two results:
- the lender refuses to extend credit to the applicant; or
- the lender will extend credit only at a higher price or on other less favorable terms.

It is fairly easy to recognize discriminatory actions when questions specifically prohibited by the Equal Credit Opportunity Act have been asked. Beyond this, it may be difficult to determine what factors prompted a denial of credit. The following example will show how ambiguous such a situation can become:

> Mae Borrow is a 29-year-old black female. She has two children, ages 12 and 9. Mae has been working as an associate for a medium-size law firm for six months and earns $13,000 per year. She has been divorced for about a year and receives $250 per month from her ex-husband. Mae rents an apartment in a predominantly black part of town. She does not own a car. Recently she applied for a Cornucopia Charge Card and was refused.

Many questions need to be answered to determine whether Mae was a victim of discrimination. Does Cornucopia normally extend credit to people who make $13,000 per year? Have they properly considered the child-support income? Do they normally extend credit to persons who have been employed for only six months? Amount of income and duration of employment are legitimate credit considerations. If these factors did not influence Cornucopia's denial of application, what did? Was it because she is black, or female, or unmarried? How does she find out?

The Equal Credit Opportunity Act facilitates such an investigation by requiring a creditor to notify an applicant formally of the reasons for denial.[5] As a general rule, the four most important reasons for denial must be identified. The Federal Reserve Board has provided a model "statement of reasons" for the denial of credit:

STATEMENT OF CREDIT DENIAL, TERMINATION, OR CHANGE

DATE _____

Applicant's Name: _____
Applicant's Address: _____
_____

Description of Account, Transaction, or Requested Credit:
_____
_____

Description of Adverse Action Taken:
_____
_____

PRINCIPAL REASON(S) FOR ADVERSE ACTION CONCERNING CREDIT

__ Credit application incomplete
__ Insufficient credit references
__ Unable to verify credit references
__ Temporary or irregular employment
__ Unable to verify employment
__ Length of employment
__ Insufficient income
__ Excessive obligations
__ Unable to verify income
__ Inadequate collateral
__ Too short a period of residence
__ Temporary residence
__ Unable to verify residence
__ No credit file
__ Insufficient credit file
__ Delinquent credit obligations
__ Garnishment, attachment, foreclosure, repossession, or suit
__ Bankruptcy
__ We do not grant credit to any applicant on the terms and conditions you request.
__ Other, specify: _____

DISCLOSURE OF USE OF INFORMATION OBTAINED FROM AN OUTSIDE SOURCE

__ Disclosure inapplicable

___ Information obtained in a report from a consumer reporting agency
Name _____

Street address: _____

Telephone number: _____

___ Information obtained from an outside source other than a consumer reporting agency. Under the Fair Credit Reporting Act, you have the right to make a written request, within 60 days of receipt of this notice, for disclosure of the nature of the adverse information.
Creditor's name: _____
Creditor's address: _____

Creditor's telephone number: _____

Creditors may use this model or formulate their own statements.

Despite the comprehensiveness of this statement, it will not be helpful in all cases of credit denial. In some cases, however, it may raise a reasonable suspicion of discrimination. For example, income and length of employment may have been identified as the primary reasons for Mae's denial. If Mae discovered that a male co-worker who was employed at the same time as she received credit from Cornucopia, she would be justified in suspecting discrimination.

How does a creditor decide whether to extend or deny credit?

The statement of reasons in the form above looks relatively simple. However, a method of evaluating credit applications called "credit scoring" clouds the picture. In a credit scoring system, the applicant is given negative or positive points for each characteristic in the application. The points are then added up. Those applicants scoring above a certain sum are given credit; those scoring below are not.

This sounds innocent enough, but let's take a look at Mae's application. Suppose that Cornucopia has assigned negative points because of her zip code, which represents a predominantly black neighborhood. This practice has the *effect* of discriminating against blacks.

To determine the legality of such indirect discrimination, a judicial rule called the "effects test" has been developed. The effects test involves a weighing of the discriminatory effect, on the one side, against the statistically provable value of a given factor in predicting the likelihood of repayment, on the other.

The practice of credit scoring and the "effects test" lend an element of uncertainty to credit discrimination claims. This certainly weakens the Act. However, despite the Act's awkwardness and loopholes, it still provides valuable protection. By declaring credit discrimination to be illegal, the Act encourages conscientious creditors to treat people equally and provides for penalties against those who continue to discriminate.

What can I do if I suspect that I have been wrongfully denied credit?

Consumers who feel they have been the victims of credit discrimination should take action similar to those who have purchased a defective product (see *Chaper 5, Warranties*). The first step is to speak to the credit manager. The statement of reasons for credit denial discussed above is usually your basis of argument. If you haven't been provided with one, demand it. Then point out how it inaccurately reflects your ability to repay.

If you do this in writing, keep copies of all correspondence. If you do it in person, take notes of the time, date, place, persons with whom you spoke, and what they said. Always make it clear that you are aware of your rights under the Equal Credit Opportunity Act. The second step is to correspond with the president or owner of the business to which you are applying for credit.

These steps may get results. If they don't several types of organizations may be able to help. Non-governmental organizations may provide you with advice or lead you to an attorney. Consumer groups also may provide valuable assistance. See *Chapter 20, Consumer Assistance Agencies* for a list of these groups. Women's organizations, groups of retired people, and minority organizations may also be helpful, as may state and federal agencies. Since the Equal Credit Opportunity Act is enforced by a hodgepodge of regulatory agencies whose jurisdiction depends on the type of creditor involved, it may take a little searching to find the appropriate agency.

Equal Credit Opportunity 157

Many of these cases are complicated and difficult to pursue, making self-help in this area difficult. Therefore, an attorney's assistance is likely to be necessary at some point. See *Chapter 19, Lawyers* for advice on how to select appropriate counsel. If you win the suit, the Equal Credit Opportunity Act provides for actual damages, punitive damages and attorney fees.

Chapter 14
Repossession

You lost your job two months ago and have missed two car payments. The bank says you must catch up within ten days or your car will be repossessed. What, exactly, are they talking about?

Usually when a loan is made, the creditor will try to assure repayment by designating specific property as *collateral*. The rights the creditor and the debtor have in the collateral are set out in a document called a *security agreement*. The most common example of this arrangement is in the purchase of a car. The buyer takes possession of the car after making a down payment, and the creditor takes a security interest in the car (the collateral). Repossession, then, is the taking of property in which the creditor has a security interest.

Under what conditions may a creditor repossess property?

In order for the creditor to repossess your property, you must have signed a written security agreement giving the creditor a security interest in the property.[1] Therefore, if a sale has been entirely oral or if there is merely a receipt without a security agreement, the creditor has no right to repossess the property. It has not become collateral. Likewise, a lender of money can repossess only that property in which the lender has been given a written security interest. Otherwise, the only way payment can legally be forced is through a lawsuit. After obtaining a judgment in a lawsuit, the creditor may then seize any non-exempt property you may have to satisfy the judgment. See *Chapter 15, The Homestead and Other Judgment Exemptions* for a discussion of what property can and cannot be seized to satisfy a judgment.

A second requirement for repossession is that you must be in *default*. This usually means that one or more payments have been missed, but many other types of default (for example, not keeping the collateral insured) are usually listed in the security agreement. What constitutes default is not always clear. A creditor who has made a habit of accepting payments late may be found to have "waived" the right to have them made on time; or there may be a question as to whether the creditor has done something (such as failing to deliver what was promised) that allows you to quit paying.

In most cases, the creditor must make a *demand* for payment of the overdue installments in order to accelerate the balance of the debt (make it all due at once).[2] Although acceleration is not a legal requirement for repossession, it is a requirement for conducting a valid sale of the collateral after repossession. Until acceleration has been accomplished, you have a right to get the collateral back by catching up on payments and paying the cost of the repossession. Therefore, in the unlikely event that a creditor should repossess without first making a demand for delinquent installments, you may be able to get the collateral back. In this case, if the creditor does not agree to give back the collateral in return for your paying back payments and repossession costs, see an attorney.

What kind of notice must a creditor give me before repossessing my property?

The creditor is not required to give you any notice before repossessing property. In fact, creditors carefully avoid telling when and where they will strike to avoid running into debtors personally.

What are the legal restrictions on repossession procedure?

The only legal restriction on repossession is that it must be done *without breach of the peace*.[3] Repossession of a car from in front of your home in the middle of the night is the tactic preferred by many creditors, and it is legal.[4] On the other hand, it constitutes a "breach of the peace" to enter a building by picking a lock,[5] to grab car keys from the owner,[6] or to initiate a physical fight.[7]

Where property cannot be taken stealthily and you refuse to give it up peacefully, a court-supervised procedure called *sequestration* may be used.[8] After the creditor files a suit, but without giving you notice, the creditor may obtain a writ of sequestration ordering the sheriff or constable to seize the property. You will be subject to arrest if you resist the sheriff or constable. Many technical rules apply to this procedure, including those giving the debtor the right to regain the property under certain conditions. An attorney should be consulted if matters become this involved. However, this procedure is not ordinarily used in consumer collections.

What can I do to prevent a repossession?

In most cases, negotiation is the first order of business. Most creditors do not want to go through with a repossession and will accept an agreement to catch up on payments within a certain period of time — especially if this is accompanied by partial payment.

162   Buying, Renting & Borrowing in Texas

The law places some restrictions on how you, as a debtor, may treat property subject to a security interest. *You may not destroy, remove, conceal, encumber, transfer, or otherwise harm or reduce the value of the property with intent to hinder enforcement of the security interest.*[9] As this book goes to press, the Texas Court of Criminal Appeals has just rendered a decision that may mean that simply refusing to deliver the property to the creditor when the debt is overdue is a "concealment" under this law. *Anzaldua v. State,* No. 64,066 (Tex. Crim. App. June 11, 1980). If that decision is not changed or reversed, creditors will be able to have a debtor *charged* with a criminal offense for refusing to deliver the property to the creditor upon demand at a time when the debt is overdue. It would still be possible for the debtor to prove at *trial* that such "concealment" was not "with intent to hinder enforcement of the security interest," in that the debtor thought the debt was not overdue. Consumer advocates are at this writing asking the Court of Criminal Appeals to change this decision and are considering appealing to the U.S. Supreme Court if it does not do so. Therefore, an attorney's advice will be helpful if you are considering refusing to return collateral to a creditor upon demand.

How can I recover property after it has been repossessed?

At the time the creditor decides to repossess, the due date of the debt is usually accelerated. That is, the creditor literally speeds up the date the final payment is due by withdrawing the agreement that allowed you to repay the debt over a certain period of time. Declaring the debt to be due all at once allows the transaction to be wound up immediately by repossession and resale of the property. This can be done only if there is a written agreement allowing it, but virtually all installment contracts contain such a clause.

As long as the collateral has not been sold or properly retained in satisfaction of the debt, the debtor can *redeem* it (get it back) by paying the following to the creditor: the unpaid principal of the debt; reasonable expenses of repossession and preparation for sale; and the creditor's reasonable attorney fees (if provided for in the security agreement).[11]

What will be done with the property after repossession?

If you have paid less than 60 percent of the debt, the creditor may propose to keep the property and consider the debt paid.[12] The creditor must send you a written proposal to this effect. If you do not send a written objection within 21 days after the notice was sent, the creditor may keep the property, and you will no longer owe any part of the debt.

The creditor's other option is to sell the property.[13] This may be done either at a *public sale* (advertised to the public) or a *private sale* (by bargaining with one or more particular buyers). The money paid for the collateral is applied first to the expenses of the repossession and sale, then to the debt. If something is left over (which happens very rarely), it should be paid back to you. If the debt is not fully paid off as a result of the sale, you still owe the balance, known as a *deficiency*. The creditor may then sue you to try to seize any non-exempt property you may have in an effort to collect the deficiency.

What are my rights concerning what the creditor does with my property?

Any resulting sale must be conducted in a *commercially reasonable* manner. What is commercially reasonable must be decided on a case-by-case basis. However, the fact that a better price could have been obtained at a different time or by a different method does not in itself make the sale commercially unreasonable.[14]

Except in cases involving perishable goods and goods with very standard prices, you have a right to notice of the time and place of any public sale or, if the sale is to be private, of the time after which the private sale may be held. This gives you a chance either to bid yourself or to find a buyer who will bid a reasonable price. The higher the price, the smaller the deficiency. This right of notice of the sale applies to sales of repossessed automobiles.

What can I do if my rights are violated by the repossessing creditor?

If the property has not been sold, you can sue for a court order requiring the creditor to comply with the law. Otherwise, you can sue for the actual damages resulting from the improper procedure. If consumer goods are involved, the debtor has a right to recover the finance charge plus 10 percent of the original amount of the debt.[15] In addition, the offending creditor cannot recover a deficiency judgment without proving that the sale was commercially reasonable.[16] Otherwise, if the creditor has followed the rules in repossessing and reselling, the burden is on the debtor to prove that the sale was *not* commercially reasonable.

Chapter 15
The Homestead and Other Judgment Exemptions

Texas law provides strong protection for a homestead. Perhaps this is a result of our frontier spirit. Perhaps it is because of a fear that depriving a family of its home may make the family members wards of the state. Whatever the reason, in Texas the homestead as well as certain personal property is constitutionally protected from forced sale.[1] This chapter will explain exactly what this protection means.

What is a homestead?

Homestead refers to real property, that is, land and the buildings on it. In order to be a homestead, the property must be used as the home or as the place of business of either a family or a single adult. There are limitations on the amount of land that may be claimed as homestead.

A *rural homestead* is limited to 200 acres for a family or 100 acres for a single person. The acreage need not be in one plot of land, and buildings and other improvements on the land are considered a part of the homestead. In fact, the building used as a residence must be included as part of the homestead. If a person has more than the allowable acreage, he or she may designate which tracts of land will be claimed as homestead.

An *urban homestead* consists of a lot or lots to the extent the land

166   Buying, Renting & Borrowing in Texas

was worth not more than $10,000 at the time it became homestead, if the land became homestead on or after November 3, 1970. If the land became homestead before that date, the protected amount is $5,000.[2] All buildings on the lots are also protected. However, the value of the buildings is not included in the $10,000 limitation, nor is any increase in value since the time the property became homestead.

> Earl E. Houston and his family purchased a lot on the edge of town for $4,000 in 1971. That same year they built a house on the lot. They have lived there ever since. The property is now worth $150,000. It is all homestead since the land itself was worth less than $10,000 when the family began to live there.

A *business homestead* is considered to be part of the urban homestead. A business or residential urban homestead, or both, may be claimed. However, if both are claimed, they are exempt

only to the extent that the combined value of the land on which they stand did not exceed $10,000 at the respective times of purchase (or $5,000 if acquired before November 3, 1970). A person can have a rural homestead or an urban homestead but cannot have both.

> Pluto Kratt, who is married, owns a house in town (in which he and his family live), a downtown building in which he has his investment counseling business, and a 150-acre farm with a farmhouse. Pluto can claim as his homestead his house *or* his downtown building *or* both, but he cannot claim his farm. If he moved to the farm, it would then become his only homestead.

Whether a particular piece of land is "urban" or "rural" depends on all the specific facts of the case. Land located outside city limits has been held to be "urban," and land within city limits has been held to be "rural."

How is a homestead created?

You don't have to do anything to create a homestead. Land becomes homestead automatically if it is used as a home or the place of personal or family business.

The land doesn't have to be currently occupied to be considered homestead under these conditions:

- if there is an intention to use it as a home or business; *and*
- if there is some overt evidence of that intention.

> Quagmira Marsh lives in a rented garage apartment. She has purchased a lot in the suburbs, hired an architect and builder, and begun construction of her new home. Her suburban lot is a homestead even though she still lives in the garage apartment.

Homestead status of property comes into existence automatically. You are required to do something to assert your right to a homestead exemption only if someone attempts to force a sale of your home. However, if you have a rural homestead and own more than 200 acres (100 acres if you are single), you may voluntarily designate which land you want to claim as homestead by filing a form with the county clerk. This allows you to put a lien on the excess (non-homestead) land if you want to, without the restrictions that apply to putting a lien on a homestead.

How is the homestead exemption ended?

Once created, a homestead retains its character until it is *abandoned*. This means more than leaving the homestead. It includes an intent not to use the land as homestead any longer. Temporary renting of the homestead will not change its status. Thus, a person who leaves a homestead while on an extended vacation has not abandoned it. The law also states that a homestead cannot be considered abandoned while the family is still living there. So, if Quagmira lived in a home she owned during construction of a new home, the old home rather than the new one would be her homestead until she sold the old house or moved into the new one.

The proceeds of a voluntary sale of a homestead remain protected for six months. This is intended to give the previous owner a chance to relocate onto another homestead. Property received in exchange for a homestead is exempt for the same reason, as are the proceeds of insurance resulting from damage to or destruction of the homestead.

What happens if urban land is worth more than $10,000 when it becomes homestead?

Urban land does not entirely lack homestead protection just because it is worth more than $10,000 (or $5,000 if it became homestead before November 3, 1970). Instead, its protection is limited to that proportion of the total value at the time of enforcement of the judgment that the exempt amount bore to the value of the land at the time the property became homestead.[3]

> Homer and Marsha Stead bought a lot worth $13,000 in 1969 and built their home on it. In 1980, Family Security Bank won a judgment against the Steads for $40,000. At that time their home (including both lot and house) was worth $40,000. Their homestead was exempt only to the extent of $5/13$ (that is, $5,000 \div 13,000$) of its current value. Therefore, the court ordered that the Steads could keep their home by paying $8/13$ of the $40,000 judgment (that is, $24,615.38); but, if they failed to pay it, their

home would be sold and $^8/_{13}$ of the proceeds of that sale would be paid to Family Security Bank.

If the Steads had bought their lot after November 3, 1970, they would have been able to keep their home by paying only $^3/_{13}$ of the judgment, because the exempt amount would have been $10,000. The $13,000 value of the lot would have exceeded the exempt amount by only $3,000 instead of by $8,000.

What legal protection does homestead property have?

A homestead is generally exempt from sale without the owner's consent. There are three very important exceptions, however:

• A homestead is not protected from foreclosure of a lien (mortgage) to secure a debt for the purchase of the property. This *purchase money mortgage* is ordinarily created whenever you finance the purchase of a home.[4]

• A homestead is not protected from foreclosure of a lien (mortgage) to secure a debt for the purchase of improvements to the property.[5] This *mechanic's and materialman's lien* is ordinarily created whenever you finance home improvements. See *Chapter 3, Buying Home Improvements* for further discussion of this type of lien.

• A homestead is not protected from forced sale for payment of overdue property taxes on the homestead, or for payment of federal income taxes.

The protection provided for a homestead (and other *exempt* property discussed below) is still quite substantial. A homestead may not, for example, be sold in a forced sale to pay a judgment resulting from a negligence suit (including a suit for damages caused by an automobile accident); nor a business venture that fails; nor a default on any loan (except when properly secured by a purchase money lien or mechanic's and materialman's lien). This protection is one very good reason to own rather than rent a home. However, if someone takes a judgment against you, they will probably record it in the real estate records even if all you own is your homestead. Since such recording will sometimes cause title companies to refuse to insure the title, it may make your home more difficult to sell.[6]

What personal property is exempt from forced sale?

Texas law also gives homestead-type protection to certain personal property, that is, property other than real estate. Unlike the homestead exemption, the exemption on personal property can be given up voluntarily by a written agreement to create a lien for any purpose. Recall that the only purpose for which liens may be created voluntarily on a homestead are for purchase money and for home improvements. As with homestead property, exempt personal property may be taken for failure to pay federal income taxes.

The maximum value of exempt personal property is $15,000 for a single adult and $30,000 for a family. At any time prior to the time of the forced sale, a debtor who owns more than $15,000 worth of property eligible for exemption may designate which property he or she wishes to exempt, as long as the items designated are contained on the list below. The following types of personal property are exempt from forced sale except by reason of a voluntary lien or failure to pay federal income taxes:

- furnishings of a home, including family heirlooms, and provisions for consumption;
- all of the following which are reasonably necessary for the family or single, adult person, not a constituent of a family — implements of farming or ranching; tools, equipment, apparatus (including a boat), and books used in any trade or profession; wearing apparel; two firearms; and athletic and sporting equipment;
- all passenger cars and light trucks[7] that are not held or used for production of income or, whether held or used for production of income or not, any two of the following categories of means of travel — two animals from the following kinds with a saddle and bridle for each: horses, colts, mules, and donkeys; a bicycle or motorcycle; a wagon, cart, or dray, with harness reasonably necessary for its use; an automobile or station wagon; a truck cab; a truck trailer; a camper-truck; a truck; a pick-up truck;
- livestock and fowl not to exceed the following in number and forage on hand reasonably necessary for their consumption — 5 cows and their calves, one breeding age bull, 20 hogs, 20 sheep, 20 goats, 50 chickens, 30 turkeys, 30 ducks, 30 geese, 30 guineas;
- a dog, cat, and other household pets;
- the cash surrender value of any life insurance policy in force for more than two years to the extent that a member or members of

The Homestead and Other Judgment Exemptions

the family of the insured person or a dependent or dependents of a single, adult person, not a constituent of a family, is beneficiary thereof;

- current wages for personal services.[8]

The last category, current wages, is the most important. *In Texas, current wages may not be garnished.* Wage garnishment requires an employer to pay part of a debtor's wages directly to the creditor. In other states, this practice has proven to be oppressive and unjust. The employer often will fire an employee rather than go through the trouble of complying with a garnishment. This is especially true among low-income and unskilled workers. Because wage garnishment is illegal in Texas, any threat to garnish wages would be in violation of the Texas Debt Collection Practices Act. See *Chapter 16, Debt Collection Practices.*

Much of the property described above is also exempt from the landlord's lien on a tenant's property. The landlord's lien is discussed in detail in *Chapter 2, Renting Homes and Apartments.*

How does a creditor take property to satisfy a debt?

When personal property is taken by a creditor under the authority of a lien without a court order, it is said to be *repossessed.* See *Chapter 14, Repossession.* When a court order has been legally obtained, the taking of property by a creditor is called *execution, garnishment, attachment* or *sequestration,* depending on what procedure the creditor chooses.

Writs of sequestration[9] and *attachment*[10] are court orders that instruct a law enforcement officer to take property and hold it until further order of the court pending the outcome of a lawsuit. These orders may be granted at the time a suit is filed or at any time while the suit is pending. Both require a sworn claim that the person whose property is to be taken is indebted to the person requesting the writ. Property taken under either of these types of orders may be sold before judgment if the creditor can prove to the judge that the property is perishable or subject to a rapid decrease in value.

The difference between these two orders is that a writ of sequestration is proper when the credit has some existing legal interest in the property. In consumer transactions, the existing legal interest usually consists of a lien. Sequestration usually comes into play in a consumer transaction when a creditor has been unable to repossess the collateral without breaching the peace. See *Chapter 14, Repossession*. A writ of attachment is proper, on the other hand, if the creditor does not have a lien on the property.

The proper purpose of sequestration and attachment proceedings is simply to make sure that particular property will be available to satisfy a judgment in case the plaintiff wins. Therefore, these proceedings are not proper unless the plaintiff (usually a creditor) swears to some facts making it reasonably appear that the defendant (usually a debtor) will conceal, damage, destroy, or dispose of the property, or take it out of the county. Usually a creditor trying to collect on a consumer debt doesn't have such information. Consumers and their attorneys should be alert to their right to ask for a hearing to show that the creditor's claims in this regard are false, if that is the case, and to get the property back.

A *writ of garnishment* is a court order that instructs someone else who has possession of your property to give that property to your creditor. For example, a bank may be ordered to turn over your savings to a creditor. Garnishment may be requested either while a lawsuit is pending or after judgment.

Pre-judgment garnishment, sequestration and attachment must be ordered by the judge after a hearing. The hearing may be conducted without your being present. If the writ is granted, a copy of the writ must be given to you. The writ must include the following statement in bold type:

> TO: _____ , DEFENDANT
>
> YOU ARE HEREBY NOTIFIED THAT CERTAIN PROPERTIES ALLEGED TO BE CLAIMED BY YOU HAVE BEEN SEQUESTERED.* IF YOU CLAIM ANY RIGHTS IN SUCH PROPERTY YOU ARE ADVISED:
>
> YOU HAVE A RIGHT TO REGAIN POSSESSION OF THE PROPERTY BY FILING A REPLEVY BOND. YOU HAVE A RIGHT TO SEEK TO REGAIN POSSESSION OF THE PROPERTY BY FILING WITH THE COURT A MOTION TO DISSOLVE THIS WRIT.
>
> *(The words garnishment or attachment will appear when applicable.)

In other words, you may post bond to get the property back from the sheriff or constable, file a motion to remove the writ if it is not proper, or allow the property to be taken.

The Homestead and Other Judgment Exemptions 173

A *writ of execution* orders the seizure and forced sale of a person's property after that person has lost a lawsuit. The exemptions discussed in this chapter apply to writs of execution.

If there is an immediate possibility of forced sale of your property and you feel that this action is not justified, it is time to get the help of an attorney. This is especially true if your home is threatened. Even if you owe on a debt, it may not be proper for the creditor to take your homestead. It is important to understand the exemptions discussed in this chapter so that you don't voluntarily let somebody take property that is exempt, or feel undue pressure from someone threatening to foreclose on exempt property.

Chapter 16
Debt Collection Practices

A recent news item told of a debt collector who equipped himself with dead fish and Limburger cheese when he went out on the job. He said he found that if he made himself offensive enough debtors would pay up just to get rid of him. This technique may be imaginative and funny, but the harassment and trickery of some unscrupulous collectors is all too real. It is not a bit funny to their victims.

Why should I be concerned with how those people who fail to pay their debts are treated?

When someone fails to pay a debt, there is usually a reason other than simple irresponsibility. That person may feel cheated in the deal, or his or her ability to pay may have been reduced by illness or loss of a job. Even those who simply get "over their heads" in debt usually do not do so intentionally.

In other words, there are two sides to every default story. Creditors, naturally, understand their own side most clearly — someone owes them money and isn't paying. Sometimes they are tempted to do whatever seems necessary to frighten or coerce a defaulting debtor into paying. This approach, however, may serve only to aggravate whatever problems caused the debtor to default in the first place. Ultimately, this vicious cycle injures both business and consumers. Various laws, therefore, place limits on debt collection practices.

How do creditors collect debts?

Debt collection techniques are of infinite variety. Generally, however, they follow a pattern of putting more and more pressure on the debtor as time goes by and the overdue debt remains unpaid. This makes sense, because the techniques that apply more pressure are more costly to the creditor, both in expense and in goodwill. Accordingly, debt collection campaigns usually begin with personal requests for payment. If necessary, the campaign then progresses to the taking of property without court action. Finally, as a last resort, it ends with court action.

By personal requests for payment. Creditors usually begin with polite written reminders that a payment is overdue. If that produces no results, they make progressively more insistent demands, sometimes including telephone calls, personal contacts, and contacts with employers. How far creditors may go at this stage in applying pressure and threats, and still remain within the law, is the subject of this chapter.

By taking property without court action. If the creditor has a security interest in specific property to secure the debt, the creditor may try to take away the property when the debt is not paid. This is called *repossession* if the property is not real estate, and *foreclosure* if the property is real estate. See *Chapter 4, Foreclosure on Homes,* and *Chapter 14, Repossession.*

By court action. The creditor may file a civil lawsuit. This procedure allows the debtor to argue in court that the debt has been paid or should not be collected for some legal reason. If the creditor obtains a judgment, the judge will order the sale of some of the debtor's property (if there is any) that is not *exempt* from such a sale. See *Chapter 15, The Homestead and Other Judgment Exemptions.* The judge will also order the sale of any of the debtor's property on which the creditor has a lien, if the creditor has not already obtained all such property by foreclosure sale or repossession.

THE TEXAS COURT-MADE LAW OF UNREASONABLE DEBT COLLECTION PRACTICES

Since the mid-1950's, Texas courts, in some cases, have awarded damages to the victims of unreasonable debt collection practices.[1] To succeed in one of these suits, the debtor must prove that the collector conducted a *campaign of unreasonable collection practices*. The harassed debtor must also show that he or she suffered physical or financial injury as a result of that campaign.

Harassment — by its very nature — usually causes mental, rather than physical, suffering. Because of this, the requirement of showing physical or financial injury is often an unfair barrier to a debtor's recovery of damages for unreasonable collection practices.[2] Recently, however, this legal barrier has been breaking down. If the debtor can show *any* amount of physical damage, he or she may also recover monetary damages for mental suffering. Fairly minor physical injuries, such as costs of accepting collect long distance calls or medicine to calm nerves, may open the door to collecting damages for mental anguish as well as for physical injuries. The trend in many other states is not to require the existence of physical injury for recovery of a judgment based on debtor harassment. This trend may spread to Texas in the near future.

What collection practices are unreasonable?

A second problem with Texas court-made law concerning debt collection practices is that it does not define precisely what constitutes a "campaign of unreasonable collection practices." Many factors may be taken into account, including vulnerability of the debtor, specific conduct of the debt collector, and validity of the debt. To some extent, this broad definition is helpful, because it does not contain clearly marked loopholes for evading the law.

Vulnerability of the debtors was an important factor in the case of *United Finance & Thrift Corp. v. Smith*.[3] Constant creditor harassment of Mr. and Mrs. Smith at their home in Tyler and on their jobs resulted in Mr. Smith's blacking out on the job. Mr. Smith apparently suffered a nervous breakdown. He spent time in the hospital and was later bedridden at home. Mr. Smith's creditors, however, did not abandon him in his time of trouble. They continued to visit him at home, demanding payment and making threats. Finally, they came to his home with a truck and threatened to take all his furniture unless he paid up. Eventually, the court awarded Mr. Smith about $6,500 in damages.

Length and intensity of a debt collection campaign are other factors that determine whether it is unreasonable. In one case, a finance company's twenty-point collection campaign was found to be unreasonable. Some of its highlights included the following:
- daily telephone calls;
- statements to neighbors that the debtors were "deadbeats";
- threats that the creditor would cause them to lose their jobs;
- numerous telephone calls to one debtor's place of employment; and

- threats to garnish the debtors' wages (which is not allowed in Texas).[4]

On the other hand, a campaign of harassment may be compressed into a short period of time. In one case, the creditor actually chased the debtor in his automobile, attempting to force her off the road. He then claimed to have a warrant for her arrest and tried to put handcuffs on her. She was finally rescued by her husband's employer.[5]

These three cases demonstrate the extremes to which some creditors will go. Most of the reported cases are based on such extreme abuses. For this reason and because this is an issue each judge and jury may decide differently, the cases do not tell us precisely what constitutes an unreasonable campaign of harassment.

THE TEXAS DEBT COLLECTION PRACTICES ACT

The Texas Debt Collection Practices Act adds to the court-made law discussed above by prohibiting specific debt collection practices.[6] When one of these specific practices has been proven, the Act provides for recovery by the injured debtor of attorney fees and court costs in addition to actual damages.

What specific debt collection practices are prohibited by the Texas Debt Collection Practices Act?

The lists of specific prohibited practices below are in almost the same language as the statute. We have translated some of the "legalese," however, where this would make the meaning clearer to nonlawyers. Where the wording in the list below is unclear, the original statutory language is also unclear. In such cases, lawyers are equally uncertain about the meaning.

A debt collector may not collect or attempt to collect a debt by *threats* or *coercion* employing any of the following practices:

- using or threatening to use violence or other criminal means to cause harm to the person or property of any person;
- accusing falsely or threatening to accuse falsely any person of fraud or any other crime;
- representing or threatening to represent to anyone that a con-

sumer is willfully refusing to pay a non-disputed debt when the debt is in dispute for any reason and the consumer has notified such debt collector in writing of the dispute;

• threatening falsely to assign the credit contract so as to cut off the consumer's legal defenses to paying the debt, or so as to subject the consumer to illegal collection attempts;

• threatening that the debtor will be arrested for nonpayment of an alleged debt without proper court proceedings (but nothing prevents a debt collector from warning that the debtor may be arrested after proper court proceedings in cases where the debtor has violated the criminal laws of this state);

• threatening to file charges, complaints, or criminal action against a debtor when in fact the debtor has not violated any criminal laws; provided, however, nothing herein shall prevent a debt collector from threatening to institute civil lawsuits or other judicial proceedings to collect a debt;

• threatening that nonpayment of an alleged debt will result in the seizure, repossession, or sale of the debtor's property without proper court proceedings (however, the debt collector may exercise or threaten to exercise any rights of seizure, repossession, or sale which do not require court proceedings); or

• threatening to take any action prohibited by law.

A debt collector may not *harass or abuse* any person by collection methods employing any of the following practices:

• using profane or obscene language or language that is intended to unreasonably abuse the hearer or reader;

• placing telephone calls without disclosure of the name of the individual making the call, and with the willful intent to annoy or harass or threaten any person at the called number;

• causing expense to any person in the form of long distance telephone tolls, telegram fees, or other charges incurred by a medium of communication, without first disclosing the name of the person making the telephone call or transmitting the communication;

• causing a telephone to ring repeatedly or continuously, or making repeated or continuous telephone calls, with the willful intent to harass any person at the called number.

A debt collector may not collect or attempt to collect a debt by *unfair or unconscionable* means employing the following practices:

- seeking or obtaining any written statement or acknowledgment that the debt was incurred for necessaries of life where this was not the case; or
- collecting or attempting to collect any interest or other charge, fee, or expense incidental to the obligation unless such interest or incidental fee, charge, or expense is expressly authorized by the contract or legally chargeable to the consumer. (However, creditors may charge reasonable reinstatement fees as consideration for renewal of a real estate loan or contract of sale, after default, if the additional fees are included in a written contract executed at the time of renewal.)

A debt collector may not collect or attempt to collect a debt or obtain information concerning a consumer by any *fraudulent, deceptive or misleading representations* employing the following practices:

- using any name while engaged in the collection of debts, other than the true business or professional name or the true personal or legal name of the debt collector;
- failing to maintain a list of all business or professional names known to be used or formerly used by individual persons collecting debts or attempting to collect debts for the debt collector;
- falsely representing that the debt collector has information or something of value for the consumer in order to obtain information about the consumer;
- failing to clearly disclose, in any communication with the debtor, the name of the person to whom the debt has been assigned or is owed at the time of making any demand for money (however, this does not apply to persons servicing or collecting real estate first lien mortgage loans);
- failing to clearly disclose, in any communication with the debtor, that the debt collector is attempting to collect a debt, unless such communication is for the purpose of discovering the whereabouts of the debtor;
- using any written communication which fails to clearly indicate the name of the debt collector and the debt collector's street address, when the written notice refers to an alleged delinquent debt (but this does not require disclosure of names and addresses of employees of debt collectors);
- using any written communication which demands a response

to a place other than the debt collector's or creditor's street address or post office box (but this does not require response to the address of an employee of a debt collector);

• misrepresenting the character, extent or amount of a debt against a consumer, or misrepresenting its status in any judicial or governmental proceeding;

• falsely representing that any debt collector is vouched for, bonded by, affiliated with, or an instrumentality, agent, or official of this state or any agency of federal, state or local government;

• using, distributing, or selling any written communication which simulates or falsely represents that it is a document authorized, issued, or approved by a court, an official, a government agency, or any other governmental authority, or which creates a false impression about its source, authorization, or approval;

• using any seal or insignia or design which simulates that of any governmental agency;

• claiming that a debt may be increased by the addition of attorney fees, investigation fees, service fees, or other charges when there is no written contract or statute authorizing such additional fees or charges;

• representing that a debt will *definitely* be increased by the addition of attorney fees, investigation fees, service fees, or other charges when the award of such fees or charges is *discretionary* by a court of law;

• falsely representing the status or true nature of the services rendered by the debt collector or his business;

• using any written communication which violates or fails to conform to U.S. postal laws and regulations;

• using any communication which purports to be from any attorney or law firm, when in fact it is not;

• representing that a debt is being collected by an attorney when it is not; or

• representing that a debt is being collected by an independent, bona fide organization engaged in the business of collecting past due accounts when the debt is being collected by a subterfuge organization under the control and direction of the person to whom the debt is owed; however, this does not prohibit a creditor from owning or operating its own bona fide debt collection agency.

In addition, no one may use the terms "credit bureau," "retail merchants," or "retail merchants' association" in a business name unless the person actually gathers and distributes favorable as well as unfavorable information about credit worthiness. Finally, no creditor may knowingly use any independent debt collector who repeatedly and continuously violates the Texas Debt Collection Practices Act.

What types of debt collectors are covered by the Texas Debt Collection Practices Act?

The Texas Debt Collection Practices Act covers anyone who tries to collect a debt. Unlike the federal Fair Debt Collection Practices Act, the Texas law covers not only those collecting the debts of others, but also those collecting their own debts.

What are the penalties for violating the Texas Debt Collection Practices Act?

This law allows anyone injured as a result of a violation of the Act to sue for actual damages plus court costs and attorney fees, as well as for a court order to make the debt collector stop violating the Act. Some experts maintain that it is not necessary to show physical harm in order to recover under the Act for mental suffering.

THE FEDERAL FAIR DEBT COLLECTION PRACTICES ACT

The federal Fair Debt Collection Practices Act became effective in March 1978.[7] Because Texas already had strong collection practices legislation, the federal law had less of an effect here than elsewhere. However, it does provide consumers with some additional protections.

How does the federal Fair Debt Collection Practices Act help debtors?

Under this federal law, the debt collector may not contact the debtor at inconvenient or unusual times or places. The debt collector is required to assume, unless he or she has information otherwise, that any time before 8:00 a.m. and after 9:00 p.m. is inconvenient.[8] Also, the collector may not contact the debtor at work if the debtor's employer prohibits such contact.

The debtor may stop the collector from making any contact at all. You may do this simply by notifying the collector in writing that you don't want to hear from the collector any more. Once the debtor has done this, the collector can make contact only to advise that no further contact will be made, or to advise what action will be taken next. Of course, the collector may go ahead and repossess or file a lawsuit, as long as the jawboning stops.

The collector must inform the debtor of the amount of the debt and the name of the creditor to whom the payments are currently owed. The collector must also give written notice informing the debtor that if he or she disputes the debt within 30 days, the collector will obtain written verification of the debt and provide a copy of the verification to the debtor. If the debtor disputes the validity of the debt, the creditor must stop collection efforts until the debt has been verified. Within 30 days of the debtor's receipt of this notice, the collector must also, upon written request, supply the name of the orignal creditor, if different from the creditor to whom the debt is now owed.

The collector is limited in communicating with people other than the debtor. When trying to determine the debtor's location, the person doing the collecting may not state that the debtor owes anything, may not let it be known who the creditor works for, unless asked, may not communicate with anyone more than once unless there is reason to believe that more information may be obtained, and may not send any mail indicating on the outside that it relates to collection of a debt.

The collector may not engage in harassing or abusive conduct. Like the Texas Debt Collection Practices Act discussed above, the federal law contains a list of *specific* prohibited practices. However, unlike the Texas law, the federal law has a *general* prohibition against "any conduct the natural consequence of which is to harass, oppress, or abuse any person in connection with the collection of a debt."

The collector may not make false or misleading representations. Again, specific actions are prohibited, but the federal law also prohibits generally "any false, deceptive, or misleading representations or means in connection with the collection of any debt."

The collector may not use unfair or unconscionable practices. Similarly, besides a specific list of prohibited practices, the federal act also prohibits generally all "unfair or unconscionable means to collect or attempt to collect any debt."

What types of debt collectors are covered by the federal Fair Debt Collection Practices Act?

Although the federal law is very comprehensive, there is a serious hitch: *it applies only to collection agencies.* It does *not* apply to creditors collecting their *own* debts, nor to attorneys acting on behalf of creditors.

Buying, Renting & Borrowing in Texas

What are the penalties for violating the federal Fair Debt Collection Practices Act?

The Act provides for actual damages, plus an additional penalty of up to $1,000 (depending on how bad the violation is). It also provides for recovery of court costs and attorney fees in a suit brought successfully by a debtor.

STATUTES OF LIMITATIONS

If a creditor waits so long to sue in collecting a debt that the *statute of limitations* has run, the case can be thrown out of court. This happens quite frequently. By knowing the rules below, a debtor can sometimes put an end to a creditor's demand by pointing out that it is *barred by limitations*.

What is the statute of limitations on a written contract?

Four years is the applicable limitation period on a suit for a debt "evidenced by or founded upon any contract in writing."[9] Thus, if you agree in writing on January 1, 1981 to pay on February 1, 1981 the total price of a car, limitations will have run on February 1, 1985. Remember that the four years begins to run on the date the payment is due, *not* on the date the contract is signed.

What is the statute of limitations on an oral contract?

Two years is the limitation period on a suit for a debt not evidenced by a contract in writing.[10] The most common consumer debts of this type are for medical expenses and loans made by personal friends.

How can a debt that is barred by limitations *become enforceable again?*

After a debt is barred by limitations, it can become fully enforceable again only if the debtor signs a *written* acknowledgment of the debt.[11] Once such an acknowledgment has been signed, the limitation period begins to run again from the date of signing. A creditor whose debt is barred by limitations will sometimes attempt to persuade the debtor to sign a written agreement to pay in easy installments. By refusing to sign, the debtor can avoid paying the debt at all.

When a debt is barred by limitations, is it gone for all purposes?

A debt that is barred by limitations can still be collected in court if the debtor fails to file a written defense based on limitations. Therefore, a debtor whose debt is barred by limitations will need some legal assistance.

The courts have characterized a debt barred by limitations as a "moral obligation" that cannot be enforced legally. The most important practical effect of such a debt is that it can be placed on the debtor's credit record by a credit bureau. See *Chapter 12, Credit Bureaus.* Since any valid entry in a person's credit record will remain there for seven years, this action may have serious long-term consequences.

SELF-DEFENSE STEPS FOR HARASSED DEBTORS

As we suggested earlier, few people *intentionally* get behind in their payments. Defaults usually result from illness, unemployment, breakup of families, and unintentional overuse of credit. Debt collectors, however, tend to treat every debtor as being simply irresponsible until (if ever) they are shown otherwise. Therefore, the following self-defense suggestions are offered for debtors who mean to pay when they can, but are simply unable to at the moment:

- Do not ignore a debt collector's initial contact.
- Determine whether the debt is valid. If you are not certain, make a written request for validation of the debt to the person attempting to collect. Keep a copy of this request.
- If the debt is valid, try to work out a reasonable payment plan. Do not sign post-dated checks. Do not make promises you can't keep.
- If the debt is not valid, demand in writing that the collector stop collection efforts at once. Provide the collector with copies of evidence — for example, cancelled checks. Keep the originals.
- Keep records of all communications with the debt collector. Agreements and communications should be in writing. You should

always know the names of persons with whom you are dealing.

- Know your rights concerning exempt property, repossession and foreclosure. See *Chapter 4, Foreclosure on Homes, Chapter 14, Repossession,* and *Chapter 15, The Homestead and Other Judgment Exemptions.*
- Do not ignore or try to avoid service of legal papers. Obey all orders to appear in court, either by going yourself or by hiring an attorney.
- If you feel that a debt collector is trying to harass or trick you, or has violated the laws described in this chapter, you should contact an attorney, the Federal Trade Commission, or some other appropriate agency. See *Chapter 20, Consumer Assistance Agencies.* For more suggestions on how to be your own advocate in consumer complaints, see *Chapter 18, Self Help.*

Debt collectors have a right to apply reasonable pressure on overdue debtors. Too often, however, righteousness and greed move them beyond pressure to oppression. At that point, they usually violate one of the specific provisions in the Texas or federal debt collection practices acts, and they violate the Texas court-made law against unreasonable debt collection practices. These laws should be enforced more often to provide needed protection for harassed debtors and to improve the general business climate.

Chapter 17
Financers' Responsibilities

You bought a used car last month at Blue Sky Auto Sales and signed a contract to pay installment payments to Blue Sky. The contract contains a written warranty that the engine will perform properly under normal conditions for 90 days or 5,000 miles, whichever comes first. Now, a month later, the engine has less than 60 percent compression in all cylinders and is failing fast. Meanwhile, Blue Sky Auto Sales has sold your contract to a bank and has gone out of business.

Must you keep paying installments to the bank? Until very recently, the answer would have been, quite simply, "Yes." Because of recent changes in the law, however, the answer now in most cases is "No." Usually it is easy to tell whether you are obliged to continue making payments because a notice now required by the Federal Trade Commission (FTC) will be printed in your contract. This notice and its implications will be discussed later in this chapter.

Even if this notice is not contained in the contract, a good consumers' attorney can usually find a way to hold the financer responsible. This chapter will summarize some of the legal rules for doing just that. It will also sketch a general picture of the legal and financial relationships between retail businesses and the banks and other lenders that keep them financially afloat.

The Blue Sky Auto Sales problem raises a related issue: even assuming that the business to which you owe a debt is *responsible* for product defects and other complaints, when does that give you the right to quit making payments? Some complaints are so minor that the law allows you only to require that the product be repaired or that damages be paid. This issue of what legal *remedies* you have against whoever is responsible is discussed in *Chapter 5, Warranties* and *Chapter 6, Deceptive Trade Practices.* This chapter will attempt to answer only the following question:

Under what circumstances can a consumer make complaints against the financer as well as the seller?

Since this chapter deals with some fairly complex rules, a simplified summary is provided at the end. It may be helpful to read the summary first.

HOW CONSUMER FINANCE WORKS

The simplest means of financing a consumer purchase is for the seller to "carry the note." In this situation, the seller and the consumer actually make two agreements. One is the sales agreement — for a price, the seller will provide a product or service to the consumer. The second agreement is the financing agreement — the seller will allow the consumer to pay the price over a period of time. In exchange, the consumer agrees to pay a *finance charge* (in effect, interest) in addition to the purchase price (the principal of the debt). As part of the financing agreement, the consumer also signs a security agreement, which allows the seller to repossess certain property (*collateral*) if the debt is not paid.

Both of these agreements involve the same two parties and stipulate certain obligations from each. The fact that the seller is required to fulfill his or her part of the agreement is of particular importance to the consumer.

> Gil Lubel purchased two-year subscriptions to several national magazines from C. D. Subscription Service, Inc. The sale was made at Gil's home, where he signed several documents. One was a promissory note in which he promised to pay C. D. $25 per month for two years. Gil

received the magazines for a few months, but after that they seldom came.

Gil would be able to notify C. D. Subscription Service that he was not satisfied with their performance under the agreement, stop paying on the subscriptions, and demand his money back. Why? Because his promise to pay (the financing agreement) is directly linked to C. D.'s promise to perform (the sales agreement).

This example, however, doesn't reflect what actually occurs in financing most consumer purchases. Usually, the seller converts the sale into cash immediately. The seller, for a price, *assigns* to a *financer* the right to receive payments from the consumer as well as all other rights under the financing agreement. Basically, this is how most retail businesses obtain the funds to buy inventory and to pay operating expenses.

After assignment of the debt, the consumer is involved in a legal and financial relationship with *two* businesses. The sales agreement remains with the seller, who has certain obligations under it (such as honoring warranties). The financing agreement is with the financer, to whom the consumer now owes the money.

Another way to accomplish the same thing financially is for the financer to make a direct loan to the consumer for the purchase of goods from the seller. The financer and seller may cooperate very closely in such an arrangement. The seller may refer the consumer to that financer or may even fill out the financer's papers so that the consumer never even visits the financer.

In our example, assume that C. D. Subscriptions assigned the promissory note and security agreement to Benevolent Finance Co. in return for cash. Gil would then be obligated to make his monthly payments to Benevolent instead of to C. D. If C. D. didn't send the magazines, could Gil quit paying? Read on.

LEGAL WAYS FINANCERS CAN AVOID RESPONSIBILITY

Widespread sale of consumer goods on credit is a twentieth century phenomenon that has reached a massive scale since the Second World War. This rapid change in business practices has outrun the established legal rules of commerce.[1] Therefore, we have consumer credit transactions that are governed by rules developed during the Middle Ages to regulate transactions between far-flung merchants. This situation generally suits present-day entrepreneurs quite well, since it gives them an edge over their customers. Consumers, however, have not been so happy with this situation. Many of the recent "consumer protection" laws — which are frequently condemned by lobbyists as "interfering" with business — have been designed to bring the law up to date with present business realities.

The credit laws developed during the Middle Ages were designed to encourage assignments of debts. In those days, merchants' notes were about the only form of currency available for international trade, so those notes had to be easy to sell if commerce were to flourish. To facilitate assignment of debts, the law granted (and still grants) to certain financers a protected status called *holder in due course*. The holder in due course is not responsible for most of the legal claims the debtor may have against the seller, because the debtor's (buyer's) claims and defenses against the seller, in effect, have been "cut off" by the sale of the credit contract to the holder in due course.[2]

Under the holder-in-due-course doctrine, Gil Lubel would still be obligated to pay Benevolent Finance even though C.D. Subscription Service was not sending the magazines. Gil's only choice would be to keep on paying Benevolent and to sue C. D. for damages. It's easy to see how this doctrine encourages assignment: C. D. has cash; Benevolent has a virtually indisputable right to receive payments; and all Gil has is a debt and the right to sue C. D. It's also easy to see how this doctrine can have harsh and unjust results. The consumer usually does not have the resources to sue the seller, who may be insolvent or may have disappeared by the time problems with the sale arise.

Not all financers, however, are entitled to this special status. The law provides that in order to become a holder in due course, the financer must have purchased the contract under the following conditions:

• *for value,* meaning something must have been paid or traded for it;

• *in good faith,* meaning that the transfer must not have been made in an attempt to defraud anyone; and

• *without notice,* meaning that the financer must have purchased the contract without having received any notice of a dispute between the purchaser and the seller.[3]

The harsh results of the holder-in-due-course doctrine can sometimes be avoided by proving the financer did not meet these requirements. If such failure can be proven, the financer is not entitled to the special status accorded a holder in due course. The result is that all the legal claims the consumer may have against the seller are good against the financer also. Thus, if you can prove the financer did not meet the requirements for being a holder in due course, you will be able to hold the financer responsible for your complaints against the seller.

The problem with this legal theory is that it can be applied only on a case-by-case basis. Since the reported cases involve grossly unjust situations, no real standard exists upon which a consumer can rely. In the above example, Gil could stop making payments if Benevolent was not a holder in due course. However, he would need an attorney to make this determination, and the attorney's opinion might prove wrong.

LEGAL WAYS TO HOLD FINANCERS RESPONSIBLE

As poor Gil's situation shows, the holder-in-due-course rule can be very unfair to consumers. Several arguments exist for placing some of the risk of unfair or deceptive trade practices on the financers. One is that the lending institutions keep the merchants financially afloat, making it only fair that the financers accept some of the risks as well as the rewards. Another reason is that the lending institutions hold the power to shut down businesses guilty of unfair and deceptive practices by simply refusing to finance them. Financers, therefore, should be given every incentive to take an active role in policing the marketplace, since this will save taxpayers the expense of sending platoons of prosecutors and police officers in pursuit of the sharp operators.

Federal Trade Commission Rules
Holding Financers Responsible

In 1976, the Federal Trade Commission (FTC) passed a rule that protects consumers from much of the harshness of the holder-in-due-course doctrine.[4] The purpose of this rule is to ensure, in most cases, that the consumer's duty to pay on a credit purchase is not separated from the seller's duty to provide goods and services as

194   Buying, Renting & Borrowing in Texas

promised. Thus, when the rule applies, the consumer's rights are not cut off by assignment of the debt to a financer. The FTC rule mentioned above has two parts: the holder-in-due-course rule and the purchase-money loan rule.

The FTC holder-in-due-course rule. The first part of the FTC rule protects the consumer whose debt is to be assigned by requiring the seller to include in the retail installment agreement the following notice:

NOTICE
ANY HOLDER OF THIS CONSUMER CREDIT CONTRACT IS SUBJECT TO ALL CLAIMS AND DEFENSES WHICH THE DEBTOR COULD ASSERT AGAINST THE SELLER OF GOODS OR SERVICES OBTAINED PURSUANT HERETO OR WITH THE PROCEEDS HEREOF. RECOVERY HEREUNDER BY THE DEBTOR SHALL NOT EXCEED AMOUNTS PAID BY THE DEBTOR HEREUNDER.[5]

Financers' Responsibilities

What all this legal jargon means is this: whenever this notice appears, your rights will be protected against both the seller and the financer. For example:

> After four months, Gil has paid $100 to Benevolent Finance and still owes $500 under the contract. C. D. hasn't complied with the agreement, so Gil has a *defense* (a legal reason to stop making payments on the $500 he owes to Benevolent). Gil also has a *claim* against both C. D. and Benevolent to get back the $100 he has already paid. However, the last sentence of the required notice means that other claims he may have against C. D., such as the $10,000 for mental anguish he suffered by missing the Super Bowl edition of *Sports Verbalized,* are not valid against Benevolent.[6]

The FTC purchase-money loan rule. The second part of the same FTC rule provides protection, in some cases, for the consumer who finances a purchase with a direct loan from a bank or other lending institution. This part of the rule applies *only* if the financer is *affiliated* with the seller, or if the seller *refers* the consumer to the financer. In either case, the following notice must appear in the financing papers:

> *NOTICE*
> ANY HOLDER OF THIS CONSUMER CREDIT CONTRACT IS SUBJECT TO ALL CLAIMS AND DEFENSES WHICH THE DEBTOR COULD ASSERT AGAINST THE SELLER OF GOODS OR SERVICES OBTAINED WITH THE PROCEEDS HEREOF. RECOVERY HEREUNDER BY THE DEBTOR SHALL NOT EXCEED AMOUNTS PAID BY THE DEBTOR HEREUNDER.[7]

Affiliation requiring this type of notice exists if the seller and the financer are under the same ownership, or if some formal or informal contract exists between them regarding sales or financing practices. If the seller fills out the loan contract or loan forms for you, or gets a commission from the lender, then the necessary affiliation probably exists.

Texas Laws Holding Financers Responsible

Financers may, in some cases, try to evade responsibility by slipping through loopholes in the FTC rule. For example, uncertainty exists over what the legal consequences might be for failure to provide the notices required by the FTC. Several Texas laws help plug such potential loopholes.

Notice of assignment or negotiation. In installment sales of goods and services, your claims and defenses cannot be cut off unless the financer gives you a "Notice of Assignment or Negotiation." The notice should look something like this:

NOTICE

IF YOU HAVE ANY COMPLAINT OR OBJECTION REGARDING THE GOODS OR SERVICES COVERED BY THE CONTRACT IDENTIFIED IN THIS NOTICE, OR ANY CLAIM OR DEFENSE RELATING TO SUCH CONTRACT, YOU MUST NOTIFY US WITHIN 30 DAYS FROM THE DATE THIS NOTICE WAS MAILED.[8]

The law requiring this notice came into existence before the FTC rule applying to financers' responsibilities. It represents only a *small* step toward making financers responsible for consumers' claims because it protects only claims which came into existence during the 30 days following receipt of the notice. The FTC rule now provides much stronger protection. However, if you have a complaint against the seller at the time you receive a notice of assignment, you should notify the financer in writing of that complaint. This will help ensure that your rights regarding the complaint will not be cut off.

Certificate of completion: Another Texas law that existed prior to the FTC rule applies to home repair contracts. That law requires the seller to obtain a "Certificate of Completion or Satisfaction" signed by the consumer when all the improvements have been completed. This certificate should contain the following notice:

WARNING TO BUYER — DO NOT SIGN THIS CERTIFICATE UNTIL ALL SERVICES HAVE BEEN SATISFACTORILY PERFORMED AND MATERIALS SUPPLIED OR GOODS RECEIVED AND FOUND SATISFACTORY.[9]

Confusion often exists regarding the purpose and effect of the certificate of completion. It is important to know that if you sign the certificate, you do not waive any warranties or other rights. Also, the credit agreement remains valid whether or not you sign the certificate. The practical purpose of the certificate of completion is to assure the financer that the work has been done, so that funds may be released to the contractor.

Since the FTC rule is stronger, your claims will be preserved automatically whenever it applies. However, the certificate of completion is still important. The financer generally will not release funds to the contractor until the certificate is signed. Therefore, your signature on the certificate can be an excellent bargaining tool in conflicts you may have with a contractor. Simply *refuse to sign the certificate of completion until the contractor has done everything required by the contract.*

SUMMARY OF FINANCERS' RESPONSIBILITIES

Let's return to the question set out at the beginning of this chapter:

Under what circumstances can a consumer make complaints against the financer as well as the seller?

In the most common consumer credit arrangement, in which an installment contract with the seller is later assigned to the financer, the notice required by the FTC rule makes the financer subject to all the consumer's claims and defenses up to the amount of the debt. Most such contracts signed since May 14, 1976 (effective date of the rule) contain this notice. Contracts signed since that date that do not contain the required notice may nevertheless be treated by the courts as if they did contain it.[10] In addition, the consumer still may be protected when a court determines that, for one or more of the reasons discussed above, the financer does not have holder-in-due-course status.[11]

In the case of a purchase-money loan, the FTC rule has the same effect as long as the seller and the financer are *affiliated* or the seller has *referred* the consumer to the financer. On the other hand, if the consumer obtains financing with a lender unconnected with the seller, without being referred by that seller, the consumer must usually pay the debt no matter how bad the product or service may turn out to be. This suggests one advantage of obtaining financing through the seller. Usually, however, "credit shopping" at banks, credit unions, etc. will produce savings that more than outweigh this consideration. See *Chapter 11, Calculating the Costs of Credit* for further discussion of shopping comparatively for credit.

PART FOUR
ENFORCING THE CONSUMER'S RIGHTS

Chapter 18
Self Help

Since the primary purpose of this book is to inform Texas consumers about their legal rights, it wouldn't be complete without a discussion of how to enforce those rights. This chapter will make some suggestions about how to resolve your own complaints and disputes without professional assistance. *Chapter 19, Lawyers* will discuss hiring and using a lawyer, if your case comes to that. *Chapter 20, Consumer Assistance Agencies* will provide a list of organizations that provide help with many types of consumer problems. At the end of the book, a list of *Suggested Readings* will guide you to publications which provide more detailed advice on how to assert your legal rights.

What can I do to help myself on basic legal problems?

As an informed consumer, you can take several steps toward resolving your own legal problems: investigate, read, question, and write.

Investigate. You can avoid many problems by checking on products before you buy. Printed sources include consumer information publications such as the monthly magazines *Changing Times* and *Consumer Reports,* the annual *Consumer Reports Buyer's Guide,* and specialty magazines such as *Modern Photography* and *Stereo Review.* Publications such as these compare and rate a variety of products and provide detailed information to allow you to make your own comparisons. Services such as home and auto repair also

202   Buying, Renting & Borrowing in Texas

can be investigated by asking for references and checking these out. Finally, don't overlook family and friends as a source of first-hand information on all types of products and services.

Read. The necessity of reading all contracts and documents before signing or buying anything can't be stressed too heavily. Don't overlook warranties; they're not all alike. See *Chapter 5, Warranties.* If you don't like the terms you read, ask that they be changed.

Question. Many people are embarrassed to question business people about things they don't understand. Overcoming this embarrassment can be a great step toward avoiding consumer problems. If you don't understand a contract or a warranty, don't feel bad. Just remember the words of Will Rogers:

> The minute you read something and you don't understand it, you can almost be sure it was drawn up by a lawyer. Then if

you give it to another lawyer to read and he doesn't know just what it means, why then you can be sure it was drawn up by a lawyer.[1]

We do not advocate taking Will Rogers literally, and throughout this book we have suggested using lawyers to clarify and resolve problems and conflicts. Perhaps you will be less hesitant to ask questions, however, if you know that this might be the first thing a lawyer would do in your place. Ask questions about whatever you'd like to know, whether it concerns the papers you are to sign or the product you are buying.

Write. When promises are made, whether at the time of a sale or during a later dispute, you should get them in writing. Formal contracts are nice, but they are neither required nor practical in many situations. Many promises can simply be written on a receipt. When you can't get a promise in writing, you should at least learn the name and position of the person who makes the promise and record this information for possible future reference.

What steps should I follow to make a consumer complaint?

The very first thing you should do if you are dissatisfied with a product or service is to be sure that your complaint is justified in your own mind. Then, complain first to the person with whom you did business. At this stage, the complaint may be made in person or by telephone. Subsequent communications should be in writing or followed up by a letter.

The initial complaint may fail to yield results. In that case, complain to one or more of the following:

- the owner of the business;
- the district or regional manager of a chain;
- the president of a corporation; or
- the manufacturer of the item purchased.

There are a number of ways to find out the names of these people and how to contact them. The simplest way is to ask the person to whom you first complained. Corporate registers and numerous consumer complaint guides contain this information. These can probably be found in your local library.[2] Some libraries have research services that will provide such information over the telephone.

A letter of complaint should be in the form of a forceful yet polite business letter. The sample letter below and the comments on the next page illustrate the information this letter should contain.

April 6, 1990

Thurgood Trudge
1234 Winding Rd.
Suburb, Texas 77777

Placid Leisure, Inc.
Box 1087
Los Angles, California 88888

To Placid Leisure, Inc.:

[A]On April 1, 1990, I purchased a pair of Float Running Shoes at Colossus Sports Shop in Houston, Texas.

[B]I purchased the shoes because of claims that millions of tiny air bubbles in the soles would protect a runner's feet from hard pavement.

[C]The very next day I was taking my usual jog when I had a blowout in my right shoe. [D]I returned to Colossus and was told that they would neither exchange the shoe nor refund my money. They also informed me that there is no such thing as a spare sole.

These shoes are totally useless now. [E]I am returning them to you along with this letter and a copy of my receipt. [F]I would like to have my money refunded or the shoes replaced with a pair that will last a reasonable length of time.

[G]I look forward to your response and will wait two weeks before taking any further action.

Sincerely yours,

Thurgood Trudge

[H]cc: Attorney General of Texas
    Consumer Protection Division
    P.O. Box 12548
    Austin, Texas 78711

[I](Certified No. 12345678)

> ᴬIdentify the product about which you are complaining. State when and where it was purchased.
>
> ᴮTell why you purchased the product. If you have been satisfied with the product or the company in the past, you might mention that.
>
> ᶜState in your complaint exactly why you are dissatisfied.
>
> ᴰDescribe what steps you have already taken to remedy the problem and why you have not been successful (or what it cost).
>
> ᴱAttach copies of receipts, cancelled checks or other evidence. Keep the originals of these documents. If the item is totally useless, you may want to return it to display your seriousness.
>
> ᶠMake a demand. What do you want to have done to resolve the problem?
>
> ᴳGive a deadline.
>
> ᴴIt may be effective to send copies of this letter to regulatory agencies or consumer protection agencies. On the other hand, you may want to give the manufacturer or dealer a chance to satisfy your demands before making such complaints.
>
> ᴵSending the letter by certified mail, return receipt requested will give you a way of proving later that you made your complaint within a "reasonable time," as required by law.

What should I do if my first complaint letter gets no results?

If your first letter of complaint gets no results, you may want to take the "shotgun approach" of complaining to every regulatory body, public consumer protection agency, industry or trade organization, consumer group and media representative you think might listen. A letter to the company with copies to all of these organizations is one method of accomplishing this. Many of these agencies are listed in *Chapter 20, Consumer Assistance Agencies.*

Complaints to public agencies and business-sponsored self-policing organizations are effective against businesses that want to avoid controversy. However, when a business doesn't care about its reputation and wants to be difficult, these agencies are often ineffec-

tive. Self-policing groups, such as the Better Business Bureau and trade/professional associations, have no legal authority and frequently have no particular interest in being aggressive. Public agencies are limited by funds, staff and jurisdiction.

You should complain to these organizations anyway. Your problem may be one of broad, general concern that will cause a public agency to use its authority or will stir a private agency to effective action. If not, your complaint will at least help the agencies to identify patterns of deceptive business practices.

What further action can be taken without seeking legal advice?

The next and final stage in the consumer complaint process is to file a lawsuit. In general, lawsuits are time-consuming, frustrating and costly. There is no prohibition against self-representation in a lawsuit, but in any court except small claims court it is not ordinarily advisable to sue without the services of an attorney. Even an informed consumer is no match for a skilled attorney. We therefore suggest you consider suing in small claims court, where both parties generally represent themselves.

What is a small claims court?

Small claims courts were created early in this century to provide a speedy, informal and inexpensive system of justice for those who cannot afford a lawyer. Today, most states have some form of small claims court. In Texas, such courts are presided over by the local justices of the peace.

Small claims courts have great potential for providing redress of grievances to consumers. In practice, however, they haven't lived up to this potential, and numerous problems have been found to exist:

• Not enough people are aware of the existence or function of small claims court.

• The courts often operate only during regular business hours, making them inaccessible to many working people.

• The maximum amount for which one can sue is too low.

• Collecting a judgment can sometimes be a problem.[3]

Despite these shortcomings, small claims courts can provide effective remedies in certain cases. Several studies have shown that consumer-plaintiffs win in the vast majority of suits they bring in small claims courts.[4]

What is the difference between "small claims court" and "justice of the peace court" in Texas?

What is technically called "small claims court" in Texas is simply the familiar justice of the peace court supposedly operating under different rules. The judge of the "small claims court" is the justice of the peace, and the only differences between filing in "small claims court" and "justice of the peace court" are these:

• Filing and service fees are lower in "small claims court" — $3 for filing and $5 for service of one citation, as opposed to $15 for filing and $8 for service of one citation in regular "justice of the peace court."

• The rules of evidence and procedure are supposed to be informal in "small claims court." In the regular "justice of the peace court," the rules of evidence and civil procedure are supposed to apply. As a practical matter, however, these formal rules are not applied in most regular "justice of the peace courts" either.

- Jurisdiction of "small claims court" is only of claims not over $150 (or $200 for wage claims). Jurisdiction of regular "justice of the peace courts" is of claims not over $500.

Therefore, if your claim is for not over $150 (or $200 if it is a wage claim), tell the clerk or the justice of the peace that you want to file in "small claims court," as this will save a few dollars in fees. If your claim is for more than that but not over $500, file it as a regular civil case in "justice of the peace court." Although some justices of the peace may follow formal rules more strictly in cases not designated for "small claims court," the distinction is probably more technical than practical for most of them. Most justices of the peace are not lawyers and are not particularly familiar with the formal rules. In addition, a party appealing a decision from either "small claims court" or "justice of the peace court" gets a whole new trial, so procedural errors at the earlier trial are never pointed out.

What is the procedure for filing a small claim in Texas?

Ordinarily, it makes no practical difference, except for the amount of the filing fee, whether a case is filed in a "justice of the peace court" or in "small claims court." The discussion below will therefore apply to all claims for $500 or less filed with a justice of the peace.

Before filing suit, you must know the correct legal name and address of the person you are going to sue. If this is a business, you will want to know the name of the owner as well as the business name. You may be able to get this information simply by asking or by observing signs, stationery or business cards. In other cases, you may have to refer to the "assumed names records" which list people who do business in names other than their own. The office of the county clerk at your county courthouse will be able to assist you in using these files.

If the owner is a corporation, call the Secretary of State in Austin at 512/475-3551 and ask for the names and addresses of the president, vice president, and registered agent for service of process. Suit should be filed in the name of the corporation, but the citation is served on any one of these three persons.

When you have this information, you must then determine what county precinct to sue in. The best way to find this out is to call the office of the justice of the peace nearest you. Someone in that office will be able to tell you if you can sue in that precinct or whether you must sue in another.

The most beneficial characteristic of the justice court is its informality. Once you have determined which precinct to sue in, simply go down to the court and tell the justice of the peace or the clerk that you want to file a claim. They will then help you fill out a petition.

A pamphlet prepared by the State Junior Bar of Texas advises that the following steps be taken:

1. Give the clerk the following information:
    (a) your complete name and address,
    (b) the name and address of each person or business your claim is against,
    (c) the amount of money your claim is for,
    (d) the basis of your claim,
    (e) the amount of money you properly owe the defendant, if any.
2. Swear under oath that this small claims statement is true.
3. Pay the clerk the filing fee. If you want a jury trial you must pay extra. All these costs may be recovered at trial if you win your suit.
4. Ask the clerk to issue a subpoena (which will order a witness to appear at trial) for anyone you need to prove your claim and who you think may not come if you ask them to do so. You will need only the witness' full name and street address for a subpoena to be issued. There will be a small charge.
5. Tell the clerk where the defendant may be found and the approximate time of day he or she is likely to be found at that location. This is important since *the defendant must be served with a citation before the suit can begin.*
6. Call the clerk in 2 or 3 days to make sure the defen-

dant has been served and *find out the exact date of service*. This date is important because it will be used to calculate the trial date.

7. *Calculate the trial date* as follows: From the time of service, count 10 days; the next Monday after the expiration of the 10-day period is the first day on which the trial *may* be held. Check with the clerk or justice of the peace to determine the exact date and time on which the trial *will* be held. Also be sure the defendant has notice of the trial date, either from the clerk or by your sending the defendant a certified letter. Don't give the defendant any excuse for not showing up at the trial. Of course, you must be there, with all your evidence (such as witnesses, papers, the defective product, photographs, etc).[5]

The amount of your claim must not be more than $500. The basis of your claim should be stated briefly and concisely in your own words. No formal "pleadings" are necessary. You need not claim that the defendant violated a specific statute. In fact, in most cases you should beware of specifically pleading that the defendant violated the Consumer Protection Act. Some judges will refuse to hear the case if the possibility of multiple damages under the statute appear to put your claim over the $500 mark, even if you don't request multiple damages.

You, as plaintiff, have the burden of proving that you were harmed by the defendant. You must be prepared to demonstrate this to the judge (or jury). Be prepared. Bring all relevant documents with you and have them organized. Make sure all the important witnesses are there.

If one of your witnesses absolutely cannot be present, try to get a signed statement from that person. The statement, called an affidavit, must be sworn to and notarized. Such affidavits are not technically admissible at trial in "justice of the peace court" but probably are admissible in "small claims court." The following is a sample:

> I, Will B. Witness, was present when Otto Buyer purchased a 1977 Dodge from Fast Fred's Used Cars. At that time I personally heard Fred promise Mr. Buyer that if he

had any problems with the car within six months, he could bring it back for repair at no charge.

_____
Will B. Witness

Signed and sworn to before me on this the _____ day of _____ , 198__ .

_____
Notary public in and for _____ County, Texas.
My commission expires _____.

If such a key witness cannot be at the trial at that time, you may want to ask the judge to change the trial date. Your chances will be better if you present an affidavit from the witness regarding what his or her general testimony would be, and why the witness cannot be present at the time for which the trial has been set.

On the day of the hearing you must be in the court on time. The judge will usually call the names of all the cases to be heard on that day. If you are not present at this "docket call," your case will probably be dismissed.

If the defendant is not there, you should win by default. This is not necessarily good news. Studies indicate that plaintiffs generally have more difficulty collecting the money awarded when the defendant has defaulted than when there has been a trial.

The hearing itself is informal.[6] When the judge asks you to start, simply tell your story briefly, and in an organized manner. Don't try to put on a show of emotional outrage. Just tell your story, and the feelings you express naturally and genuinely will provide plenty of emotional persuasion. The other side will then be allowed to question you. Answer them briefly and politely. It won't do you any good to interrupt or get into an argument.

If the judge decides in your favor, your problems may still not be over. In many instances, the losing party will pay you immediately or soon after the hearing. However, studies indicate that 30 to 40 percent of victorious consumer-plaintiffs have some difficulty collecting their judgments.[7] You may have to make several demands for the payment. Finally, you may have to go back to the court and ask the clerk to prepare a *writ of execution* This document orders the constable to obtain the money. You must wait ten days before seeking a writ of execution. During that period, the losing party has the right to appeal the decision or seek a new trial. The writ costs about $4.00 and is good for only 90 days. If the 90 days passes and the constable hasn't collected the money, you must pay an additional fee for another writ or drop your efforts.

Even if you are unable to collect through the writ of execution, you should at least have the clerk prepare an *abstract of judgment* to be filed in the county records. This will give official notice of your lien on all the defendant's property, other than that which is judgment exempt, as discussed in *Chapter 15, The Homestead and Other Judgment Exemptions*. Then, before the defendant can sell any non-exempt real property, the buyer or title company will sometimes require that your judgment be paid. Your lien is good for ten years from the date of judgment and may be renewed indefinitely. Thus, if your patience is great enough, you should be able to collect from any defendant who ever owns any non-exempt property. Unfortunately, however, many people don't own any such property. In this case, your victory may be only a moral one.

One of the benefits of small claims court is that the threat of a lawsuit often encourages a business to settle. As the hearing date nears, settlement becomes ever more attractive. You should be aware of this. The trouble of going to court may be avoided if both parties are open to reasonable compromise.

With the help of the State Junior Bar pamphlet (cited at note 5), and a helpful justice of the peace or clerk, most consumer small claims can be processed without a lawyer's assistance. It may, however, be worthwhile to go over your case with a lawyer for suggestions on how to present your case in court. Especially if you are "stuck" on questions you have about what to do, the lawyer's advice may enable you to carry on successfully instead of giving up.

Chapter 19
Lawyers

The practice of law is a skilled profession. It is also a business. When a person who has a consumer complaint seeks legal advice, he or she again becomes a consumer. Thoughtful comparison shopping for legal services and careful evaluation of each lawyer will help avoid a second consumer complaint.

This chapter does not propose a foolproof method for choosing a lawyer. That would probably be impossible. The following discussion will simply present the authors' ideas about how to find lawyers who will take consumer complaints and will handle them well. It also offers suggestions as to how to maintain a productive and satisfactory relationship with the chosen lawyer.

Problems in finding a good consumer lawyer can arise out of some basic characteristics of the legal profession as well as from the nature of most consumer complaints:

• Most consumer claims are small by ordinary lawyers' standards. Some lawyers tend to put aside such smaller cases in favor of their big money-makers, if they even take the smaller cases at all.

• Most of the law governing consumer complaints is new. Some lawyers who are generally competent have neither the ready know-how to handle a consumer claim efficiently, nor the willingness to dig into an unfamiliar area of law.

• The legal profession, like all other professions, trades and businesses, has some unscrupulous members of whom the public must be wary.

What are the traditional ways of finding a lawyer?

Some people "have a lawyer" either personally or in their businesses. If you are one of these people, your usual lawyer may be the best person to handle your consumer complaint. If your lawyer doesn't do consumer cases, he or she should recommend someone who does. However, most people don't have an ongoing business relationship with a lawyer. There are several traditional methods by which most of those people find a lawyer.

Some people find a lawyer through the yellow pages. Obviously, this method is nothing but pot luck and not a good way to find legal counsel.

Bar studies indicate that most people find a lawyer through the *recommendations of a friend or relative.* This may be a very good method. However, you should make sure that the person making the recommendation has actually employed the lawyer and been satisfied. It is also important to know what kind of case the person making the recommendation had. Tactfully quiz the person to determine if he or she got a fair deal. Surprisingly, people will sometimes recommend a lawyer even if they weren't completely satisfied with the service they received.

Many local or county bar associations in Texas have a lawyer referral service. This simply refers clients to lawyers who have signed up for referrals on a rotating basis. Any lawyer who is a member of the bar association can be listed. The bar association makes no assurances about the quality of service provided. Lawyers may list themselves as being interested in certain types of cases, but they are not required to comply with any special standards to receive such referrals. The lawyer referral service requires that an attorney give the prospective client an initial interview for a set fee (frequently $10). That fee ultimately goes to the referral service, not to the attorney. In general, lawyer referral services are not much better than the yellow pages.

Many clients end up with a lawyer as a result of *referral by another attorney.* Consumers should be aware that much of the business of some lawyers is essentially that of acting as a broker by making referrals. Referral fees are customary among lawyers. Theoretically, these should not increase the fee paid by a specific client. However, they do increase the across-the-board costs to consumers of legal services. You have a right to know if a referral fee is being paid.[1]

In 1977 the United States Supreme Court issued an opinion which opened the door to lawyer advertising.[2] Advertising benefits consumers of legal services by providing information for comparison shopping. However, permissible lawyer advertising of fixed fees is limited to very routine matters, such as uncontested divorces, wills and name changes. Thus, its impact for people with consumer problems is not very great.

All advertising has a potential for being misunderstood. You should read lawyers' ads very carefully. For example, a lawyer who advertises "Uncontested divorces, $99 plus costs" will charge considerably more if a dispute develops; and the costs can be more than the attorney fee if it is difficult to serve the papers on the other spouse or if other pretrial procedures become necessary.

Are there any less conventional ways to search for a good consumer lawyer?

The traditional methods of finding a lawyer only assure that the attorney found is competent and has a generally good reputation. This is a required starting point, but for most consumer cases you need more information. This need stems from the fact that most consumer claims are relatively small, thus requiring efficient handling in order to be profitable for the lawyer.

As a businessperson, a lawyer will be motivated to pursue a case only if the case is likely to yield a reasonable fee. Small cases usually yield a reasonable fee only if they fit into a streamlined office practice that turns over numerous similar small cases efficiently and profitably. Few attorneys have such an office system set up to handle consumer claims.

It is normal and proper for a lawyer to discuss with his or her client the chances of making a profit on a particular case. Such forthrightness is in the client's interest, because the client not only wants the attorney to take the case but also wants the case pursued diligently. Whether the attorney will be economically motivated to do so is an important consideration.

However, a lawyer may be motivated by considerations other than economics. Lawyers who are committed to representing individuals in consumer rights cases do exist. A consumer who can find one has taken a great step toward solving the problem of attorney motivation.

At this time no consumer group in the state has a formal lawyer referral service. However, a contact with one or more such groups may yield helpful referrals to lawyers. Contact with other civil libertarian, environmentalist, feminist, and minority organizations may also yield results. News stories also provide information on those lawyers and public agencies that represent consumers.

Some lawyers have developed good reputations for handling "products liability" cases. These are cases in which someone has suffered personal injuries (physical injury or death) that may have been caused by a defective product. Such attorneys may or may not be good at handling the more ordinary consumer disputes discussed in this book. The reason for this is that products liability cases require expertise in an area of consumer law (*strict liability*) that applies only when someone is injured physically, and in proving damages resulting from such personal injury. Thus, products liability attorneys, in general, are not much more likely than any other lawyer to have interest or expertise in the ordinary consumer law of buying, renting and borrowing, although some may be very good at it.

Lawyers

How can I use the initial attorney-client interview to evaluate a lawyer?

The suggestions made thus far will help you determine which lawyer to contact first. It is sometimes wise to identify several prospects and have an interview with each. Many attorneys will agree to an initial consultation at no charge. However, some will not give specific legal advice at such an initial consultation.[3]

One purpose of the initial interview is to present the facts of the case to the lawyer. However, another purpose is for you to discover as much as you can about the lawyer:

- Is the lawyer competent to handle a consumer problem such as yours?
- Is the lawyer likely to pursue your case diligently?
- What will be the fee and the method of payment?

An attorney's competence is very difficult to judge from a personal interview. Some of the most trustworthy lawyers come across as thoughtful but unsure of themselves; and some of the least trustworthy appear to have all the answers and to be ready to take on anything. One thing you can do is to ask if the lawyer has done any cases similar to yours. You might also test his or her familiarity with concepts in this book that appear to apply to your case. Otherwise, an attorney's reputation, not his or her conversational ability, is the best guide to a lawyer's competence.

You may want to ask whether the lawyer you talk with is a member of the Consumer Law Section of the State Bar of Texas. Membership in that section, which has several thousand members, does not assure any particular degree of competence in consumer law. It does, however, indicate that the member is interested in this area of law. It also means that the lawyer is receiving a newsletter that provides an update on recent developments in consumer law.

What are the customary arrangements for paying attorney fees in consumer cases?

Always agree at the initial interview how much you will pay in attorney fees, and what the terms will be. This is essential to avoid misunderstandings and disagreements later. Three basic types of fee arrangements that may be offered for a consumer case will be discussed below.

One arrangement is the *hourly rate*. Lawyers generally charge between $40 and $150 per hour. They generally bill in increments of one-tenth or one-quarter hour. A five-minute phone call or one-paragraph letter may cost you as much as $37. In addition, the lawyer may request a *retainer* fee, which is a front-end payment. An hourly fee arrangement gives the lawyer much discretion in deciding how much of the lawyer's time — that is, how much of your money — the case is worth as it progresses. However, this arrangement can tempt the attorney to over-work the case in order to earn a steady fee. Even when this is not happening, the client may suspect that it is. Therefore, the hourly fee arrangement is usually best confined to attorney-client relationships of long standing and high confidence.

A second type of fee arrangement is the *flat fee*. This is simply an agreement to pay a certain fixed amount for a certain job. This fee arrangement is more applicable to simple divorce suits, wills and other routine matters than to consumer cases. This is what appears in lawyers' ads. In all flat fee arrangements, the consumer should understand from the beginning exactly what services the flat fee covers and how the fee is to be paid.

The *contingent fee* is the most common type of fee arrangement in consumer cases. In a contingent fee arrangement, the bulk of the lawyer's fee is dependent on winning the case. The lawyer will usually require a retainer fee to be paid when the case is opened. The amount of the retainer varies so much that there is no way to indicate what a usual retainer would be. This front-end fee is negotiable. The remainder of the lawyer's fee comes as a percentage of the amount of money the consumer wins (40 percent is typical) or from the attorney fees the court may award under many consumer protection statutes. The lawyer will usually be guaranteed an amount equal to a certain percentage of the judgment. The attorney fees awarded by the court are then replaced by or set off against this amount. If, for example, the consumer receives a judgment of $1,000 and the attorney is guaranteed a contingent fee of at least 40 percent of the judgment, the exact amount the attorney receives will depend on the amount awarded by the court as "attorney fees," as follows:

1. judgment awarded = $1,000
   attorney fees awarded = -0-
   consumer receives = 600
   attorney receives = 400
2. judgment awarded = $1,000
   attorney fees awarded = 400
   consumer receives = 1,000
   attorney receives = 400
3. judgment awarded = $1,000
   attorney fees awarded = 200
   consumer receives = 800
   attorney receives = 400
4. judgment awarded = $1,000
   attorney fees awarded = 600
   consumer receives = 1,000
   attorney receives = 600

Of course, this isn't the only type of contingent fee arrangement. Some lawyers will suggest that their percentage come from the gross award (that is, the judgment awarded to the client plus the attorney fees awarded). In example 2 above, this method would result in the lawyer receiving $560 and the consumer receiving $840.

There should also be an agreement between the lawyer and the client as to who will pay what expenses — for example, filing fees, the fee of the court reporter at pre-trial depositions, and expert witness fees. Most often, the client agrees to pay these fees as they are incurred. Then, if the client wins the case, the other (losing) party will have to pay many of these fees as "court costs." If the client loses, then the client will have to pay his or her own court costs, plus the court costs incurred by the other (winning) party.

Customary practices with regard to fees differ from one area of the state to another. At the present time, for example, it is much easier to find an attorney in Austin or San Antonio who will handle a typical consumer case on a contingent fee than it is to find one in Houston. It may even be worthwhile for you to retain a lawyer outside your home area to handle a sizable case, if a suitable lawyer cannot be found in the local area. Wherever you may live in Texas, however, the fundamental principles are the same. Your choice of a lawyer should be *informed,* and your agreement with that lawyer should be *clear.*

How can I tell if my lawyer is doing a good job?

It's very difficult to determine if a lawyer is doing a proper job, especially if you are having trouble communicating with your lawyer. Bar associations claim that most problems between attorneys and their clients stem from failure to communicate. Establishing a pattern of communication will help you determine if the attorney is diligently progressing with your case.

It is important to realize that your case is not the only one for which the attorney is responsible. It is also important to realize that the legal process is excessively slow. However, you do have a right to know what has happened with your case, what should happen next, and when it should happen.

Some attorneys intentionally avoid communication with some clients. If you hire an attorney who won't return your phone calls and is never in, it's a sure sign that you've hired one who's not really interested in your case. On the other hand, some attorneys consider it good business to send the client a copy of every piece of paper used in the case. This is a good practice, but it doesn't tell you much about what to expect next and when.

We suggest that you discuss communications at the initial consultation. Tell the lawyer you understand that the legal process is slow, but that you want to be kept aware of what to expect in the progress of your case. Then, each time you communicate with the lawyer, ask what is likely to happen next and when. This should enable you to be informed without becoming a "problem client."

Lawyers take a very dim view of clients who call or visit constantly without good reason. On the other hand, lawyers whose office procedures are inadequate and whose caseloads are too high sometimes need to be reminded of cases. It ought not to be so, but sometimes it is. Use your common sense and judgment to determine whether and when to ask how your case is coming along.

Lawyers

What can I do if I believe my lawyer is not doing satisfactory work?

If you're unhappy with the work your lawyer is doing, and if you have made reasonable efforts to resolve your complaint through communication, about the only thing you can do is fire that lawyer and find another. If you feel that your lawyer has been so slow or unfair as to be unethical, a complaint to the bar association grievance committee would be proper.

A lawyer is ethically required to withdraw from a case when requested to do so by the client, no matter what the client's reason may be for making the request. However, if the lawyer has in fact served the client properly, the client will be liable for damages resulting from the lawyer's withdrawal — for example, for the reasonable value of the time the lawyer has spent on the case. If the lawyer has delayed too long or otherwise improperly handled the case in violation of the agreement with the client, then the lawyer cannot recover anything from the client.

Are there any types of legal services other than the traditional private general-practice law office?

There's not a lot of variety in the types of legal services available. One new type of law office is the *legal clinic* which provides routine services at relatively low cost. Legal clinics depend on high volume and quick turnover to operate successfully.[4] Unfortunately, consumer cases do not fit neatly into this pattern. Therefore, there is no point in going to a legal clinic with a consumer complaint unless you have reason to believe that someone there practices consumer law.

Another innovative idea is the *prepaid legal services* plan. This is a form of insurance similar to health insurance. It is usually offered as an employee benefit. Prepaid legal services plans are not widespread in Texas, but the idea seems to be growing. If you are covered by such a plan, then by all means consult first with your prepaid attorney.

Legal aid offices provide free legal services for persons of very low income. If you think you may qualify, call the office nearest you (see the list of offices in *Chapter 20, Consumer Assistance Agencies)* and ask what the income limit is for someone with your size family or for a single person. If the office is outside the county of your residence, ask also if that office serves those who reside in your county. Then, if you appear to fall within the income and residency requirements, set up an appointment. The office may still deny your request for service if they decide your case is not worth the resources necessary to handle it; but even then, you are likely to obtain some helpful advice or a knowledgeable referral to a private attorney. If your case is accepted, then you will have a free attorney. Most legal aid offices are funded primarily by the Legal Services Corporation from annual appropriations by Congress.

Chapter 20
Consumer Assistance Agencies

The first step in obtaining assistance in a consumer case is to try self help. See *Chapter 18, Self Help*. This approach usually works, and you may be surprised how your self-confidence is helped along with your legal problem. Sometimes, however, you may need additional help or advice, and that is what this chapter is about.

Unfortunately, getting help on a consumer problem can be as frustrating as buying a good used car. It's easy to find the dealers, but plan on contacting several before you buy. Similarly, while this list of consumer assistance agencies and organizations will give you a start, you may have to make several calls before finding the best one for your particular problem.

If the first office you call cannot help, they may be able to refer you to someone who can. Although these offices are often overworked and understaffed, they do offer the services of able people willing to assist the consumer.

GENERAL COMPLAINT HANDLING

Federal Agencies:

Federal Trade Commission
2001 Bryan
Suite 2665
Dallas, TX 75201

214-767-0032

State Agencies:

Attorney General's Office
Consumer Protection Div.
P.O. Box 12548
Austin, TX 78711

512-475-3288

Attorney General's Office
Consumer Protection Div.
701 Commerce, Suite 200
Dallas, TX 75202

214-742-8944

Attorney General's Office
Consumer Protection Div.
4824 Alberta, Suite 160
El Paso, TX 79905

915-533-3484

Attorney General's Office
Consumer Protection Div.
312 County Office Bldg.
Lubbock, TX 79401

806-747-5238

Attorney General's Office
Consumer Protection Div.
Houston Bar Center Bldg
Houston, TX 77002

713-228-0701

Consumer Assistance Agencies

Attorney General's Office
Consumer Protection Div.
4313 N 10th Suite F
McAllen, TX 78501

512-682-4547

Attorney General's Office
Consumer Protection Div.
200 Main Plaza #400
San Antonio, TX 78205

512-225-4191

County Agencies:

Bexar County District Attorney
Consumer Fraud Div.
Office of Criminal District Attorney
San Antonio, TX 78205

512-224-1007

Dallas County District Attorney
Consumer Fraud Div.
500 Stemmons Tower East
Dallas, TX 75207

214-630-6300

El Paso County District Attorney
Consumer Fraud Div.
City-County Bldg. #401
El Paso, TX 79901

915-543-2860

Harris County District Attorney
Consumer Fraud Div.
201 Fannin Bank Bldg.
Houston, TX 77002

713-221-5836

Tarrant County District Attorney
200 W. Belknap
Fort Worth, TX 76102

817-334-1261

Travis County Consumer Affairs
624 N. Pleasant Valley
Austin, TX 78702

512-474-6554

Waller County District Attorney
County Courthouse
Box 171
Hempstead, TX 77423

713-826-3335

City Offices:

Austin Consumer-Vendor Affairs Office
City Attorney's Office
Municipal Building
Austin, TX 78767

512-477-6511

Dallas Dept. of Consumer Affairs
City Hall, Room 108
Dallas, TX 75201

214-744-1133

Fort Worth Office of Consumer Services
1800 University Dr., Room 218
Fort Worth, TX 76107

817-335-7211 ext. 209

San Antonio Office of Consumer Services
Dept. of Human Resources
600 Hemisfair Way, Bldg. 249
San Antonio, TX 78205

512-299-7140

Consumer Assistance Agencies 227

GENERAL CONSUMER INFORMATION

Government Agencies:
Federal Information Centers:
  Austin 512-472-5494
  Dallas 214-749-2131
  Fort Worth 817-334-3624
  Houston 713--226-5711
  San Antonio 512-224-4471

County Agricultural Extension Agents — Offices are located in all counties in Texas. Consult the county offices listed in your telephone book.

Private Organizations:
Texas Consumer Association
302 W. 15th, Suite 202
Austin, TX 78701

512-477-1882

Better Business Bureaus:

Better Business Bureau of
Abilene, Inc.
P.O. Box 3275
Abilene, TX 79604

915-677-8071

Better Business Bureau of
The Golden Spread, Inc.
518 Amarillo Bldg.
Amarillo, TX 79101

806-374-3735

Better Business Bureau
720 American Bank Tower
Austin, TX 78701

512-476-6943

Better Business Bureau of
Southeast Texas, Inc.
P.O. Box 2988
Beaumont, TX 77704

713-835-5348

Better Business Bureau of
Brazos Valley, Inc.
202 Varisco Bldg.
Bryan, TX 77801

713-823-8148

Better Business Bureau of
Corpus Christi, Inc.
403 North Shoreline #100
Corpus Christi, TX 78401

512-888-5555

Better Business Bureau of
Metropolitan Dallas, Inc.
1511 Bryan Street
Dallas, TX 75201

214-747-8891

Better Business Bureau of
El Paso, Inc.
2501 N. Mesa St., Suite 301
El Paso, TX 79902

915-533-2431

Better Business Bureau of
Fort Worth & Tarrant Co.
709 Sinclair Bldg.
Fort Worth, TX 76102

817-332-7585

Better Business Bureau of
Metropolitan Houston, Inc.
533 Main Bldg, 1212 Main
Houston, TX 77002

713-868-9500

Better Business Bureau of
South Plains, Inc.
P.O. Box 1178
Lubbock, TX 79401

806-763-0459

Better Business Bureau of
The Permian Basin, Inc.
P.O. Box 6006
Midland, TX 79701

915-563-1882

Better Business Bureau
337 W. Twohig
San Angelo, TX 76903

915-653-2318

Better Business Bureau of
San Antonio, Inc.
406 W. Market St. Suite 301
San Antonio, TX 78205

512-225-5833

Better Business Bureau of
Waco, Inc.
P.O. Box 7203
Waco, TX 76710

817-772-7530

HELP WITH SPECIFIC CONSUMER PROBLEMS

Advertising:
Federal Trade Commission
2001 Bryan
Suit 2665
Dallas, TX 75201

214-767-0032

Buying, Renting & Borrowing in Texas

Attorneys:
Office of General Counsel
State Bar of Texas
P.O. Box 12487
Capitol Station
Austin, TX 78711

512-475-1234

Automobiles:
Dealer Complaints
AutoCAP
1108 Lavaca
Austin, TX 78701

512-476-2686

Mechanic Complaints
Independent Garagemen's Association
8311 Shoal Creek
Austin, TX 78758

512-454-3392

Recalls
National Highway Traffic Safety Administration
Dept. of Transportation
Washington, D.C. 20590

1-800-424-9393

Titles
Texas Dept. of Highways and Public Transportation
1106 Clayton
Suite 110 W
Austin, TX 78723

512-475-7445

Warranties on New Cars
Texas Motor Vehicle Commission
National Bldg., Suite 200
815 Brazos St.
Austin, TX 78768

512-476-3587

Consumer Assistance Agencies

Banks:
National
Comptroller of Currency
1201 Elm St.
Suite 3800
Dallas, TX 75270

214-767-4400

Federal Reserve Board
Division of Consumer Affairs
Washington D.C. 20551

202-452-3946

State
State Dept. of Banking
2601 N. Lamar
Austin, TX 78705
512-475-4451

Credit:
Credit Counseling Services
Consumer Credit Counseling Service
509 San Antonio
Austin, TX 78701

512-474-5542

Consumer Credit Counseling Service
4447 N. C. Expressway #310
Dallas, TX 75205

214-521-1560

Consumer Credit Counseling Service
2103 Belknap
Fort Worth, TX 76102

817-334-1788

Consumer Credit Counseling Service
MHMR Center
2323 W. Front
Tyler, TX 75702

214-597-1637

Family Debt Counselors
3210 Reid Dr.
Suite 8-A
Corpus Christi, TX 78404

512-853-9869

Complaints About Credit Transactions

Consumer Credit Commissioner
1011 San Jacinto
P.O. Box 2107
Austin, TX 78767

512-475-2111

Federal Trade Commission
Division of Credit Practices
Washington, D.C. 20580

202-724-1181

Credit Unions:

National Credit Union Administration
Division of Consumer Affairs
Washington, D.C. 20456

202-254-8760

Dentists:

Texas State Board of Dental Examiners
718 Southwest Tower
211 E. Seventh St.
Austin, TX 78701

512-475-2443

Energy:

Department of Energy
Office of Consumer Affairs
Washington, D.C. 20585

202-252-5141

Food:

Labeling and Quantity
Texas Dept. of Agriculture
P.O. Box 12847
Capitol Station
Austin, TX 78711

512-475-6577

Also offices in major Texas cities

Quality
Texas Dept. of Health
1100 W. 49th St.
Austin, TX 78756

512-458-7248

Or contact city or county health department.

Funeral Homes:
State Morticians Board
1513 S. Interregional Highway
Austin, TX 78704

512-442-6721

Federal Trade Commission
(See Advertising)

Gasoline — quality, water in:
Weights and Measures Division
Texas Dept. of Agriculture
P.O. Box 12847
Capitol Station
Austin, TX 78711

512-475-6577

Also offices in major Texas cities.

Health and Safety:
Texas Dept. of Health
(See Food Quality or contact city
or county health department)

Hearing Aids:
Texas Board of Examiners in the Fitting and
   Dispensing of Hearing Aids
1212 Guadalupe, Suite 105
Austin, TX 78701

512-475-3429

Homes:
Manufactured Homes
Texas Dept. of Labor and Standards
P.O. Box 12157
Capitol Station
Austin, TX 78711

512-475-5712

Home Warranties
Texas Real Estate Commission
P.O. Box 12188
Capitol Station
Austin, TX 78711

512-822-6693

Also offices in Corpus Christi, El Paso, Fort Worth, Houston, Lubbock, Richardson, and San Antonio

Insurance:
State Board of Insurance
Claims and Complaints
1110 San Jacinto
Austin, TX 78786

512-475-2444

Magazine Subscriptions:
Publisher's Clearinghouse
Magazine Action Line
382 Channel Dr.
Fort Washington, N.Y. 11050

516-883-5432

Mail Fraud, Mail Order:

Direct Selling Association
1730 M St., N.W.
Suite 610
Washington, D.C. 20036

202-293-5760

U.S. Postal Inspectors — call your local post office to register a complaint

Mobile Homes:

Texas Dept. of Labor and Standards
(See Manufactured Homes)

Moving:

Intrastate

Railroad Commission
Transportation Div.
P.O. Box 12967
Capitol Station
Austin, TX 78711

512-445-1340

Interstate

Interstate Commerce Commission
Office of Consumer Affairs
Room 1211
Washington, D.C. 20423

1-800-424-9312

Nursing Homes:

Texas Dept. of Health
Long Term Care Division
1100 W. 49th St.
Austin, TX 78756

512-458-7706

Optometrists:

Texas Optometry Board
5555 N. Lamar
Suite H-101
Austin, TX 78751

512-458-2141

Buying, Renting & Borrowing in Texas

Pharmacists:

Texas State Board of Pharmacy
Southwest Tower, Suite 1121
211 East Seventh Street
Austin, Texas 78701

512-478-9827

Physicians:

Texas State Board of Medical Examiners
Southwest Tower, Suite 900
211 East Seventh Street
Austin, Texas 78701

512-474-6335

Plumbers:

State Board of Plumbing Examiners
204 John H. Reagan Building
Austin, Texas 78701

512-472-9221

Product Safety:

Consumer Product Safety Commission
Consumer Services Board
Washington, D.C. 20207

1-800-638-8326

Public Accountants:

Texas State Board of Public Accountancy
940 American Bank Tower
Austin, Texas 78701

512-476-6971

Real Estate:

Texas Real Estate Commission
4920 N. Interregional Highway
Austin, Texas 78751

512-475-4247

Consumer Assistance Agencies 237

Renting:

Austin Tenant's Council
1619 E. First
Austin, TX 78702

512-474-1961

Dallas Tenant's Union
3525 State St.
Dallas, TX 75204

214-823-6510

Dallas Texas Tenant's Union
107 Collett
Dallas, TX 75214

214-827-0406

Fort Worth Texas Tenant's Union
1400 Hemphill
Fort Worth, TX 76104

817-923-5071

Harris County Tenant's Alliance
4600 Main #205
Houston, TX 77002

713-528-0192

River City Tenant's Center
1512½ S. Congress
Austin, TX 78704

512-441-8660

Savings and Loans:

Consumer Division
Office of Community Investment
Federal Home Loan Bank Board
Washington, D.C. 20552

202-377-6237

Securities:

State Securities Board
L.B.J. Building, Seventh Floor
P.O. Box 13167, Capitol Station
Austin, Texas 78711

512-475-4561

Travel:

Air:

Civil Aeronautics Board
Bureau of Consumer Protection
P.O. Box 1689
Ft. Worth, TX 76101

817-625-0402

Interstate by Bus and Rail:

Office of Communications and Consumer Affairs
I.C.C.
Room 1211
Washington, D.C. 20423

1-800-424-9312

Intrastate by Bus and Rail:

Railroad Commission
(See Moving, Intrastate)

Utilities:

Electricity and water: in incorporated areas — contact city.

Electricity and water: in unincorporated areas —

Public Utility Commission
Consumer Affairs Section
7800 Shoal Creek Blvd., Suite 400
Austin, TX 78757
512-458-0100

Telephone: Public Utility Commission

Gas:
Railroad Commission
Gas Utilities Div.
P.O. Box 12967
Capitol Station
Austin, TX 78711

512-445-1145

Veterinarians:
Texas Board of Veterinary Medical Examiners
603 Capital National Bank Building
Austin, Texas 78701

512-475-3571

LEGAL AID OFFICES

Bexar County Legal Aid Association
434 S. Main St., Suite 300
San Antonio, Texas 78204
512-227-0111

Bexar County Legal Aid Association
131 Walgreen Plaza
Las Palmas
San Antonio, Texas 78237
512-434-5528

Bexar County Legal Aid Association
1520 Guadalupe St.
San Antonio, Texas 78207
512-222-0103

Bexar County Legal Aid Association
1910 East Houston St.
San Antonio, Texas 78202
512-226-9356

Bexar County Legal Aid Association
728 S.W. Military Dr.
San Antonio, Texas 78221
512-924-7113

Coastal Bend Legal Services
901 Leopard St., Room 105
Corpus Christi, Texas 78401
512-888-0282

Coastal Bend Legal Services
200 N. 6th Street
Robstown, Texas 78380
512-387-2867

Coastal Bend Legal Services
117 W. Sinton
Sinton, Texas 78387
512-364-3805

Coastal Bend Legal Services
404 W. Jackson
Beeville, Texas 78102
512-358-5165

Coastal Bend Legal Services
507 E. Commercial
Victoria, Texas 77901
512-576-3300

Dallas Legal Services
  Foundation, Inc.
810 Main St., Suite 320
Texas Bldg.
Dallas, Texas 75202
214-742-1631

East Texas Legal Services
125 N. Fredonia
Nacogdoches, Texas 75961
713-560-1455; 560-1850

East Texas Legal Services
527 Forsythe
Beaumont, Texas 77704
713-835-4971

East Texas Legal Services
P.O. Box 8
Jasper, Texas 75851
713-384-3479

East Texas Legal Services
208 North Green, Suite 600
Longview, Texas 75601
214-758-9123

East Texas Legal Services
1425 New Boston
Texarkana, Texas 75501
214-793-7661

Consumer Assistance Agencies

East Texas Legal Services
P.O. Box 337
Tyler, Texas 75710
214-595-4781

El Paso Legal Assistance Society
109 N. Oregon, Suite 1500
El Paso, Texas 79901
915-533-1942

El Paso Legal Assistance Society
7678 Alameda St.
El Paso, Texas 79915
915-778-6431

El Paso Legal Assistance Society
2023 Myrtle Ave.
El Paso, Texas 79901
915-533-1937

Gulf Coast Legal Foundation
2601 Main St., Room 400
Houston, Texas 77002
713-651-9080

Gulf Coast Legal Foundation
2314 Cochran
Houston, Texas 77009
713-228-0091

Gulf Coast Legal Foundation
4401 Lovejoy, Room 13
Houston, Texas 77003
713-237-8061

Gulf Coast Legal Foundation
4534 Griggs Rd.
Houston, Texas 77021
713-748-0532

Gulf Coast Legal Foundation
503 National Hotel Bldg.
2221 Market St.
Galveston, Texas 77550
713-763-0381

Gulf Coast Legal Foundation
16811 El Camino Real
Suite 126, Alpha Bldg.
Clear Lake City, Texas 77058
713-486-9682

Gulf Coast Legal Foundation
900 Morton Street
Richmond, Texas 77469
713-342-9201

Laredo Legal Aid Society, Inc.
1019 Convent
Laredo, Texas 78040
512-722-7581

Legal Aid Society of Central Texas
500 Perry Brooks Bldg.
8th and Brazos
Austin, Texas 78701
512-476-7244

Legal Aid Society of Central Texas
509 Spring Lane
Bastrop, Texas 78602
512-321-3925

Legal Aid Society of Central Texas
512 S. Main
Belton, Texas 76513
817-939-5773

Texas Rural Legal Aid, Inc.
103 E. Third St.
Weslaco, Texas 78596
512-968-9574; 383-0461

Texas Rural Legal Aid, Inc.
306 E. Main
Alice, Texas 78332
512-664-0171

Texas Rural Legal Aid, Inc.
1154 E. Elizabeth, Suite 502
Brownsville, Texas 78520
512-546-5558

Buying, Renting & Borrowing in Texas

Texas Rural Legal Aid, Inc.
101 Kerr
Cotulla, Texas 78014
512-879-3508

Texas Rural Legal Aid, Inc.
600 John F. Kennedy
Crystal City, Texas 78839
512-374-3428

Texas Rural Legal Aid, Inc.
309 Cantu
Del Rio, Texas 78840
512-775-1535

Texas Rural Legal Aid, Inc.
558 Madison
Eagle Pass, Texas 78852
512-773-6151

Texas Rural Legal Aid, Inc.
216 N. Closner
Edinburg, Texas 78539
512-383-5673

Texas Rural Legal Aid, Inc.
305 E. Jackson, Suite 206
Harlingen, Texas 78550
512-423-3111

Texas Rural Legal Aid, Inc.
P.O. Box 188
Hebbronville, Texas 78361
512-527-4771

Texas Rural Legal Aid, Inc.
1406 W. Hwy. 60
Hereford, Texas 79045
806-364-3961

Texas Rural Legal Aid, Inc.
1206 17th St.
Hondo, Texas 78861
512-426-3787

Texas Rural Legal Aid, Inc.
504 Sidney Baker St.
Kerrville, Texas 78028
512-896-4316

Texas Rural Legal Aid, Inc.
712 N. 3rd
Kingsville, Texas 78363
512-492-3306; 668-8742

Texas Rural Legal Aid, Inc.
1106 Scott
Laredo, Texas 78040
512-727-5191

Texas Rural Legal Aid, Inc.
411 N. Willow
Pearsall, Texas 78061
512-334-4261

Texas Rural Legal Aid, Inc.
700 E. 3rd St.
Rio Grande City, Texas 78582
512-487-2593

Texas Rural Legal Aid, Inc.
103 N. Piper
Uvalde, Texas 78801
512-278-4449

Texas Rural Legal Aid, Inc.
P.O. Box 1104
Zapata, Texas 78076
512-765-5251

Waco-McLennan County Legal Aid
214-216 N. 6th St.
Waco, Texas 76701
817-752-7796

West Texas Legal Services
Lawyer's Bldg.
100 Main Street
Fort Worth, Texas 76102
817-336-3943

Consumer Assistance Agencies 243

West Texas Legal Services
221 Oak Street
Abilene, Texas 79602
915-677-8591

West Texas Legal Services
504 S. Polk, Suite 102
Amarillo, Texas 79101
806-373-6808

West Texas Legal Services
114 Center St., Suite 402
Brownwood, Texas 76801
915-643-3581

West Texas Legal Services
223 W. Hickory
Denton, Texas 76201
817-383-1407

West Texas Legal Services
1601 Metro Tower
Lubbock, Texas 79401
806-763-4557

West Texas Legal Services
108 E. Louisiana
Midland, Texas 79701
915-463-0090

West Texas Legal Services
1415 W. Fifth St.
Plainview, Texas 79072
806-293-8491

West Texas Legal Services
First Savings Bldg., #400
San Angelo, Texas 76903
915-653-6982

West Texas Legal Services
917 Seventh St.
Wichita Falls, Texas 76301
817-723-5542

West Texas Legal Services
304 E. Main
Eastland, Texas 76448
817-629-8521

Notes

Self-help on consumer issues can consist of looking up the statutes, court decisions, and legal articles to find out what the law may be. Listed below by chapter are citations to various laws referred to throughout this book. Legal citations may appear to be written in an unintelligible language, but they are not as complicated as they may at first seem to be. Anyone with a solid high school education can quickly learn to use a law library, and looking up citations is the easiest part. The following discussion will explain how to read a legal citation and where to find the appropriate material. This discussion, however, will not make a lawyer out of anyone.

Finding items in a law library is very much like looking for things in any other library. A variety of reference services, indexes, and other finding aids are generally available and prominently displayed. In addition, law librarians, like all librarians, can be of great assistance in locating books, periodicals, etc. and in providing other useful information. Increasingly, many law librarians are also lawyers. Such lawyer-librarians can be especially helpful in your search for the law.

The law is written primarily in the following documents: constitutions (state and federal), statutes (legislative law), cases (judicial law), regulations (administrative law), law reviews (periodicals) and encyclopedias, treatises and digests (summaries). The discussion below will show how the most common of these are usually abbreviated. Most abbreviations and rules governing legal references can be found in a little book called the Uniform System of Citation (or Harvard Blue Book).

Constitutions. The only constitutions which a Texas resident will generally need to consult are the United States Constitution and the Constitution of Texas. These documents are abbreviated as follows:
- United States Constitution — U.S. CONST. amend. XIV, § 2;
- Texas Constitution — TEX. CONST. art. XVI, § 50.

Constitutions generally consist of articles (art.), sections (§), and amendments (amend.). These documents provide the general foundation upon which all other laws are based.

Statutes. Statutes relating to consumer law have been passed at both the federal and the state level. Federal statutes are most widely available in the United States Code Annotated (abbreviated U.S.C.A.). Texas statutes are organized into general statutes and various codes. Of most interest to consumers are these:
- general statutes — Texas Revised Civil Statutes Annotated (TEX. REV. CIV. STAT. ANN.), sometimes referred to as Vernon's Annotated Texas Statutes (V.A.T.S.);
- business and commercial code — Texas Business and Commercial Code Annotated (TEX. BUS. & COMM. C.);
- insurance code — Texas Insurance Code Annotated (TEX. INS. C.).

Citations to statutes will generally appear in this fashion: Federal Truth in Lending Act, 15 U.S.C.A. § 1601. There are many titles in U.S.C.A., and most titles are contained in several volumes. The relevant volume can be found by checking the information on the spine of each book.

Case law. Texas cases are found in the Southwestern Reporter System, which is abbreviated S.W. or S.W.2d (for the second series). Federal cases are found in the National Reporter System, which consists of the following reporters:
- United States Reports (U.S.);
- Supreme Court Reporter (S.Ct.);
- Supreme Court Reports — Lawyer's Edition, with second series (L.Ed., L.Ed.2d);
- Federal Reporter, with second series (F., F.2d);
- Federal Supplement (F.Supp.).

All cases are referred to with a citation similar to the following and appear after the names of the parties involved:

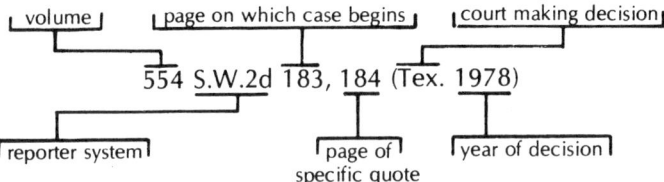

Administrative law. References to administrative law are not as standard. The most common citations are to the Code of Federal Regulations (C.F.R.). You may need the help of a librarian to find an administrative regulation.

Law reviews. Law review articles may be located in the *Index to Legal Periodicals.* This reference book is similar to the *Reader's Guide to Periodical Literature.* In the *Index to Legal Periodicals,* law review articles are referred to as follows:

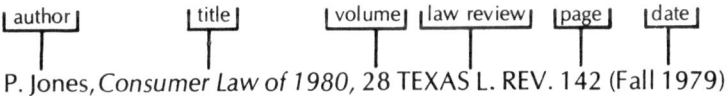

Summaries. Encyclopedias, treatises, and digests are sets of books summarizing various areas of the law. They are organized by subject and usually have a detailed index. They, like law reviews and this book, are secondary sources that discuss and analyze the primary sources of law (such as constitutions, statutes and cases).

With this information at hand, now, the interested reader should be able to find any of the sources cited below. Understanding the law as it applies to your particular situation, however, is a task you must assume yourself, with or without a lawyer's help.

Notes to Chapter 1
BUYING AND SELLING HOMES

[1] TEX. REV. CIV. STAT. ANN. art. 6573a, § 3.

[2] TEX. REV. CIV. STAT. ANN. art. 6573a, § 1(b).

[3] Gerald M. Steiner, *Home for Sale by Owner* (New York: Hawthorne, 1976, $7.95); Louis Gilmore, *For Sale by Owner* (New York: Simon & Schuster, 1973, $3.95).

[4] TEX. REV. CIV. STAT. ANN. art. 3995. There is an "equitable exception" in certain cases. See 26 TEX. JUR. 2d 272; *Hooks v. Bridgewater*, 229 S.W. 1114 (Tex. 1921).

[5] TEX. FAM. CODE § 5.22(c); *Cooper v. Texas Gulf Industries*, 513 S.W.2d 200 (Tex. 1974).

[6] TEX. REV. CIV. STAT. ANN. art. 6626.

[7] Olds, *The Scope of the Texas Recording Act*, 8 S.W.L.J. 36, 39 (1954).

[8] *De Leon v. Aldrete*, 398 S.W.2d 160 (Tex. Civ. App.—San Antonio 1966, writ ref'd, n.r.e.).

[9] TEX. REV. CIV. STAT. ANN. art. 1301b; Mixon, *Installment Land Contracts: A Study of Low Income Transactions*, 7 HOUSTON L. REV. 523, 550 (1970).

[10] *Wentworth v. Medellin*, 529 S.W.2d 125 (Tex. Civ. App.—San Antonio 1975, no writ); *Marshall v. Garcia*, 514 S.W.2d 513 (Tex. Civ. App.—Corpus Christi 1974, writ ref., n.r.e.); but see *Pratt v. Story*, 530 S.W.2d 325 (Tex. Civ. App.—Tyler 1975, no writ).

[11] TEX CONST. art 5, § 8; TEX REV. CIV. STAT. ANN. art. 2387; TEX R. CIV. P. 746; 7 HOUSTON L. REV. 523, 608 (1970).

[12] *Gulledge v. White*, 11 S.W. 527 (Tex. 1889); *Rodriguez v. Sullivan*, 484 S.W.2d 592 (Tex. Civ. App.—El Paso 1972, no writ).

Notes to Chapter 2
RENTING HOMES AND APARTMENTS

[1] TEX. REV. CIV. STAT. ANN. art. 1288, 3995(4).

[2] *Miller v. Nacol*, 224 S.W.2d 734 (Tex. Civ. App.—Fort Worth 1949, no writ).

[3] *Davis v. City of San Angelo*, 376 S.W.2d 949 (Tex. Civ. App.—Waco, 1974, no writ).

[4] 35 TEX. JUR.2d Landlord and Tenant § 61.

[5] *Maple Terrace Apartment Co. v. Simpson*, 22 S.W.2d 698 (Tex. Civ. App.—Texarkana 1929, no writ).

[6] TEX. REV. CIV. STAT. ANN. art. 5236f § 2(c).

[7] *Kamarath v. Bennett*, 568 S.W.2d 658 (Tex. 1978).

Notes 249

[8] TEX. REV. CIV. STAT. ANN. art. 5236f § 1 et seq.

[9] TEX. REV. CIV. STAT. ANN. art. 5236e § 3(a).

[10] *Sims v. Century Kiest Apartments,* 567 S.W.2d 526 (Tex. Civ. App.— Dallas 1978, no writ).

[11] 35 TEX. JUR.2d Landlord and Tenant § 93.

[12] TEX. REV. CIV. STAT. ANN. art. 5236a.

[13] Our definition is not the traditional definition of a periodic tenancy. We are, rather, using the term "periodic tenancy" to describe the type of tenancy regulated by Art. 5236a. In Texas, the only tenancies of any practical importance are that type of tenancy and the tenancy for a fixed term. We therefore deviate from the traditional classifications of tenancies in the interest of clarity and practicality.

[14] TEX. REV. CIV. STAT. ANN. art. 5236a.

[15] TEX. REV. CIV. STAT. ANN. art. 3975a.

[16] 35 TEX. JUR.2d Landlord and Tenant § 26; *Willeke v. Bailey,* 189 S.W.2d 477 (Tex. 1945).

[17] 35 TEX. JUR.2d Landlord and Tenant § 130.

[18] 36 TEX. JUR.2d Landlord and Tenant § 254.

[19] *Wendandt v. Sommers Drug Stores,* 551 S.W.2d 488 (Tex. Civ. App.— Austin 1977, no writ).

[21] 35 TEX. JUR.2d Landlord and Tenant § 129; *Rohrt v. Kelly,* 349 S.W.2d 95 (Tex. 1961).

[21] *Thrift v. Johnson,* 561 S.W.2d 864 (Tex. Civ. App.—Houston 1977, no writ).

[22] 35 TEX. JUR.2d Landlord and Tenant § 69.

[23] *Thrift v. Johnson, supra.*

[24] TEX. REV. CIV. STAT. ANN. art. 5237.

[25] 35 TEX. JUR.2d Landlord and Tenant § 228.

[26] TEX. REV. CIV. STAT. ANN. art. 5236c § 2.

[27] TEX. REV. CIV. STAT. ANN. art. 5236c § 1.

[28] TEX. REV. CIV. STAT. ANN. art. 3973-3994; TEX. R. CIV. P. 738-755.

[29] TEX. REV. CIV. STAT. ANN. art. 3975b.

[31] TEX. REV. CIV. STAT. ANN. art. 3975a.

[31] *Gulf Oil Corp. v. Smithey,* 426 S.W.2d 262 (Tex. Civ. App.—Dallas 1968, writ dism'd).

Notes to Chapter 3
BUYING HOME IMPROVEMENTS

[1] TEX. CONST. art. 16, § 50; TEX. REV. CIV. STAT. ANN. art. 5460.
[2] TEX. REV. CIV. STAT. ANN. art. 5452.
[3] TEX. REV. CIV. STAT. ANN. art. 5069-5.01 et seq.
[4] TEX. REV. CIV. STAT. ANN. art. 5069-6.06(4).
[5] 15 U.S.C.A. § 1635; 12 C.F.R. § 226.9.
[6] TEX. CONST. art 16, § 50; TEX. REV. CIV. STAT. ANN. art. 5069-6.08.

Notes to Chapter 4
FORECLOSURE ON HOMES

[1] TEX. REV. CIV. STAT. ANN. art. 3810.
[2] 39 TEX. JUR.2d 270.
[3] *Whalen v. Etheridge,* 428 S.W.2d 824 (Tex. Civ. App.—San Antonio 1968, writ ref'd n.r.e.).
[4] *Joy Corp. v. Nob Hill North Properties, Ltd.,* 543 S.W.2d 691 (Tex. Civ. App.—Tyler 1976, no writ); *Covington v. Burke,* 413 S.W.2d 158 (Tex. Civ. App.—Eastland 1967, writ ref'd n.r.e.). It is probably necessary also for the creditor to be certain the debtor understands that if the debtor fails to pay the overdue installments, the balance will be accelerated. *Lockwood v. Lisby,* 476 S.W.2d 871 (Tex. Civ. App.—Fort Worth 1972, writ ref'd n.r.e.); *Jernigan v. O'Brien,* 303 S.W.2d 515 (Tex. Civ. App.—Austin 1957, no writ).
[5] 39 TEX. JUR.2d 208; *Crow v. Heath,* 516 S.W.2d 225 (Tex. Civ. App.—Corpus Christi 1974, writ ref'd n.r.e.).

Notes to Chapter 5
WARRANTIES

[1] TEX. BUS. & COMM. C. § 2.313, official comment no. 3; *General Supply and Equipment Company v. Phillip,* 490 S.W.2d 913 (Tex. Civ. App.—Tyler 1972, writ ref'd n.r.e.).
[2] TEX. BUS. & COMM. C. § 2.314.
[3] *Chag Oil Company v. Gardner Machinery Corp.,* 500 S.W.2d 877 (Tex. Civ. App.—Houston [14th Dist.]1973, no writ).
[4] TEX. BUS. & COMM. C. § 2.316.
[5] TEX. REV. CIV. STAT. ANN. art. 5221f.
[6] 15 U.S.C. § 2301 et seq.; 16 C.F.R. § 701.1 et seq.
[7] TEX. BUS. & COMM. C. § 2.601.
[8] TEX. BUS. & COMM. C. § 2.608.

⁹TEX. BUS. & COMM. C. § 2.508. See *Chapter 6, Deceptive Trade Practices* for a discussion of the additional requirements regarding giving notice before filing suit under the Texas Deceptive Trade Practices—Consumer Protection Act, including suits for breach of warranty brought under that act.

Notes to Chapter 6
DECEPTIVE TRADE PRACTICES

¹TEX. BUS. & COMM. C. § 17.41 *et seq.*

²TEX. BUS. & COMM. C. § 17.44.

³TEX. BUS. & COMM. C. § 17.46(b). Copies of the Consumer Protection Act may be obtained from the Attorney General's Consumer Protection Division, P.O. Box 12548, Austin, Texas 78711. See the Act itself for the entire "laundry list."

⁴Free pamphlets explaining pyramid and ponzi schemes can be obtained from the Consumer Information Center, Pueblo, Colorado 81109, or the U.S. Securities and Exchange Commission, Office of Public Affairs, Washington, D.C. 20049.

⁵TEX. BUS. & COMM. C. § 17.50(a) (1).

⁶TEX. BUS. & COMM. C. § 17.45(5), 17.50(a) (3).

⁷TEX. BUS. & COMM. C. § 17.50(a) (2).

⁸TEX. BUS. & COMM. C. § 17.50A.

⁹10 TEX. JUR.2d Building Contracts § 17 (Supp. 1979); *Certain-Teed Products Corp. v. Bell,* 411 S.W.2d 596 (Tex. Civ. App. — Amarillo 1966), aff'd, 422 S.W.2d 719 (Tex. 1968).

¹⁰TEX. REV. CIV. STAT. ANN. art. 5503, 5504.

¹¹TEX. PENAL C. § 31.04.

Notes to Chapter 7
DOOR-TO-DOOR SALES AND MAIL ORDERS

¹D. Caplovitz. *The Poor Pay More.* New York: The Free Press, 1967.

²Texas Home Solicitation Sales Act, TEX. REV. CIV. STAT. ANN. art. 5069-13.01 *et seq.;* 16 C.F.R. Part 429.

³Under the Texas statute, a sale under $200 need not include the notice if the buyer may at any time cancel the order, refuse to accept delivery, or return the goods without charge. TEX. REV. CIV. STAT. ANN. art. 5069-13.02(e). No such exception exists under the FTC rule.

⁴TEX. REV. CIV. STAT. ANN. art. 5069-13.02(c), 1303(a).

⁵TEX. REV. CIV. STAT. ANN. art. 5069-13.03(b).

⁶TEX. REV. CIV. STAT. ANN. art. 5069-13.03(a).
⁷TEX. REV. CIV. STAT. ANN. art. 5069-13.03(b).
⁸FTC trade regulation rule concerning undelivered mail order merchandise and services, 16 C.F.R. § 435.

Notes to Chapter 8
BUYING AUTOMOBILES AND OTHER GOODS

¹TEX. REV. CIV. STAT. ANN. art. 6687-1 § § 33, 53, 62; art. 6687-5.
²TEX. REV. CIV. STAT. ANN. art. 6687-1 § 36.
³TEX. REV. CIV. STAT. ANN. art. 6687-1 § 39.
⁴Interstate compacts pursuant to art. 6675a-16.
⁵15 U.S.C.A. § 1981 et seq.; 49 C.F.R. § 580.1 et seq.
⁶TEX. BUS. & COMM. CODE § 2.201.
⁷TEX. BUS. & COMM. CODE § 2.202.
⁸*United Postage Corp. v. Kammeyer,* 581 S.W.2d 716 (Tex. Civ. App.— Dallas 1979).

Notes to Chapter 9
CREDIT AND COLLATERAL

¹*Cantrell v. First National Bank of Euless,* 560 S.W.2d 721 (Civ. App. — Fort Worth 1977).
²15 U.S.C.A. § 1643(a).

Notes to Chapter 10
UNDERSTANDING THE LANGUAGE OF CREDIT

¹15 U.S.C. § 1640 et seq.; 12 C.F.R. § 226.1 et seq. ("Regulation Z" of the Federal Reserve Board).
²TEX. REV. CIV. STAT. ANN. art. 5069-1.01 et seq.
³12 U.S.C. § 2601 et seq.

Notes to Chapter 11
CALCULATING THE COSTS OF CREDIT

¹The only problem with this usage is that § 106 of the Truth-in-Lending Act and § 226.4 of Reg. Z define *finance charge* as including various fees and insurance charges, unless they are disclosed in a prescribed manner. Since they usually are so disclosed, however, the finance charge does not usually have to include them.

Notes 253

[2] RULES, RATES AND REGULATIONS OF THE TEXAS STATE BOARD OF INSURANCE RELATING TO CREDIT LIFE AND CREDIT ACCIDENT AND HEALTH INSURANCE, Rule 4.2.

[3] This is an obvious violation of the Truth-in-Lending Act and Texas Credit Code but happens so frequently that consumer attorneys routinely check on it in analyzing a contract.

[4] TEX. REV. CIV. STAT. ANN. art. 5069-7.03(1). This is calculated as follows: The Statute just cited allows a maximum add-on rate of 12.50 in credit sales of 3 year-old used cars. That means "$12.50 per $100 amount financed per year." $12.50 x 30 (hundreds financed) x 3 (years) = $1125 maximum finance charge.

[5] TEX. REV. CIV. STAT. ANN. art. 5069-4.01(1).

[6] Present interest rate limits are contained in the Texas Credit Code, TEX. REV. CIV. STAT. ANN. art. 5069-1.01 et seq. These rates are subject to change, either by amendments to the statutes or by superseding federal legislation.

[7] *Southwestern Investment Co. v. Mannix*, 557 S.W.2d 755 (Tex.1977); *Moore v. Sabine National Bank*, 527 S.W.2d 209 (Tex.Civ.App.—Austin 1975, writ ref'd n.r.e.); but with reference to transactions covered by Chapter 1 of the Texas Credit Code, see TEX. REV. CIV. STAT. ANN. art. 5069-1.07(a). Concerning what notice is required before acceleration, see notes 3 and 4 to *Chapter 4, Foreclosure on Homes*, and accompanying discussion.

[8] TEX. REV. CIV. STAT. ANN. art. 5069-6.02(13), 7.02(8).

[9] TEX. REV. CIV. STAT. ANN. art. 5069-3.15(6), 4.01(6), 5.01(4), 6.02(10), 7.04.

[10] TEX. REV. CIV. STAT. ANN. art. 5069-7.04. On sales of goods other than motor vehicles, this amount depends on the size of the sale. Art. 5069-6.02(9) (e), (10). No such deduction need be made upon prepayment of loans. If a close approximation of the amount owed is all you need, don't worry about this charge.

[11] RULES, RATES AND REGULATIONS OF THE TEXAS STATE BOARD OF INSURANCE RELATING TO CREDIT LIFE AND CREDIT ACCIDENT AND HEALTH INSURANCE, Rules 10.1(a), 10.3.

[12] TEXAS AUTOMOBILE MANUAL, Rule 11. For "Short Rate" and "Pro Rata" tables, see TEXAS AUTOMOBILE MANUAL and TEXAS GENERAL BASIS SCHEDULES, available from the State Board of Insurance.

[13] TEX. REV. CIV. STAT. ANN. art. 852a-5.07. In addition, in loans in which 10 percent or less annual percentage rate is charged and in loans secured by first liens on real estate, a penalty for prepayment may be charged; but unless the loan is made by a savings and loan association, the penalty for prepayment is counted as "interest" in determining whether the interest rate is within the applicable usury limit (if any).

[14]The interest earnings on savings shown above are computed without compounding. Savings institutions compound interest on some types of savings accounts on a daily, monthly or quarterly basis, thus giving you greater interest earnings.

Notes to Chapter 12
CREDIT BUREAUS

[1] 15 U.S.C.A. § 1681 et seq.
[2] Many credit bureaus are members of a trade association, Associate Credit Bureaus, Inc., 6767 Southwest Fwy., Houston, Texas 77074.
[3] 15 U.S.C.A. § 1681b.
[4] 15 U.S.C.A. §§ 1681b, 1681f.
[5] 15 U.S.C.A. § 1681c.
[6] 15 U.S.C.A. § 1681d(b).
[7] 15 U.S.C.A. § 1681m(a).
[8] 15 U.S.C.A. § 1681m(b).
[9] 15 U.S.C.A. § 1681g.
[10] 15 U.S.C.A. § 1681j.
[11] 15 U.S.C.A. § 1681i(a).
[12] 15 U.S.C.A. § 1681i(d).
[13] 15 U.S.C.A. § 1681i(b), (c).

Notes to Chapter 13
EQUAL CREDIT OPPORTUNITY

[1] 15 U.S.C. § 1691 et seq.; regulations at 12 C.F.R. Part 202.
[2] 12 C.F.R. § 202.4(d) (3).
[3] 12 C.F.R. § 202.5(c) (2) (iv).
[4] 12 C.F.R. § 202.6(b) (5).
[5] 15 U.S.C. § 1691(d).

Notes to Chapter 14
REPOSSESSION

[1] TEX. BUS. & COMM. CODE, § 9.203(A) (1).
[2] *Allen Sales & Servicenter, Inc. v. Ryan*, 525 S.W.2d 863 (Tex. 1975).
[3] TEX. BUS. & COMM. CODE § 9.503.
[4] *Phil Phillips Ford, Inc. v. St. Paul Fire & Marine Insurance Co.*, 454 S.W.2d 465 (Tex. Civ. App.—San Antonio 1970), aff'd., 465 S.W.2d 933.

⁵*Gulf Oil v. Smithey,* 426 S.W.2d 262 (Tex. Civ. App.—Dallas 1968, writ dism'd).
⁶*Pryor v. Universal C.I.T. Credit Corp.,* 253 S.W.2d 493 (Tex. Civ. App.—San Antonio 1952, no writ).
⁷*Godwin v. Stanley,* 331 S.W.2d 341 (Tex. Civ. App.—Amarillo 1959, writ ref'd n.r.e.).
⁸TEX. REV. CIV. STAT. ANN. art. 6840.
⁹TEX. PENAL CODE § 32.33.
¹⁰TEX. A.G. Op. H980.
¹¹TEX. BUS. & COMM. CODE § 9.506.
¹²TEX. BUS. & COMM. CODE § 9.505.
¹³TEX. BUS. & COMM. CODE § 9.504.
¹⁴TEX. BUS. & COMM. CODE § 9.507(b).
¹⁵TEX. BUS. & COMM. CODE § 9.507(a).
¹⁶*O'Neil v. Mack Trucks,* 533 S.W.2d 832 (Tex. Civ. App.—El Paso 1975), rev'd on other gds., 542 S.W.2d 113; *United States v. Whitehead Plastics,* 501 F.2d 692 (5th Cir. 1974), cert. den., 471 U.S. 912. **But see** *First State Bank of Keene v. Northrup,* 519 S.W.2d 161 (Tex. Civ. App.—Waco 1975, no writ), which suggests that the offending creditor has no right to a deficiency judgment at all.

Notes to Chapter 15
THE HOMESTEAD AND OTHER JUDGMENT EXEMPTIONS

¹TEX. CONST. art XVI, §§ 49, 50, 51; TEX. REV. CIV. STAT. ANN. art. 3833-3836.
²*Valley Bank of Nevada v. Skeen,* 401 F.Supp. 139 (N.D. Tex. 1975), aff'd w/o op., 532 F.2d 185 (5th Cir. 1976), cert. den., 429 U.S. 834 (1976).
³*Valley Bank of Nevada, supra; Hoffman v. Love,* 494 S.W.2d 591 (Tex. Civ. App.—Dallas 1973), aff'd per curiam, 499 S.W.2d 295 (Tex. 1974).
⁴TEX. CONST. art. XVI, § 50.
⁵TEX. REV. CIV. STAT. ANN. art. 5460.
⁶Charles H. Bell, *Texas Real Estate,* 3d ed. (Houston: Gulf Publishing Co., Inc., 1977), p.129.
⁷See definition of passenger cars and light trucks, TEX. REV. CIV. STAT. ANN. art. 6701d, § 2.
⁸TEX. CONST. art. XVI, § 49; TEX. REV. CIV. STAT. ANN. art. 3836.
⁹TEX. REV. CIV. STAT. ANN. art. 6840; TEX. R. CIV. P. 696-716.
¹⁰TEX. REV. CIV. STAT. ANN. art. 275-282; TEX. R. CIV. P. 592-609.

Notes to Chapter 16
DEBT COLLECTION PRACTICES

[1] This law was developed by the courts in lawsuits rather than by the Legislature in statutes. *Duty v. General Finance Company*, 273 S.W.2d 64 (Tex. 1954).

[2] R. Anderson, *Coercive Collection and Exempt Property in Texas: A Debtor's Paradise or a Living Hell,* 13 HOUSTON L. REV. 84 (1975).

[3] *United Finance & Thrift Corp. v. Smith,* 387 S.W.2d 752 (Tex. Civ. App.—Tyler 1965, writ ref'd, n.r.e.).

[4] See note 1 above.

[5] *Lubbock Bail Bond v. Joshua,* 416 S.W.2d 523 (Tex. Civ. App.—Amarillo 1967, no writ).

[6] TEX. REV. CIV. STAT. ANN. art. 5069-11.01 *et seq.*

[7] 15 U.S.C.A. § 1692, *et seq.*

[8] 15 U.S.C.A. § 1692c(a) (1).

[9] TEX. REV. CIV. STAT. ANN. art. 5527(1).

[10] TEX. REV. CIV. STAT. ANN. art. 5526(4).

[11] TEX. REV. CIV. STAT. ANN. art. 5539.

Notes to Chapter 17
FINANCERS' RESPONSIBILITIES

[1] TEX. BUS. & COMM. CODE ANN., Chapter 3.

[2] Where holder-in-due-course status is achieved, the sale of the contract is technically a *negotiation* rather than an *assignment*.

[3] TEX. BUS. & COMM. CODE ANN. § 3.302.

[4] Federal Trade Commission Rule 433, 16 C.F.R. § 433 (effective May 14, 1976). This will be referred to as "the FTC rule" throughout this Chapter.

[5] The notice is found in 16 C.F.R. § 433.2.

[6] This limitation does not apply to recovery under other statutes, such as the Truth-in-Lending Act, which themselves extend liability to assignees. See Chapter 10, *Understanding the Language of Credit.*

[7] 16 C.F.R. § 433.2.

[8] TEX. REV. CIV. STAT. ANN. art. 5069-7.08(4). This particular notice is required with regard to motor vehicle sales. A similar notice required with regard to other sales of goods is at art. 5069-6.07.

[9] TEX. REV. CIV. STAT. ANN. art. 5069-6.06(4).

[10] The consumer's attorney may, for example, argue that the financer does not have the protected status of a holder in due course because the financer should have known that the contract was in violation of the law

for failing to contain the notice, and therefore, the financer did not purchase it "in good faith," "without notice of any defense or claim."

[11] Under TEX. BUS. & COMM. CODE ANN. § 9.318 and the common law, an assignee who does not have the protected status of a holder in due course takes the contract subject to all claims and defenses arising out of the terms of the contract. See also, Boyle, *Preservation of Claims and Defenses Under the Texas Business and Commerce Code and Under the Consumer Credit Code,* 8 ST. MARY'S L.J. 679 (1977).

Notes to Chapter 18
SELF HELP

[1] Dr. Lawrence J. Peter, *Peter's Quotations* (New York: William Morrow & Co., 1977), p. 293.

[2] Richard George, *The New Consumer Survival Kit* (Boston: Little, Brown & Co., 1978).

[3] Phyllis Funke, "Do Small Claims Courts Really Work for You?" *Coronet Magazine* (November 1972).

[4] "Redress of Consumer Grievances," Report of the National Institute for Consumer Justice (1973).

[5] *How to Sue in Small Claims Court,* a pamphlet prepared by the State Junior Bar of Texas. Individual copies are available free of charge from the Sales Desk, State Bar of Texas, P.O. Box 12487, Capitol Station, Austin, Texas 78711.

[6] Attorneys are allowed to represent parties in small claims court in Texas. When one side is represented by an attorney, the intended simplicity is often lost. Some other states do not allow attorneys to practice in small claims courts.

[7] David Gould, "Staff Study for the Institute for Consumer Justice on Small Claims Courts" (August 15, 1972), p. 184.

Notes to Chapter 19
LAWYERS

[1] Disciplinary Rule 2-107(A) of the State Bar of Texas provides as follows: "A lawyer shall not divide a fee for legal services with another lawyer who is not a partner in or associate of his law firm or law office, unless: (1) The client consents to employment of the other lawyer after a full disclosure that a division of fees will be made; [and] (2) The division is made in proportion to the services performed and responsibility assumed by each,

or is made with a forwarding lawyer; [and] (3) The total fee of the lawyers does not clearly exceed reasonable compensation for all legal services they rendered the client." (emphasis added)

[2]*Bates v. State Bar of Arizona,* 433 U.S. 350 (1977).

[3]"How to Choose a Lawyer (And What to Do Then)," *Consumer Reports* (May 1977), p.284.

[4]For a discussion of legal clinics, see "Paying Less for a Lawyer," *Consumer Reports* (September 1979), p.522.

Suggested Readings

Free Publications

Consumer Information Catalog. Published quarterly by the Consumer Information Center, Pueblo, Colorado 81009. Lists booklets, most of which are free, that are available from federal agencies.

Consumer's Resource Handbook. Published by the White House Office of the Special Assistant for Consumer Affairs. A "what-to-do, where-to-go manual for resolving consumer problems." Available free from the Consumer Information Center, Dept. 532G, Pueblo, Colorado 81009.

Books

Barkas, J.L. *The Help Book.* New York: Charles Scribner's Sons, 1979.

Bragg, David F., Maxwell, Philip K., and Longley, Joe K. *Texas Consumer Litigation.* Austin: Texas Law Institute, 1978.

Bell, Charles H. *Texas Real Estate.* 3rd ed. Houston: Gulf Publishing Co., 1977.

Cartwright, Joe, and Patterson, Jerry. *Been Taken Lately?* New York: Grove Press, 1974.

Charell, Ralph. *How I Turn Ordinary Complaints Into Thousands of Dollars.* New York: Dell, 1973.

Consumers Union. *Consumer Reports Buying Guide Issue 1980.* Mount Vernon, N.Y.: Consumers Union, 1980.

Fargis, Paul, ed. *The Consumer's Handbook.* New York: Hawthorn Books, Inc., 1974.

Fields, Phillip G. *Car Buyer Beware Or Be Ripped Off!* Houston: The Phantom Press, 1977.

George, Richard. *The New Consumer Survival Kit.* Boston: Little, Brown and Company, 1978.

Hill, John L. *Texan's Guide to Consumer Protection.* Houston: Gulf Publishing Co., 1979.

National Street Law Institute. *Street Law: A Course in Practical Law.* St. Paul, Minn.: West Publishing Co., 1975.

Office of Consumer Affairs. *Guide to Federal Consumer Services.* Washington, D.C.: U.S. Government Printing Office, 1971.

Rosenbloom, Joseph. *Consumer Complaint Guide 1979.* New York: Macmillan Information, 1979.

Tobias, Andrew. *The Only Investment Guide You'll Ever Need.* New York: Harcourt Brace Jovanovich, 1978.

Walker, Glen. *Credit Where Credit is Due.* New York: Holt, Rinehart and Winston, 1979.

Wishard, William R., and Felder, Frederick E. *Credit and Borrowing in Texas: Consumers' Rights and Duties.* San Francisco: Cragmont Publications, 1978.

Wasserman, Paul, and Morgan, Jean, eds. *Consumer Sourcebook: A Directory and Guide.* 2 vols. 2nd rev. ed. Detroit: Gale Research Co., 1978.

Index

a

Abandonment of homestead, 168
Abstract company, 11
Abstract of judgment, 212
Abstract of title, 11
Acceleration, 20, 60, 133, 191
Acknowledgement of contract, 19
"Add-on" interest, 118, 129-31, 133
Affiliation, 195
Annual percentage rate, 118, 130-133
Appraisal, 6
Assignment of right to receive payments, 114
Assumption, 9, 15
Attorneys, 213-222
    fees, contingent, 218
    fees, flat, 218
    fees, hourly, 218
    fees, retainer, 218
    how to find an, 214-216
    in consumer complaints, 206-207, 212
    in credit discrimination, 157
    in credit disputes, 116
    in deceptive trade practice cases, 81-83
    in foreclosure, 57
    in holder-in-due-course, 193
    in home repair financing, 50, 55, 56
    in landlord-tenant disputes, 29, 32, 44-45
    in real estate transactions, 6, 10-11, 12, 19, 20
    in repossession, 161, 162
    interviewing an, 217
    performance, assessing, 220
    retainer fee, 218

Automobile repair practices
    deceptive, 83-86
    legislation, need for, 84-86
    mechanics' rights, 84
Automobile sales
    contracts in, 104-106
        oral, 104-106
        parole evidence rule, 105-106
        written, 104-106
    odometers, 102-104
    paperwork, 94-102
    terminology, legal
        certificate of title, 93
        goods, 93
    title, 93-102
        certificate of, 93, 102
        history of, 104
        obtaining Texas certificate of, 102
        reissuing certificate of, 101
        replacing certificate of, 100
        transferring certificate of, 94-100

b

Breach of rental agreement
    by tenant, 22-23, 34, 36, 39-40
    by landlord, 23, 35-36, 43
Broker, real estate, 5-7, 9, 12, 13

c

Call clause, 17
Certificate of title, 93
Closing, 6, 12-17
Collateral
    legal documents pertaining to, 110
    protecting security interest in, 111
    securing a debt by, 110-113
    securing future debts, 111
Commercial banks as source of real estate loans, 9
Commercially reasonable sale, 163
Completion certificate, 52, 53
"Cooling off period," 87-89
Constructive eviction, 24, 36
Consumer complaints
    problems in finding a good consumer attorney, 213
    consumer assistance agencies, 223-240
Consumer finance, legal terminology in
    affiliation, 195
    assignment of the debt, 191
    assignment of right to receive payments, 114-115

Index

  carrying the note, 190
  cosigner, 115
  financer, 191
  holder-in-due-course, doctrine, 192-193
  loan, 113
  maker, 114
  note, 114-115
  payee, 114
  signature loan, 115
  surety, 115
Consumer laws. See Federal consumer laws; Texas consumer laws
Consumer Protection Act (Texas), Deceptive Trade Practices, 48, 210
Consumer Protection Division, Office of the Attorney General, State of Texas, 83
Consumer remedies
  breach of warranty, 70-75
  deceptive trade practices, 81-83
Contract
  acknowledgement of, 19
  charge accounts, 113
  closed-end credit, 113
  consumer rights determined by terms of, 71
  credit, 110
  earnest money, 7-9, 18
  executory contract for conveyance, 18
  for deed, 17-20
  in automobile sales, 104-106
  in door-to-door sales, 87-91
  in home improvement sales, 52
  installment land, 18
  of sale, 18
  open-end credit contracts, 113
  sample consumer, 120-121
  terms in basic consumer contracts, 119
  violation of Truth-in-Lending Act, 122-123
Contract for deed, 18
Contract of sale, 18
Conventional loan, 10
Covenant of "quiet enjoyment," 23
Cosigner, 115
Credit
  comparison shopping for, 118-122, 129
  extension of, 155-156
  denial of, 155-159
  saving money on purchase of, 128-130
  wrongful denial of, 156-157
Credit, calculating the cost of
  acceleration, 133
  add-on-rate, 129, 131, 133
  annual percentage rate, 130-133
  computing amount actually owed, 133-136

        credit accident and health insurance, 127, 135
        credit life insurance, 126-127, 135
        finance charge, 126, 128-140
        interest, 126, 130, 131
        miscellaneous fees, 128
        physical damage insurance, 127-128
        prepayment, 133-137
        rule of 78s, 134-135
        sum of periodic balances, 134
        time-price differential, 126
        unearned finance charges, 133-137
        unearned premiums on insurance, 135, 136
        using cash versus credit, 137-140
Credit, extension of
    by lenders, 114-116
    by sellers, 113-114
    consumer's remedies for violations in, 122-123
    disclosing terms of, 118-119
    Truth-in-Lending Act (federal), 117, 118-123
Credit accident and health insurance, 127
Credit application, 52
Credit bureau, 142
Credit cards, 113
    lost or stolen, 116
Credit life insurance, 126
Credit opportunity, equal
    legitimate questions regarding
        age, 150, 152-153
        marital status, 150, 151-152
        national origin, 150
        race, 150
        sex, 150-151
    problems of discrimination based on
        age, 150
        exercise of rights under Equal Credit Opportunity Act, 152
        marital status, 150, 151
        receipt of public assistance, 150
        sex, 150-151
    persistence of discrimination, 149
    prohibition of discrimination, 149-150
    recognizing discrimination, 153-155
    rules applicable to credit discrimination, 150-152
Credit record, 141-143, 187
    joint, 148
    right to individual, 148
Credit report, 143-147
    access to, 143-144
    consumer's right to dispute, 146-148
    consumer's right to see, 145
    contents of, 144

            denial of credit based on contents of, 144-145
            summary of, 145
Credit scoring, 152, 155
Credit transactions, legal terminology in. See Legal terminology, in credit transactions
Credit unions as source of real estate loans, 9
Cure, 9

d

Debt collection
            barred by limitations, 187
            prohibited practices, 178-183
            self-defense measures, 187-188
            statutes of limitations, 186-187
            techniques, 176
Debt Collection Practices Act (Texas), 171, 179-184, 185
Deceptive trade practices, 77-86, 106
            automobile repair practices, 83-86
            consumer remedies for, 81
            defenses to a claim of, 81
            fraud, 78
            itemization of, 79-81
            possessory lien, 84
Deed of trust, 110, 114
Deed of trust foreclosure, 20, 57, 111
Default, 110-112, 115, 160
            on homes, 57-60
            conditions constituting, 58
Deficiency, 15, 163
Disclosure statement, 52, 53
Door-to-door sales
            cancellation of, 89-91
            consumer's obligations in, 91
            consumer's remedies, 91-92
            "cooling off period," 87-89
            seller's responsibilities in, 91

e

Earnest money contract, 7-9, 18
Equal credit opportunity. See Credit opportunity, equal.
Equal Credit Opportunity Act (federal), 148, 150, 151-152, 153, 156, 157
Equitable title, 14
Equity, 19-20
Eviction
            actual, 36
            constructive, 24, 36
            forcible, 42-43
            procedures, 41-46
            protection from, 31-32

266 Index

    retaliatory (for demanding repairs), 31-32
Exclusive right to sell, 7

f

Fair Credit Reporting Act (federal), 151-152
Fair Debt Collection Practices Act (federal), 183, 184-186
    applicable only to credit bureaus, 185
    penalties for violations, 186
Federal consumer laws
    Equal Credit Opportunity Act, 148, 150, 151-152, 153, 156, 157
    Fair Credit Reporting Act, 151-152
    Fair Debt Collection Practices Act, 183, 184-186
    Magnuson-Moss Warranty Act, 67-68, 69, 70
    Motor Vehicle Information and Cost Savings Act, 103, 106
    Truth-in-Lending Act, 53, 62, 117, 118-123, 131
Federal Trade Commission (FTC) regulations on financers' responsibilities, 193-195
FHA (Federal Housing Authority), as a source of insurance for real estate loans, 10
Finance, consumer, 190-191
Finance charge, 126
Financer, 191
Financing agreement, 111
Financing consumer purchases
    financer's responsibility in home improvement finance, 56
    goods
        charge account, 113
        closed-end credit contract, 113
        cosigner, 115
        maximum finance charge, 113
        open-end credit contracts, 113
        signature loan, 115
        surety, 115
    home improvements, 49-53
    real estate, 9-10, 13, 14, 15-20
    shopping for credit, 52
    Truth-in-Lending Act (federal), 53, 62, 117, 118-123
Financers' responsibilities, 189-198
    consumer finance, 190-191
    in home improvement finance, 156
    legal ways to avoid, 191-193
    legal ways to enforce, 193-197
        FTC (Federal Trade Commission) rules, 193-195
        Texas laws, 195-197
    summary of, 197
Forcible entry and detainer suits, 45
Foreclosure
    acceleration of debt, 60
    definition of, 57
    deed of trust, 57
    legal attacks on foreclosure sale, 61-62

Index

       legal title, 57
       of a lien, 169
       on home improvement sales, 50-51, 52, 55
       on homes, 57-62
       prevention of, 60-62
       redemption of property, 59
       sales of homes, 59-62
       trustee, 57
Fraud, 78
Fraud, in automobile sales, 106
Future indebtedness security interest, 111

g

Garnishment of wages, 171
General warranty deed, 12
GI (Veterans Administration) as source of insurance for real estate loans, 10
Good-faith purchaser, 111
Goods, 93
Goods, sales of, 93, 94, 104-106, 110-111
Grantor, 14

h

Hold-over tenant, 30
Holder-in-due-course doctrine, 192-193
Home Solicitation Sales Act (Texas), 53, 87-88, 89, 90, 91-92
Home improvements
       automatic lien, 50, 52
       completion certificate, 52, 53
       contract for, 52
       credit application, 52
       disclosure statement, 52, 53
       financing of, 49-53
       illegal practices in, 53-56
       lien, 49-53
       mechanic's and materialman's lien, 50, 169
       note, 52-53
       notice of rescission, 53
       second lien, 51
Homestead
       abandoned, 168
       as judgment-exempt, 49
       creation of, 167-168
       definition of, 165-167
              rural, 165
              urban, 156-166, 168-169
              business, 166-167
       ending exemption, 168
       legal protection for, 169
       purchase money mortgage on, 169

i

Implied warranty of habitability, 66-67
Installment contracts, 112
Installment land contracts, 18
Insured loans, 10
Interest, 126

j

Judgment exemptions
    homestead, 165-169
    personal property, 170-173
Justice of the peace court, 207-208

l

Landlord's lien, 46-48
    disposal of tenant's property, 47
    procedures for enforcing, 47
    tenant's property exempt from, 46-47
Landlord's remedies
    against withholding of last month's rent, 39
    cancellation for breach of rental agreement, 35-36
    eviction, 36-37
    for tenant's withholding rent, 31
    landlord's lien, 46-48
    utility termination, 43-44
    withholding security deposit, 38
Landlord's responsibilities
    enforcement of, 27-31
    new owner, 23
    not to enter premises without permission, 23-24
    not to evict in retaliation, 30-31
    notice to terminate tenancy, 33, 34
    relating to tenant's right to "quiet enjoyment," 23-24
    rental agreement, 21-23
    to exterminate rats, roaches, 29
    to make repairs, 24-32
    to provide written list of deductions from security deposit, 39
    to satisfy housing code, 31-32
    to timely return security deposit, 37-38
    warranty of habitability, 24-25
    waiver of, 25
Landlord's rights
    in casualty losses, 31
    rental agreement, 21-23
    to collect rent, 30-31
    to retain permanent improvements to premises, 32
Lawyers. See Attorneys
Lease, 21

Legal services
    legal aid offices, 221-222
    legal clinics, 221
    prepaid legal services plan, 221
    traditional private general practices, 221
Legal terminology
    in automobile sales
        certificate of title, 93
        goods, 93
        lien, 50, 52
    in credit transactions
        acceleration, 133
        "add-on" interest, 118, 129-33
        annual percentage rate, 118, 130-133
        assignment of right to receive payments, 114
        collateral, 109, 110
        cosigner, 115
        credit accident and health insurance, 127
        credit life insurance, 126
        deed of trust, 110, 114
        deed of trust sale, 111
        finance charge, 126
        financing agreement, 111
        future indebtedness security interest, 111
        good-faith purchaser, 111
        interest, 126
        lien, 110
        loan, 113
        maker, 114
        mortgage, 110
        note, 114-115
        payee, 114
        physical damage insurance, 127
        prepayment, 133
        prepayment penalty/call clause, 137
        pro rata rebate, 135
        security agreement, 110, 114
        security interest, 110
        short rate rebate, 135
        signature loan, 115
        simple interest, 118, 131, 133
        sum of periodic balances, 134
        surely, 115
        time-price differential, 126
    in consumer finance
        affiliation, 195
        assignment of the debt, 191
        carrying the note, 190
        financer, 191
        holder-in-due-course doctrine, 192-193

Index

in debt collection
    barred by limitations, 187
    campaign of unreasonable collection practices, 177
    statute of limitations, 187
in deceptive trade practices
    fraud, 78
    possessory lien, 84
in door-to-door sales
    "cooling off period," 87-89
in foreclosure
    acceleration of debt, 60, 191
    deed of trust, 57
    deed of trust sale, 57
    legal title, 57
    redemption of property, 59
    trustee, 57
in general
    abstract of judgment, 212
    acceleration, 20
    cure, 9
    negligence, 25
    parol evidence rule, 105-106
    specific performance, 8
    statute of frauds, 104
    waiver, 35
    warrant, 12
in home improvements
    automatic lien, 49-53
    completion certificate, 52, 53
    contract, 52
    credit application, 52
    disclosure statement, 52, 53
    lien, 49-53
    mechanic's and materialman's lien, 50, 169
    note, 52-53
    notice of rescission, 53
    second lien, 51
in homestead exemptions
    abandoned homestead, 168
    purchase money mortgage, 169
in real estate and landlord-tenant relations
    abstract of title, 11
    acceleration, 20
    acknowledgement of contract, 19
    actual eviction, 36
    appraisal, 6
    assumption, 9, 15
    call clause, 17
    closing, 6, 12-17
    constructive eviction, 24, 36

Index

contract for deed, 18
contract of sale, 18
conventional loan, 10
covenant of "quiet enjoyment," 23
deed, 12
deed of trust, 14
deed of trust foreclosure, 20
deficiency, 15
earnest money contract, 7-9
equitable title, 14
equity, 19-20
exclusive right to sell, 7
executory contract for conveyance, 18
forcible entry and detainer suits, 45
general warranty deed, 12
grantor, 14
hold-over tenant, 30
installment land contract, 18
insured loan, 10
lease, 21
legal title, 14
lien, 14
liquidated damages, 40
listing agreement, 7
mortgage, 14
multiple listing, 7
negligence, 25
negotiate, 13
normal wear and tear, 25
notice, 19
open listing, 7
owner-financing, 9, 13
periodic tenancy, 32-34
possession bond, 45
promissory note, 13
quit-claim deed, 13
refinancing, 15
rental agreement, 21
security interest, 14
sovereign, 11
special warranty deed, 13
statute of frauds, 7
subleasing, 40
title insurance, 8, 10-11
title opinion, 11
title search, 8, 10-11
trustee, 14
vendor's lien, 13
waiver, 25
warrant, 12

Index

        warranty of habitability, 24
        writ of restitution, 46
    in repossession
        commercially reasonable sale, 163
        deficiency, 163
        redeeming property, 162
        writ of attachment, 171-172
        writ of execution, 171, 173
        writ of garnishment, 171, 172
        writ of sequestration, 161, 171-172

Legal title, 57
Lien, 14, 49-53, 170
Life insurance, credit, 126-127, 135
Life insurance companies as source of real estate loans, 9
Limitations, 187
Liquidated damages, 40
Listing agreement, 7

m

Magnuson-Moss Warranty Act (federal), 67-68, 69, 70
Mail order sales, laws regulating, 92
Maker, 114
Manufactured Housing Standards Act (Texas), 68
Mechanic's and materialman's lien, 50, 169
Miscellaneous fees, 128
Mortgage, 14, 110
Mortgage banks as source of real estate loans, 9
Motor Vehicle Information and Cost Savings Act (federal), 103, 106
Multiple listing, 7

n

Negligence, 25
Negotiate, 13
Norman wear and tear, 25
Note, 52-53, 114-115
Notice, 19
Notice of rescission, 53

o

Odometers, 102-104
Open listing, 7
Owner-financed, 13

p

Parol evidence rule, 105-106
Payee, 114
Periodic tenancy, 32-34
Physical damage insurance, 127

Index 273

Possessory lien, 84
Possession bond, 45
Prepayment, 133
Prepayment penalty/call clause, 137
Pro rata rebate, 135
Promissory note, 13
Purchase money mortgage, 169

q

Quit-claim deed, 13

r

Real estate appraiser, 6
Real estate sales, 5-20
    broker, 5-7, 9, 12-13
    closing, 6, 9, 12-17
    contract for deed, 17-20
    default, 16, 17, 18-20
    earnest money contract, 7-9, 18
    financing of, 9-10, 13-14, 15-20
    survey, 11-12
    title, 9, 10-11, 12-15, 19
    title company, 6, 11, 12, 17
    title examination, 10-11
Real Estate Settlement Procedures Act (federal), 117
Real estate terminology. See Legal terminology, in real estate
Redemption of property, 59, 162
Refinancing, 15
Rental agreement, 21-23, 32-33, 35, 36, 37
    cancellation of tenancy for breach of, 35-36
    enforcement of, 22
    fixed-term tenancy, 32, 34-35
    negotiating terms of, 22-23
    oral, 21-23, 33
    periodic tenancy, 32-34
    tenant's leaving before expiration of, 39-41
    termination of by eviction, 36-37
    written, 21-23, 33
Rental housing, 21-48
    consequences of breaching lease, 39-41
    eviction procedures, 41-46
    forcible entry and detainer suits, 45
    implied warranty of habitability, 66-67
    improvements, 24-31
    recovery of security deposit, 37-39
    rental agreement, 21-23, 32-33, 35, 36, 37
    repairs to, 24-32
        landlord's responsibilities, 25-27
        normal wear and tear, 25

274 Index

        requiring a landlord to make, 27-31
        security deposit, 37-39
        tenant's responsibilities, 25-27
        to satisfy housing code, 31-32
        warranty of habitability, 24-25
    tenant's right to "quiet enjoyment," 23-24
    termination of tenancy, 32-37
        cancellation for breach of rental agreement, 35-36
        fixed-term tenancy, 34-35
        notice requirement for fixed-term tenancy, 34-35
        notice requirement for periodic tenancy, 33, 34
        periodic tenancy, 33-34
        rent adjustment, 34
        termination of tenancy by eviction, 36-37
        termination of tenancy by landlord, 22-23
  See also Eviction; Landlord's remedies; Landlord's responsibilities; Landlord's rights; Rental agreement; Security deposit; Tenant's remedies; Tenant's responsibilities; Tenant's rights
Repossession, 111-113, 159-164, 171, 176
    acceleration of debt, 160, 162
    commercially reasonable sale, 163
    consumer's remedies, 163-164
    consumer's rights, 163
    default as a requirement for, 160
    deficiency, 163
    disposition of property after, 162
    obtaining judgment, 159-160
    of personal property, 171
    prevention of, 161
    procedure, 160
    recovery of property after, 162
    redeeming property, 59, 162
    requirement of written security agreement, 159-160, 162

S

Savings and loan associations as sources of real estate loans, 9
Second lien, 51
Security agreement, 110, 114, 159
Security deposit
    deductible charges, 38
    failure of landlord to itemize deductions from, 39
    failure of landlord to return, 38
    provisions regarding return of, 37-38
    time frame for return of, 37-38
Security interest, 14, 110
Self-help on consumer problems
    investigate, 201-202
    read, 202
    question, 202-203
    steps in making a consumer complaint, 203-206

Index   275

    suing in small claims court, 207-212
    write, 203
Sequestration, 161
Short-rate rebate, 135
Signature loan, 115
Simple interest, 118, 131, 133
Small claims court, 207-212
Special warranty deed, 13
Specific performance, 8
Statute of frauds, 104
Statutes of limitations, 187
    barred by limitations, 187
    debt becoming enforceable again, 186-187
    on oral contract, 186
    on written contract, 186
Subject-to financing, 16
Subleasing, 40-41
Sum of periodic balances, 134
Surety, 115

t

Tenancy, termination of
    notice requirement for fixed-term tenancy, 34-35
    notice requirement for periodic tenancy, 33, 34
    rent adjustment, 34
Tenant's remedies
    against illegal seizure of property, 48
    cancellation for landlord's breach, 35-36
    contesting an eviction, 44
    for landlord's withholding security deposit, 38-39
    lawful procedures, 27-31
    moving out, 23-24, 26-27, 31, 43
    withholding rent, 31, 39
Tenant's responsibilities
    not to terminate for landlord's breach of rental agreement, 35-36
    not to withhold rent in retaliation, 30-31
    not to remove permanent improvements on premises, 32
    notice to terminate fixed-term tenancy, 34-35
    notice to terminate periodic tenancy, 33
    rental agreement, 21-23
    to make repairs, 25-27
Tenant's rights
    in casualty losses, 31
    enforcing, 27-31
    of "quiet enjoyment," 23-24
    property exempt from landlord's lien, 46-47
    protection from unfair eviction, 30-32
    rental agreement, 21-23
    to be free of rats or roaches, 29
    to excess value of goods seized above amount owed, 47

       to physical health or safety, 25, 26, 29
       to privacy, 23-24
       to timely return of security deposit, 37
       to written list of deductions from security deposit, 39
       under new owner, 23
       waiver of, 25
       warranty of habitability, 24-25
Texas Consumer Association (TCA), 1, 226
Texas consumer laws
       Credit code, 117
       Debt Collection Practices Act, 171
       Deceptive Trade Practices-Consumer Protection Act, 77-86
       Home Solicitation Sales Act, 87-88, 89, 90, 91-92
       Manufactured Housing Standards Act, 68
Time-price differential, 126
Title. See Real estate sales; Automobile sales
Title company, 6, 11, 12, 17
Title search, 10-11
Title opinion, 11
Trustee, 14, 157
Truth-in-Lending Act (federal), 53, 62, 117, 118-123, 131

V

VA (Veterans Administration) as source of insurance for real estate loans, 10
Vendor's lien, 13

W

Wages, prohibition against garnishment of, in Texas, 171
Waiver, 25
Warranty
       breach of, 70-75, 81, 82
       disputes, 74-75, 106
       express, 65, 66
       full, 68, 69-70
       implied, 65, 66, 67
       implied warranty of habitability, 66-67
       implied warranty of merchantability, 66-67
       limited, 68, 69-70
       of title, 12
       on mobile homes, 68
       oral, 66
       reading a, 68-70
       recognizing a, 65-68
       written, 66, 68-70
Warranty of habitability, 24
Writ of attachment, 171-172
Writ of execution, 171, 211-212
Writ of garnishment, 171, 172
Writ of restitution, 46
Writ of sequestration, 171-172

ABOUT THE AUTHORS

H. Clyde Farrell received his law degree from The University of Texas School of Law in 1975. He also holds a B.A. in Political Science from The University of Texas at Austin and an M.A. in Political Science from the University of Wisconsin at Madison. From 1973 to 1975, he worked as a law clerk in Austin with attorney James G. Boyle, primarily in the consumer-law area. He has been practicing as an attorney with Texas Rural Legal Aid, Inc. since 1975. Consumer law has been a large part of his Legal Services practice, in which he has assisted Legal Services programs throughout Texas with writing, teaching and consulting. He is editor and co-author of *Texas Legal Services Manual For Routine Practice* (Austin: Texas Legal Services Center, Inc., 1980), and is author of *Texas Rural Legal Aid Mag Card Form Book* (Weslaco: Texas Rural Legal Aid, Inc., 1979) and *Consent of Minors to Medical Care: Who Has Authority in Texas?* 42 TEXAS BAR JOURNAL 25 (Jan. 1979). He is now in private practice in Austin, Texas.

Paul Kens is a graduate of The University of Texas School of Law and of Northern Illinois University. Since 1978, he has been practicing as an attorney with Gulf Coast Legal Foundation in Houston. During that time he has concentrated his practice in consumer law. From 1976 to the present, he has been a council member of the Consumer Law Section of the State Bar of Texas, and he currently chairs the Houston Bar Association Consumer Law Section. He has contributed a chapter on consumer law to the *Texas Legal Services Manual for Routine Practice* (Austin: Texas Legal Services Center, Inc., 1980) and an article to the *Texas Observer,* January 28, 1977. He is author of *Public Futility—The Status of Consumers in Light of the Public Utility Regulatory Act,* 28 BAYLOR L. REV. 953 (Fall 1976). He has also taught at the Thurgood Marshall School of Law, Texas Southern University, Houston.

YES! I do want to know the rules of the game. Please send me the following copies of **Buying, Renting & Borrowing in Texas:**

_____ copies in papaerback ($7.95 each, including tax, postage and handling)

_____ copies in hardback ($11.95 each, including tax, postage and handling)

For orders of 10 copies or more, subtract $1.00 per copy for each copy over 10. Contact TCA for special group prices for fundraising events, etc.

Name _____

Mailing Address _____ Zip _____

MAIL TO: **Texas Consumer Association, 302 West 15th Street, Suite 202, Austin, Texas 78701, 512 / 477-1882**